The Liberty FLIP Capo

IDEA BOOK

The Guitarist's Guide to the Ultimate Partial Capos

Over 70 ingenious ways to use
Liberty FLIP capos to play new music

HARVEY REID

WOODPECKER
MULTIMEDIA
York, Maine USA

www.LibertyGuitar.com

*Special deep and eternal thanks to Steve Rowley. And thanks
to Lyle Shabram for starting it all, and to Jeff Hickey for all
his effort, insights and kindred spirit all those years.*

ISBN: 978-1-63029-025-2

WOODPECKER
MULTIMEDIA

PO Box 815 York Maine 03909 USA

www.woodpecker.com

CONTENTS

2 — The Story of Liberty Capos
6 — About Partial Capos
7 — About this Book
8 — Who Are Partial Capos For?
9 — About the Diagrams in This Book
10 — Chord Voicings & Inversions

11 — ONE LIBERTY CAPO IN STANDARD TUNING

12 — 1- Drop E "Top 5" (022222)
14 — 2- Bottom 5 (222220)
16 — 3- Top 4 "Half-Open A" (002222)
21 — 4- Bottom 4 (222200)
24 — 5- E-Modal "Double-Drop E" (022220)
30 — 6- E-Suspended "Esus" (022200)
38 — 7- Open A (002220)
42 — 8- Drop C (044444)
44 — 9- Bottom 5 @4 (444440)
46 — 10- E-Modal@4 (044440)
49 — 11- Esus@4 (044400)
53 — 12- A@4 (004440)
56 — 13- Bottom 4 @5 (555500)
58 — 14- Esus@5 (055500)
60 — 15- A@5 (005550)
62 — 16- Top 5 @7 (077777)
64 — 17- Bottom 5 @7 (777770)
67 — 18- Top 4 @7 (007777)
69 — 19- Bottom 4 @7 (777700)
72 — 20- E-Modal @7 (077770)
76 — 21- Esus@7 (077700)
79 — 22- A@7 (007770)
82 — 23- Bottom 4 @9 (999900)
84 — 24- Esus@9 (099900)
87 — 25- A@9 (009990)

91 — RETUNING 1-2 STRINGS WITH 1 CAPO

92 — 26- "Double Drop" D (022222) [Drop D]
94 — 27- Drop D Bottom 5 (222220) [Drop D]
96 — 28- Drop D Top 4 (002222) [Drop D]
98 — 29- Drop D Bottom 4 (222200) [Drop D]
101 — 30- Drop D Esus (022200) [Drop D]
105 — 31- Bottom 4@4 (444400) [Drop D]
107 — 32- Bottom 4@5 (555500) [Drop D]
109 — 33- Esus@7 (077700)[Drop D]
112 — 34- A@7 (007770) [Drop D]
115 — 35- Easy-E (022200) [EADF#BE]
119 — 36- Esus Minor (022200)[EADFBE]
122 — 37- Drop A (022222) [EGDGBE]
126 — 38- Half-Open A Slide (002222) [EADGBD]
128 — 39- A Suspended (002220)[EADGCE]
135 — 40- A Drop Minor (002220) [EADGBbE]
138 — 41- "E-Modal sus" (022220)[EADGCE]
142 — 42- "Liberty" Version 1 [EADGCE]
147 — 43- "Liberty Version 2" [EADGCE]
151 — Easy Two-Finger 1-4-5 "Liberty" Chords in E
152 — Two-Finger 1-4-5 "Liberty" Chords in A
153 — Example: Why Liberty Tuning is Mysterious
154 — Playing 2 & 6 Chords
158 — Playing Minor Chords
159 — Playing Modal 7b "Drop Chords"
160 — Playing Blues in E
162 — Playing Blues in A
164 — Example: House of the Rising Sun
167 — 44- Asus @7 (007770) [EADGCE]
170 — 45- Asus @9 (009990) [EADGCE]
172 — 46- Middle 4 @9 sus (099990) [EADGCE]
175 — 47- Bottom 4 Double Drop (222200) [DADGBD]
178 — 48- Bottom 5 @5 (555550) [DADGBD]

180	49- "Low-C" (005555)[CGDGBE]
182	50- DADGCE Esus (022200) [DADGCE]
185	51- Drop D /A@7sus (007770)[DADGCE]
195	52- The Jones Esus (022200)[EADEBB]
197	53- Perfect 4ths Tuning (111100)[EADGCF]
201	**USING MULTIPLE PARTIAL CAPOS**
202	54- B6 (024444)
205	55- 044442
207	56- Drop E-Modal (244440)
209	57- 444420
211	58- Almost Open B (024442)
214	59- 044422
215	60- Esus@4 / Open A (044420)
219	61- Esus / A@4 (024440)
223	62- 066622
224	63- Esus / A@9 (029990)
228	64- 029999
230	65- EBB2 (029992)
233	66- 355530
236	67- A Minor 11 (555530)
238	68- 666640
240	69- Esus@7 / A@9 (079990)
242	70- 155530
246	71- Esus / Asus (024440)[EADGCE]
249	72- Open G 077700 [DGDGBD]
252	73- Top 4 @2 (002222)[DADGAD]
255	**APPENDIX: OTHER PARTIAL CAPO TOPICS**
256	*Simplified Guitar With Partial Capos*
257	*Using Liberty Capos on Other Instruments*
258	*Other Types of Partial Capos*
262	*Partial Capos & Notation*
266	*Some Partial Capo Math*
267	*More Guitar Resources By Harvey Reid*
270	*About the Author*

At a glance, this book may seem complicated or confusing. Even the concept of partial capos is tricky, which is probably the reason you are reading this right now. Just don't let this confusion keep you from enjoying all the great music that partial capos generate.

The complexity and confusion are the very reason that this hidden music hasn't already been played by millions of players through the centuries that guitars have been around. It's just really difficult to see the value of partial capos, to know where to put the capos or where to put your fingers. And the last thing any of us need is to be reminded that we don't understand the guitar fingerboard well enough.

Learn to embrace what's hard to see, and let me take you down this musical "rabbit hole." I will show you a "Wonderland" of new sounds that becomes instantly available to total beginners as well as novices or good players of all styles. It's taken me almost 40 years to find all these ideas, and I have learned over the years that most people just don't figure this stuff out on their own. It's practically invisible.

You don't need to understand music theory, and it won't hurt if you just start playing and ignore the explanations I try to give of what is going on. All you need to do is put the capos on, and start trying out the chord shapes. You also might end up falling in love with one or a handful of these ideas and not using the rest, which is fine too.

Whether you are a strummer, a songwriter, composer or a picker, the chord shapes in this book show you the starting point for all the new music. The new resonances, open-string effects, harmonic possibilities and cool new chords will start happening as soon as you put your fingers down. You can turn them into your own songs, accompaniments, instrumentals, or just enjoy their sound.

Your music will instantly take on a new dimension, but it's all built around the skills you already have. What could be better than a new way to immediately get great sounds, without the need to put in long hours practicing? In Vol. 2 of this book there are dozens more ideas, mostly using multiple capos, open tunings, or both together.

Harvey Reid

Model **43**

The Story of Liberty Capos

I have been studying, using and selling partial capos for almost 40 years now, and this book marks a new milestone in the evolution and development of the idea.

Since I first came across Lyle Shabram's *Chord-Forming Capo* in about 1976, I have been fascinated with the new musical possibilities that partial capos offer. The idea of using new tunings of the guitar to obtain another set of resonances and possibilities is widespread, but the shadowy world of partial capos has remained far from the mainstream, very elusive and little-understood. Capos work in a similar way as tunings, we use them for the same reasons, and they give similar results. But they are not at all equivalent to tunings, and the fresh landscape of resonances, fingerings and voicings they generate are not the same ones that tunings provide.

It's remarkable that such a powerful idea has not made it into the hands of influential and famous guitarists and subsequently spread around the guitar world. Partial capos cost about as much as a good pizza, and they unlock the door to a vast and useful musical world, yet very few guitarists own and use them, and most of the capos out there are gathering dust. Some of my best music has come from using them, and I have grown very dependent on their musical power for a large chunk of my life's work as a guitarist and songwriter. Yet as I look around me, I see them largely unused and poorly understood, even by the people who make and sell them. What is going on? Why don't people just grab them and start enjoying the new music?

First a little history. For about 20 years, there was just one partial capo, and I had nothing to do with creating it. My friend Jeff Hickey and I licensed the capo from Shabram in 1980, and I renamed it the *Third Hand Capo*. We spent years explaining, selling and promoting the idea, and got tens of thousands of them into hundreds of music stores and about 30 countries. In 1980 I published *"A New Frontier in Guitar,"* and I wrote and published a book of guitar arrangements (*Sleight of Hand*) in 1982. That same year I published another little-known book, *Duck Soup Guitar*, which first showed how to use partial capos to play simplified guitar chords.

As the years went by, the partial capo idea sprouted some new shoots and picked up converts, but never took off. I had stopped using the *Third Hand* in my own concerts because I thought it was clumsy and unsightly, and I instead found that I was happier using it for research. I used sawed-up *Shubb* capos in performances; in particular I gravitated toward the 3-string "E-suspended" or "E-sus" version that I pioneered around 1983 because I needed access to some notes that were blocked by the *Third Hand*. In 1995 *Shubb* started making their *c7b*, which was an attractive and well-made brass *Esus* capo. I used it on all my recordings and concerts until 2013. In 2002 *Kyser* released their version of this idea, the *Short-Cut*. Most of the performing guitarists who have adopted the capo idea have used one of these two capos, though steadily some new capo designs have emerged. (See appendix.)

[Interestingly, as I complete this huge research project, when I assemble my Top 10 or Top 20 lists of favorite partial capo ideas, only this old friend "Esus" uses just a single partial capo in standard tuning. The other super-charged ideas use multiple capo, altered tunings, or both...]

A confluence of events led me to put a huge amount of energy into digging much deeper into the mysteries of partial capos. The economy and the music business went into free fall, beginning around 2009, and that same year Jeff Hickey died in a car accident. My second son was born in 2008, and after over 30 years of touring and performing, I began to enjoy a family life, and was looking for ways to stay home. I decided to make a series of books and recordings to document what I knew about partial capos, to help others understand how to use them, and to get things out of my head and safely onto paper. This 5-year effort became the 9-volume set of *Capo Voodoo* books that show nearly 200 ways to use all the assorted kinds of partial capos.

As I worked on this huge project, which now totals nearly 1000 pages, I became increasingly convinced that three things were true:

- **Partial capos can be extremely valuable musically, and they can benefit all levels of players.**

- **Something about the idea of a partial capo is fundamentally opaque and confusing to even really good guitarists.**

- **Partial capo hardware needed improvement.**

I was creating amazing music with my capos, and so were some of my friends and some other pioneers, but the idea was not catching on. The list of famous or really good guitarists who have failed to find or chosen not to find great music with partial capos is sadly a long one.

The players I sent off with their *Third Hand* capos were not really discovering much, and were shaking their heads in confusion more than they were excitedly exploring and creating new music. Even Jeff Hickey, who was a fine guitarist and a very intelligent man who passionately believed in partial capos, never found a new way to use partial capos in 29 years! This fact alone should have made it crystal clear to me that people needed guidance more than just capos. When you are in the wilderness you need a map or compass more than you need encouragement or time.

So I set out to make a set of maps of the new landscape, to chart the way. The instruction sheet crammed into each *Third Hand* had been the only source of ideas of how to use the capos. My books of arrangements did not sell that well, and I realized that people wanted to make their own music and not play mine. So I chose to make chord charts the primary signposts in my guidance system. The fingering of a chord illustrates the harmonies and resonances, it puts your fingers where they need to go, and points the way to either strummed accompaniments or instrumental music. And it is a universal depiction, readable in any language and requiring no training to decode. Years earlier I had started keeping logs of my explorations, because I found that if I spent long hours working out new sounds and fingerings I would often forget what I had found. These chord logs grew into a larger and larger and increasingly bewildering library of guitar chords that now numbers nearly 20,000.

The body of knowledge outlined in these pages is more than a human brain can retain, and I will use this book myself to remind me how many of the tunings work. It's hard to learn a new tuning, and most players either know one or two tunings well, or they dabble in lots of them and play a song or two in each one. Knowing how to really play in all these capo environments is comparable to being fluent in dozens of languages.

This ridiculous picture with a C-clamp and a block of wood was actually printed in the *Journal of Research in Music Education* in 1982.

My article on how to use a partial capo for simplified guitar needed a photo, but magazine editorial policy said they could not use any photos of commercial products. Since the only partial capo in the world was the *Third Hand*, there was no other way to illustrate how to make an *Esus* capo configuration.

I'm sure it did not help spread the idea.

As I worked on my ever-growing catalog of guitar chords, my ears perked up from time to time as I found chords that sounded unfamiliar to me, yet were beautiful or interesting. When I looked closely at them, I realized that they sounded fresh to me because neither I or anyone else had ever played or heard that sequence of notes before. The next step was for me to build a complete library of all standard tuning guitar chords so I could compare my new chords against this and see what was happening. (This took about 6 months of very hard work, and turned into my epic *Troubadour Guitar Chord Book*.) As I logged each chord in my partial capo "parallel universe," I also kept track of the note names and spelled out the scale positions of every string, so I could see where the roots, fifths, 3rds, 6ths and other notes in each chord were landing. I created some primitive but very effective computer software that could instantly tell me if a chord I found was new, what other tunings or capo environments had produced that chord, and how often I was finding duplicate voicings.

I was quite startled by the results. More than half of the chord voicings I was logging were unique, and I was not finding the repetition I expected in all sorts of chords. I found about 27 ways to finger an A major chord in standard tuning, but nearly 150 distinct permutations of A-C#-E notes in my whole library, even after I ignored the useless ones that had lots of C#s and no A's. I also found that over half of the chords I was logging for my partial capo configurations were not playable voicings in standard tuning. The guitar fingerboard was indeed deeper and more varied than I realized at first, and it is probably more complex than any of us can really comprehend. **The number of ways to rearrange the notes in various chords, fretted by various combinations of fingers, on 6 strings that are tuned or capoed in some manner, is something akin to playing chess against a supercomputer.**

Then came the "kicker..."

One day in the last week of August 2011, I stumbled on something I wasn't prepared for. I thought I had explored the guitar pretty deeply, in standard tuning as well as other open tunings and dozens upon dozens of partial capo landscapes. I thought I had a pretty good sense of what was possible on the guitar. I have a good left hand, and I was using it a lot to stretch to cool new places, and in the back of my mind I was pretty sure I was aware of all the important ways that tunings and capos could make the guitar easier or more understandable.

Exploring hundreds of partial capo positions for years, among the dizzying number of ways they could be combined with various changes in tuning, I had not found any signs that there was a "hidden order" or a "master key" to mapping musical ideas onto a six-string fingerboard. Some capo environments had cool chords, some had a "drony" sound, or a big bass combined with a shimmering high end, but all of them involved basically the same complexity of fingers on my left hand to access.

That August day I almost missed the message when it was sent to me. A guitar in *Liberty Tuning* does not call out like it would in Open D or even DADGAD. It's an odd and not overly musical chord that the open strings make. The fact that it takes a particular kind of partial capo, plus you retune a string meant that no one else had found it, though it cleverly only takes about 5 seconds to get there from standard tuning. I was there by accident, but by some kind of sleepy luck I noticed that something was unusual and good. I was not looking for it when I found it. It found me.

It was early in the morning, and as I sipped my coffee and waited for my 3-year-old son to wake up, I moved my fingers around the fingerboard that I had accidentally set up in *Liberty Version 1*. Everything I played sounded good, and by the end of the day I had figured out that I could play a mind-blowing number of great chords with just 2 fingers. I was actually getting lost and confused because there were so many repeating geometric shapes, and even weeks and months later I was still finding tricky hidden fingerings I had missed. Those usual spaghetti chords and hard barre chords that had always been the center of all guitar playing had vanished, and out popped all kinds of good music with seemingly no effort.

What I found stopped me in my tracks, and changed the whole direction of my life. This weird little tuning allows you to play almost every song that matters with simple 2-finger left hand shapes. I recorded a whole album of instrumental guitar music, using only the two middle fingers of my left hand, and it basically sounds the

My box of weird capos...

same as all my other guitar albums, except many people say it sounds better. It got a 5-star rating in *Premier Guitar Magazine*.

All my life I would have smiled gently and perhaps rolled my eyes if someone who only had 2 working fingers on their left hand said they wanted to be a good guitar player. Now I would tell them to get a nice guitar and practice hard, and that they could get an instrumental gig at a restaurant if they wanted to. I have put an adult guitar in the hands of several 4-year-old children, and they were instantly able to strum full chords in the key of C, which is perfect for their voices. My kids are now 6 and 9 and they are using this idea and learning to be little troubadours, and doing what children that age have never been able to do— strumming and singing along. Have you ever noticed that kids can't do that? Not till they are 13 or so when their hands get big enough. Well, not any more.

The next step in the saga was that even though I have a box (photo) with every kind of partial capo that I keep on the coffee table in my music room, none of these capos does a satisfactory job on this powerful new thing I suddenly wanted to share with everyone. All the existing partial capos began to look worse and worse to me, and they were also not able to do this new idea properly on my guitars.

When you go high up a guitar, the neck usually gets wider and thicker. A lot of people also play nylon-string guitars, and they are used a lot in schools, and the *Kyser* and *Shubb* capos didn't work right on those necks. I realized that I did not want to ask people to put an unsightly *Third Hand* capo on their beautiful new guitar. The powerful second version of *Liberty Tuning* meant that you either needed two $35 capos that didn't quite work right, or a clumsy universal mechanism. So the *Liberty FLIP* capo was born, largely due to the genius and assistance of my friend and neighbor Steve Rowley, who is a machinist, inventor and guitar lover. We tried other mechanisms, but found that they would be too expensive and difficult to manufacture, and settled on the elegant, 2-sided reversible design that arrived in 2014.

A big part of the power of *Liberty Tuning* is that it allows people to play vastly more music than ever before with simple motor skills and essentially no difficult barre chords. This also means you have to match the chords to the singing pitch of men, women and young children. To sing a lot of songs, you need to add a full capo below the *Liberty* capo. This led to the creation of the companion *Model 65* capo. It is also a 2-sided reversible capo, with a full capo on one side and a 5-string partial on the other. **These two capos look great together, and are now in my opinion essential tools for beginning guitarists of all ages.** They are small enough to carry around in your pocket, and easy enough to operate so even young kids can tighten or remove them from a guitar. (My kids can't operate any of the other partial capos.) The *Model 65* is actually the best full capo I have ever used, and the *Model 43* is a perfect *Esus* capo, among its other uses.

The final revelation, and the underlying *raison d'étre* of this book is that these two capos are now the only ones I now keep in my guitar case, and are what I think all anyone needs. With a pair of them you can clamp 6, 5, 4 or 3 strings, plus dozens of combinations using more than one capo. This book shows over 70 possibilities.

After all my countless hours of learning to play guitar and researching what partial capos can do, I present you with 2 beautiful, well-designed, high-performance capos that are more versatile, less visible and more useful than anything else you can own. I also present you with this book, that covers more ground than any of you will ever be able to retain. You could take these capos, your guitar and this book to a desert island or monastery, and you would never reach the bottom of the pool. The handful of other extremely interesting partial capo ideas out there that you can't do with these capos are not pressing enough to warrant my energy any more, and I am now abandoning the complexity of all those piles of weird capos and encouraging you to do the same.

I have been explaining and selling all brands of partial capos for several years now to feed my family while I worked on this project, and I am now satisfied that I will be happy to shut down my partial capo store, and just preach the value of these 2 capos. As a treat to myself I will carry around two *Model 43*'s, because there are a few ideas in this book where you need two of them. I might carry a second *Model 65* also so I can use the 6-string side of it as a full capo while I sing in a higher key using my 5-string capo.

I am crossing "Research Partial Capos" off my list of things to do. I have done more than enough. I will tinker with this book, and fix errors, and maybe add a few chords here and there. I am also aware that a restless person somewhere will perhaps find an old *Third Hand* capo and discover another profoundly useful idea that can't be done with my capos, and another inventor may take partial capo guitar somewhere new that I never imagined. I hope I live to see it.

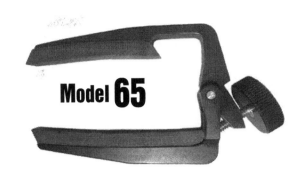

The guitar is big, and we are small, and this idea is endlessly entertaining as much as it is confusing.

It's very hard to wrap one's mind around the dimensions of this hidden world of new music that has been hiding in every guitar fingerboard for over 400 years.

But it's sure fun to try.

Harvey Reid (*York, Maine 2014*)

5

The Third Hand Capo

About Partial Capos

The use of different tunings of stringed instruments has been nearly universal throughout the history of the guitar. They change what strings can be sounded "open" or unfretted, and also the landscape of what is physically playable. Western European guitarists were using a number of "non-standard" tunings as early as the 1500's in Russia, England, France, Germany as well as Spain and Italy. The proliferation of tunings in Hawaiian slack-key guitar, American blues, folk, celtic and new age music has reached a point where individual guitarists often use dozens of tunings. Even the idea of "standard" tuning of the guitar (E-A-D-G-B-E) is eroding after a century or two of dominance, and players of many styles no longer use it. There are also dozens of banjo tunings, as well as retunings that fiddlers and even classical violinists and cellists regularly use.

> The reasons that we use different tunings are basically the same reasons you would use a partial capo, and the results are similar, but the two ideas are not at all the same.

Capos that clamp across all 6 strings have been used by nearly every guitar player for nearly 500 years. Banjo and string bass players have used small-scale versions of the partial capo for decades without the concept behind it spreading wider.

The partial capo is another quick way to change the limits of what is possible on the guitar. The reasons that we use different tunings are basically the same reasons you would use a partial capo, and the results are similar, but the two ideas are not at all the same. When different length strings are played against a fretboard, they behave differently than when the strings have been retuned.

A vital reason to use capos is that they let you enjoy the droning, open-string flavor of an open tuning, but you still have the option of sounding like you are not in a new tuning. You can always play barre chords or other familiar shapes above the capo and "erase" its effect.

Partial capos allows different open string pitches just like tunings, but fretted notes remain in the same location on the fingerboard. They allows another "dimension" of new musical possibilities on stringed instruments, roughly equivalent to that offered by different tunings, that would otherwise be impossible. It is also extremely useful and important, though also another level more confusing, to combine a partial capo with an altered tuning. You'll see these "hybrid tunings" a lot in this book, and we will combine partial capos with many different tunings that are readily achieved with normal string gauges.

Partial capo music sounds "right" to me and feels as guitaristic and natural to my hands and ears as anything else. I have written a large number of partial capo guitar pieces, and have used various capos to arrange a considerable number of traditional and popular melodies.

To date, my 30 recordings feature over 200 songs and instrumentals that use about 30 different configurations of a partial capo, dating back to 1980. Most of them are in standard tuning, though many of them combine a partial capo and a non-standard tuning. It's time to stop writing books and go record more guitar music.

> There are millions of ways to put partial capos on a guitar fingerboard, but only a small number of them are really musically useful.
>
> This book guides you through the confusing landscape of new possibilities, and shows 42 ways to use *Liberty* partial capos in standard tuning, plus 28 more ideas that combine the capos with other tunings.

The Short-Cut Capo

About this Book

This is my 19th book on the subject of partial capos. I have been studying and using them for almost 40 years, and the ideas here are almost entirely the fruits of my own research. In these pages I show you a large number of ways to use the simple and elegant *Liberty* capos to play new music, and it is almost certainly much more information than anyone can digest, including me. That's why it is a book. It's far too much data for a YouTube video, your brain or your phone. This book was even too big, so I split it into 2 books. The really far-out ideas are in Book 2.

If you give a partial capo to a guitar player, they generally don't find much, and the enormity of all its possibilities remains mysteriously invisible. How to effectively use a partial capo is just not obvious, even to a good guitarist. The man who invented, patented and manufactured the first partial capo never discovered any of the common musical uses of it. I had one of his partial capos for several years before it occurred to me to put it in the *Esus* configuration, which is now by far the most common way to use one, and something I do nearly every time I pick up a guitar. This does not mean that we were fools– it means partial capos are tricky. It has taken me decades and a lot of time and effort to find the ideas in this book, and thousands of players who already own partial capos remain unaware of most of what their capos can do.

The knowledge of what strings to capo where, as well as the understanding of where to put your fingers– is vitally important and hard to figure out. It's only after you have used one for a while that the partial capo become "obvious," and then you wonder why everyone has not been using them all along.

The partial capo is confusing enough on its own, but the idea that it is equally useful to all levels of players is also hard to understand. The truth is that beginners as well as professionals can immediately start making new music with the skills they already have. There are new places to put your fingers, and you can instantly enjoy new sounds that often result when you put your fingers in familiar places. You don't have to understand it to use it.

Guitarists who have partial capos have also discovered that there is very little good information to be found about where to put the capos and where to put their fingers, and I know players who have used an *Esus* capo for decades at fret 2 without trying anything new. Most partial capos essentially come with no instructions, and the half dozen chords they show don't do much to indicate that the capo really needs a 400 page manual. This book contains over t chords, and details over 70 different musically useful ways to play music with one or more *Liberty* capos.

The vast majority of guitarists do not read music, so I chose to fill the book mostly with chords rather than particular songs or arrangements. Players of all levels should be able to try these chords, hear what they can do, and put them to use in their own music. It's a valuable music theory lesson to study the chord structure of these chords, since each is shown with its voicing and inversion information spelled out. The letter names of each note are shown for every chord, along with the scale positions they occupy with respect to the root note of the chord.

This book is by no means a complete encyclopedia of all chords. I tried to pick out chords that were good examples of the new sounds you can get with the partial capo, and ones that best illustrated the strengths and advantages of each capo configuration. (In general, the more chords I have included, the more musically interesting I think each configuration is.)

You'll still have to do some work to find the corresponding scale patterns, and to write and arrange the songs and instrumentals you are playing. Not all songs work well with partial capos, and it takes skill, time and luck to find the ones that really shine. The chords given here should get you started, and hopefully can point you in new directions toward other ideas you can use for your own music.

This book should provide a vital piece in the puzzle of the partial capo, and I encourage everyone to roll up their sleeves and enjoy the party.

There are thousands of chords here that neither you or Mel Bay have ever heard before, and one day somebody is going to write a hit song with some of them and this idea will take off like a rocket...

All partial capo configurations are not equivalent, and some of them offer vastly more musical options than others. I rejected hundreds of other ways to use partial capos, and the ones I have included in the book are generally the ones that work better, or that illustrate a concept.

Who Are Partial Capos For?

Partial capos have significant value for players of all skill levels, and for most styles of music.

BEGINNERS & CHILDREN

Certain capo configurations allow great-sounding music to be played with simpler fingerings. Partial capos offer the most effective ways to play simplified guitar, and provide full-sounding chords and a huge repertoire of music that is newly accessible to beginners. It's not easy to find those ideas in this book, but they are here.

PICKERS & INSTRUMENTALISTS

Most players today are using more than just standard tuning, and partial capos unlock another dimension in the guitar that is as large as what altered tunings offer. You can stay in any tuning and add capos, without having to re-learn the fingerboard. Or you can go deeper, and retune some strings as well as use partial capos.

SINGERS & SONGWRITERS

This is currently the largest group of guitarists currently using partial capos. Endless opportunities abound for fresh guitar sounds that can add a distinctive flavor to almost any kind of song.

GUITAR TEACHERS

Partial capos are helpful in guitar education in a number of ways. Not only can they help people get started, but they allow easier exploration of the neck, they help teach music theory and the fingerboard, and they are immensely useful for learning right-hand skills, especially fingerpicking.

AMATEURS & HOBBYISTS

Don't get overwhelmed by all the options and the technical talk about chord theory and capo strategy. Anybody can browse through this book and try out the capo ideas and listen to the new sounds. If the chord fingering is hard, skip it. There are plenty of easy ones.

PROFESSIONALS

Just flipping through this book it should be clear that there are an almost unlimited number of new ways to pull new chords, sounds and resonances from the guitar. Composers, arrangers, songwriters and performers can all enjoy a significant new set of tools for making innovative music.

About the Diagrams in This Book

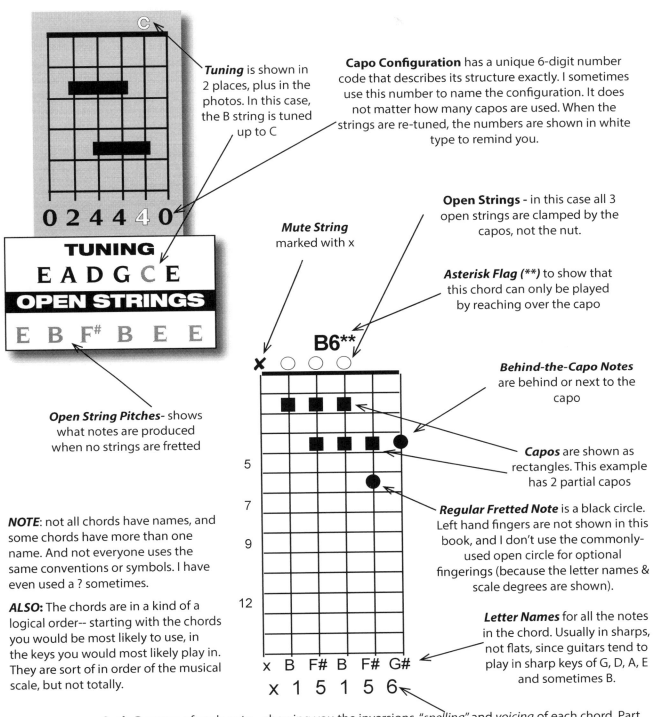

Tuning is shown in 2 places, plus in the photos. In this case, the B string is tuned up to C

Capo Configuration has a unique 6-digit number code that describes its structure exactly. I sometimes use this number to name the configuration. It does not matter how many capos are used. When the strings are re-tuned, the numbers are shown in white type to remind you.

0 2 4 4 4 0

TUNING
E A D G C E
OPEN STRINGS
E B F♯ B E E

Mute String marked with x

Open Strings - in this case all 3 open strings are clamped by the capos, not the nut.

Asterisk Flag (****)** to show that this chord can only be played by reaching over the capo

Open String Pitches- shows what notes are produced when no strings are fretted

B6**

Behind-the-Capo Notes are behind or next to the capo

Capos are shown as rectangles. This example has 2 partial capos

5

7

9

12

Regular Fretted Note is a black circle. Left hand fingers are not shown in this book, and I don't use the commonly-used open circle for optional fingerings (because the letter names & scale degrees are shown).

NOTE: not all chords have names, and some chords have more than one name. And not everyone uses the same conventions or symbols. I have even used a ? sometimes.

ALSO: The chords are in a kind of a logical order-- starting with the chords you would be most likely to use, in the keys you would most likely play in. They are sort of in order of the musical scale, but not totally.

x B F# B F# G#

x 1 5 1 5 6

Letter Names for all the notes in the chord. Usually in sharps, not flats, since guitars tend to play in sharp keys of G, D, A, E and sometimes B.

Scale Degrees of each note-- showing you the inversions, "*spelling*" and *voicing* of each chord. Part of what gives each chord its musical identity is determined by which numbers are present. The order in which they appear, and which of them are absent or *doubled* (repeated) is also a vital factor. There are many voicings of any chord, and only some of them are available on a guitar.

In this example, B is the root or 1, so the 5th of a B scale is F♯ and the 6th is a G♯. These numbers show you the structure and help you analyze and understand the sound of each chord.

5 1 1 1 1 3

5 1 1 1 3 5

1 3 6 1 2 5

5 1 1 1 5 5

5 1 1 3 4 1

1 3 5 1 3 2

1 3 5 1 3 4

5 1 3♭ 5 7 5

5 1 3♭ 5 7 6

1 3 5 1 3 7

1 3 5 1 3 7♭

1 3 5 1 5 1

1 3 5 1 5 2

1 3 5 1 5 3

Chord Voicings & Inversions

As you flip around this book, you'll see a lot of the same chord names -like E, E7, Em, A. Don't make the natural assumption that there are a lot of duplicates, and look more carefully at the scale numbers on the bottom of each chord diagram. You'll notice that the "spelling" of these different *inversions* and *voicings* are not all the same. If you compare their sound, a wealth of new harmonic subtlety opens up.

You always have different choices of chord voicings available in any guitar tuning, and how many there are depends on the tuning, the notes that make up that chord, and your left hand agility. (Many players fail to see the depth of this idea and think that there is only one E chord and a couple different C chords, for example.) There are actually about 20 playable voicings of an E major chord in standard tuning. There are over 5 or 6 times as many unique voicings of the E chord and A in this book. If you haven't ventured outside of standard tuning or used a partial capo, then almost all of them will be new to your ears.

The partial capo gives you quick access to a vast and diverse world of new chords, as well as a surprisingly large number of new ways of voicing familiar chords. Try to appreciate the complexity of all the choices and sounds that arise from the large number of new inversions and voicings of these chords, and the new musical opportunities that come with them. There are dozens of new ways to play other common chords, and a huge supply of chords you can't play any other way. You'll find some nice musical options when you are accompanying or writing a song. You may also find that particular voicings of some chords feel just right and others don't, and with some careful experimentation you can make a song really come alive.

It is a somewhat startling fact that more than half of the chords in this book are unique voicings that occur only once. Many more of them show up only a few times, and very few can be played without a partial capo.

Once you embrace this new world of harmonic ideas, your music will never sound the same again.

I thought about doubling the size of this book by putting next to each chord what the same sequence of notes would look like in standard tuning, to really hammer home what is going on inside each chord. Tunings and capo configurations are varied in how different they are from standard tuning, and some environments map to more exotic things than others.

SECTION 1

One Liberty Capo in Standard Tuning

Partial capos let you mimic the sound of open tunings, create new chords, inversions and voicings, and create other tuning-like sounds.

- Partial capos are not the same thing as an open tuning. They achieve similar results, but work differently.

- Songwriters will find fresh chords and new ideas, and new open-string resonances.

- Anyone can learn to get some new and different sounds out of their guitar, without retuning or re-learning the fingerboard.

- A world of new chord voicings become available, with fresh sounds that haven't been heard before.

- Most people think that "imitating tunings" is all a partial capo does, and are surprised to find out that they can be combined with any tuning, which we look at later.

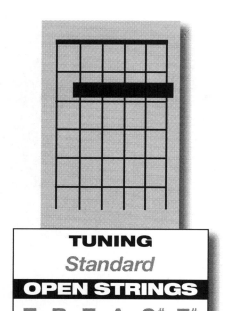

TUNING
Standard
OPEN STRINGS
E B E A C# F#

The Drop E configuration.

The 1, 4 and 5 chords in the key of D in *Drop D* tuning compared to the *Drop E* partial capo show how the chord shapes do not change with the partial capo the way they do when you retune the strings.

If you use an offset full capo to clamp only the top 5 strings, the body of the capo will probably get in your way, and block you from fretting bass strings behind the capo.

1~ Drop E "Top 5" (022222)

Important

This is conceptually the simplest way to use a partial capo, it's where the whole idea began, and it is the best introduction to the idea if you are trying to understand how partial capos work. There is an "Aha!" moment of understanding here that underlies all partial capoing. **You should engage and process this first if you are new to the partial capo.** You can do this with many types of full capos by just offsetting the capo by one string, though when you do that the body of the capo ends up on the treble side of the fingerboard, where it can get in the way of your fretting hand.

This is similar (but not identical!) to the common practice of tuning the 6th (low E) string down a whole step to D, usually called "*Drop D*" tuning. This capo configuration achieves the same result of having a low root note with a D chord, but requires less getting-used-to, since the notes on the bass string do not "move" the way they do in *Drop D* tuning. The partial capo allows you to get some richer-sounding chords in the keys of D, Dm and G without really changing the way you play. It also allows you to play in Dm and modal forms of D, since the chord shapes you would use to do that (Dm, C, Gm, F, Bb...) all play normally. None of those work as well in *Drop D* tuning, since you have to mute the bass E string.

It is useful for both instrumental music and for songs, and gives your D-based chord shapes (which sound as E) a rich open 6th string. Common chord shapes like G, C, F, Bm etc. all play normally, though they sound a whole step higher because of the capo.

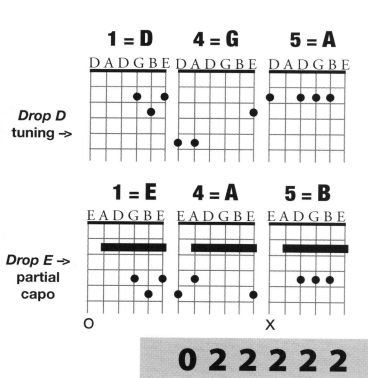

Drop D tuning →

1 = D   4 = G   5 = A

Drop E → partial capo

1 = E   4 = A   5 = B

0 2 2 2 2 2

Some Chords in the Drop E Configuration p.1
TUNING: Standard

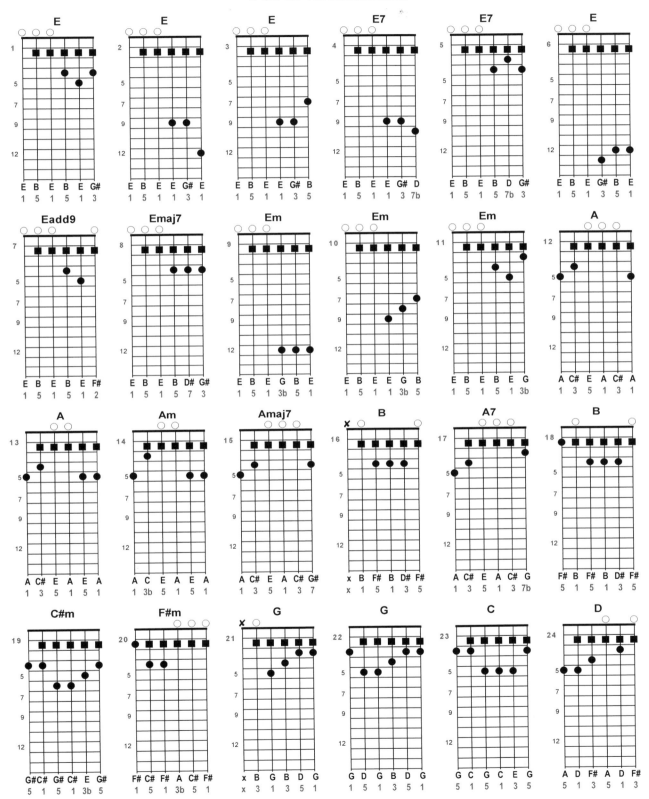

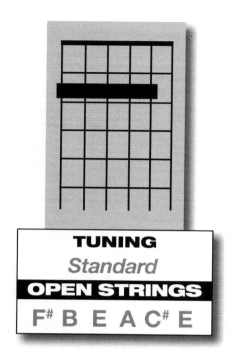

2 - Bottom 5 (222220)

This is a way to get some slightly different musical colors by adding an open high E note to chords or melodic passages.

It is useful mostly for playing songs in keys that would benefit from adding an E note. If you play in D or G position or their relative minor keys it will add a consonant note to some of your basic chords. If you play in C or Am position it will add more "colorful" notes to your chords, since you'll be adding a 9th (E) to a D chord and an 11th to a Bm.

I did that when I recorded "*Twilight*" on the *Coming of Winter* CD in 1986 in Am position. The capo colored the Am, E 7, F and G chord chords by adding an 11th on top of the Am, a 9th on the C, a 6th on the F chord, and a 7^b on the E chord. (I also used a straight capo 1 on *Twilight*, so it actually sounded in Cm.) The effect is subtle, but I never play that song without those added notes in the chords. (The most distinctive chord in that song is played as an Am with the thumb adding the 1st fret on the low E string for a low G note that is a 5$^\#$ bass note. I call it a *Bm11/G* and it is done by adding a 3rd fret G on the bottom of chord #6 just above the capo.

This is not a "deep" configuration, and it is unlikely that you would want to do more than a few songs with it. It is quick, and not that confusing. Most players can manage tunings or capo configurations where only one outer string is different from standard tuning.

As with the previous configuration, you can usually just offset a full capo, though unlike *Drop E* (#1), the capo does not get in the way of your fretting hand.

TUNING
Standard
OPEN STRINGS
F$^\#$ B E A C$^\#$ E

At the 2nd fret making the "Bottom 5" configuration.

PARTIAL CAPOS IN HISTORY

Capos have existed for centuries, but the partial capo surprisingly has not been a part of guitar playing until the last 30 years or so. I have done some historical research, and have concluded that at least a few people knew about partial capos in parts of Europe in the early 1800's, and produced the only instruments ever made with built-in mechanisms. I have posted a lengthy web page about this on **www.PartialCapo.com** in the history section.

If you find the idea of a partial capo confusing, you are in good company. Once you get used to them, the idea becomes obvious. But something has kept millions of guitarists from using this rather simple and quite useful tool for centuries. That's the biggest mystery, since different tunings and full capos have been used all along by everyone.

2 2 2 2 2 0

Some Chords in the Bottom 5 Configuration p.1
TUNING: Standard

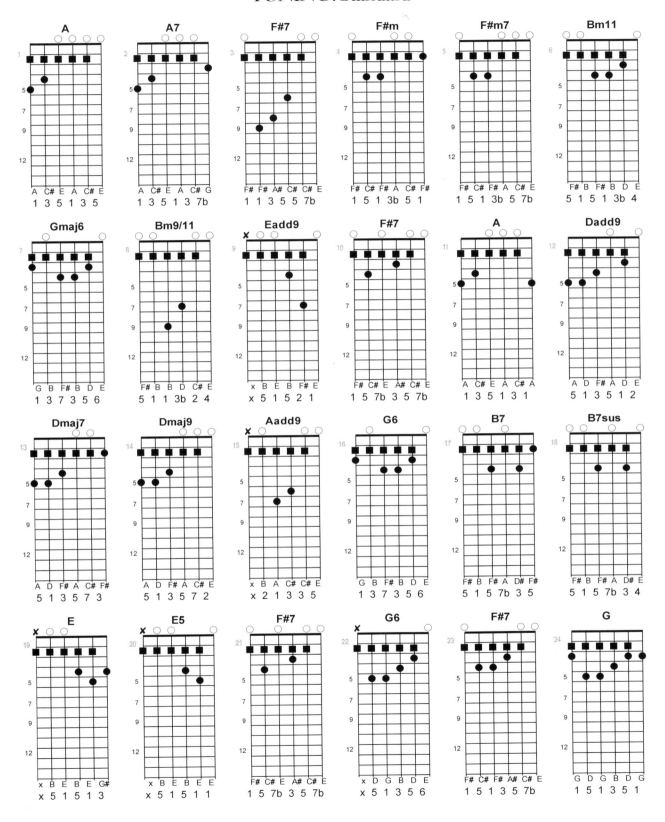

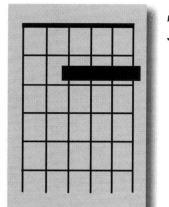

TUNING
Standard
OPEN STRINGS
E A E A C# F#

A Model 43 making Half-Open A.

3~ Top 4 "Half-Open A" (002222)

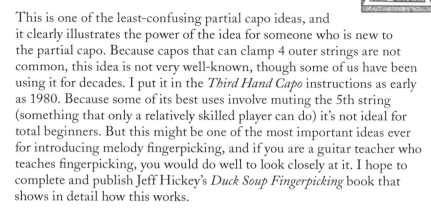

This is one of the least-confusing partial capo ideas, and it clearly illustrates the power of the idea for someone who is new to the partial capo. Because capos that can clamp 4 outer strings are not common, this idea is not very well-known, though some of us have been using it for decades. I put it in the *Third Hand Capo* instructions as early as 1980. Because some of its best uses involve muting the 5th string (something that only a relatively skilled player can do) it's not ideal for total beginners. But this might be one of the most important ideas ever for introducing melody fingerpicking, and if you are a guitar teacher who teaches fingerpicking, you would do well to look closely at it. I hope to complete and publish Jeff Hickey's *Duck Soup Fingerpicking* book that shows in detail how this works.

Most-often used for playing in G position and sounding in A, this allows you to play the basic 1, 4 and 5 chords with fewer left-hand fingers, yet full open-string bass support. It is an ideal way to simplify left-hand chording for melody fingerpicking. You can form basic chords with fewer fingers than normal, which leaves those vital "extra fingers" to play melodies around the chord positions. You can also play in C position (to sound in D) a song that needed a strong 5 chord, like *John Hardy*, the old bluegrass song.

You can do some bluegrass-style flatpicking on the top 4 strings in G position this way, and get some nice ringing bass support, and it works pretty well for banjo songs like *Old Joe Clark* that are modal and usually played in the key of A, since the 5 chord (E) is not the strongest feature of this configuration. The modal "drop chord" is just played as a normal F shape, and sounds as a G chord.

You can get a good-sounding 1 chord (you play G, it sounds as A) with one finger (chord #1), your 4 chord can be played as a usual C chord shape (#18), or with one less finger (#16). The only drawback to this configuration is that the 5 chord (D position which sounds as E) has a muted 5th string (#27), and it only really works if you have a pretty accurate right hand. You do get the open 4th and 6th strings as roots of the chord, and you can play D and D7 shapes with the left hand pretty easily. Take a good look at what I call *Drop A* (Configuration #37). It is a variant of this, and though it requires retuning a string, it has most of the advantages of *Half-Open A* plus an easy and rich 5 chord.

0 0 2 2 2 2

TUNING: Standard

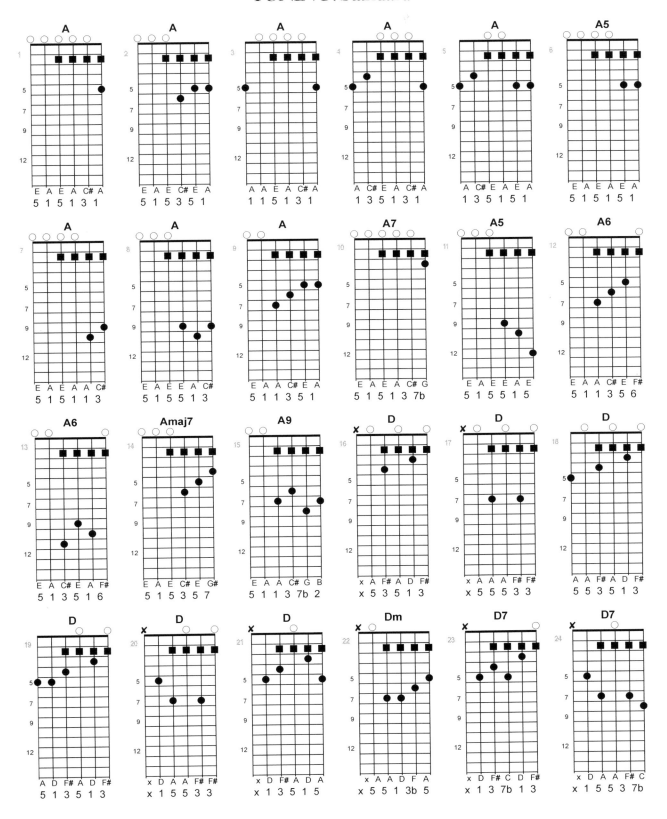

TUNING: Standard

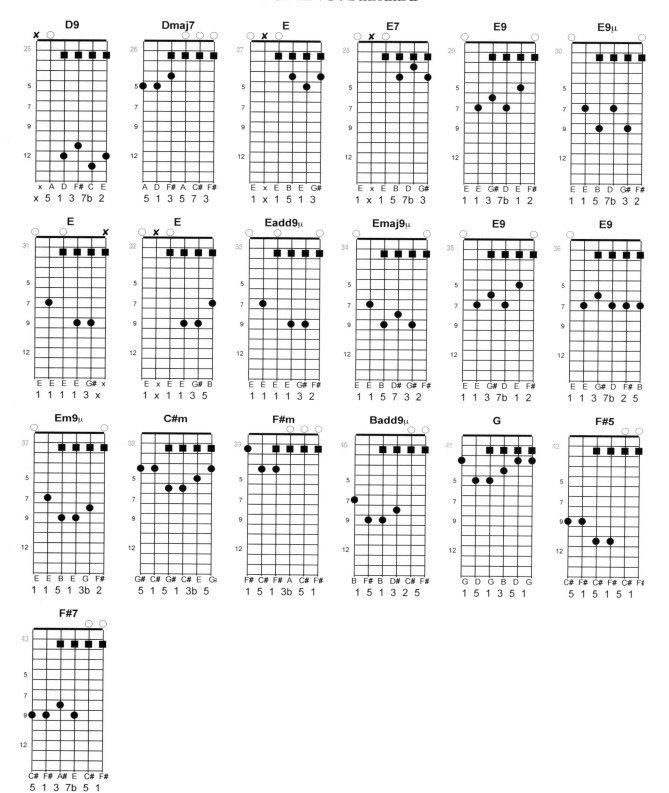

Frère Jacques (Round)

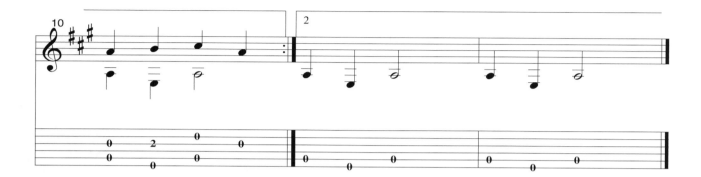

About Frère Jacques

A lot of people have convinced themselves that they don't need a partial capo, and if you are flipping through this book, wondering why such a "supposedly" valid idea is not widespread, thinking that it is not connected to any "real music" and looking over your shoulder to see if anyone else is doing it;– here is a blunt example of something that anyone can understand musically.

Everybody is familiar with the musical idea of a round, and probably everyone has sung this as a child. It is very hard to play two parts of the round on guitar without a partial capo, and quite easy if you use one. There are an amazing number of 0's (open strings) in the TAB, and even a novice fingerpicker could learn this (or most of it) in half an hour.

ABOUT NAMING CHORDS

• **Chords are usually named and described according to the "root" note**. It is not always clear what the root note is, and you might use a chord I have called "E-something" as an "A-something" chord, which would give it a different name. So feel free to disagree with the names I give some chords if you hear them differently.

• **Chords need to be described in context.** The name of a chord depends on its function in a song, and in a chord book there isn't any. The same group of notes could have a different purpose in 2 keys, and warrant different names.

• **Some common chords have more than one name.** For example, depending on the root, C6= C-E-G-A and Am7= A-C-E-G have the same notes but in a different order. And a chord with 1-3-5-6 is a 6th chord, but a 1-3-5-6-7$^\flat$ is also usually just called a 6th; also sometimes a *dominant 6th* or 6/7.

• **Omitted and doubled notes** change the sound of chord also, but there is no indication in the name of the chord to show that the 3rd or 5th might be missing, or that there might be three 5's and only one 3.

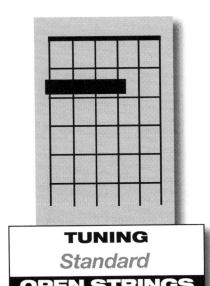

TUNING
Standard

OPEN STRINGS

F# B E A B E

The Bottom 4 configuration.

4 ~ Bottom 4 (222200)

This is a way to get some deeper chord colors by adding two open high strings to them. Like the 222220 configuration (#2), it is pretty easy to get used to, since you can pretty much play normally and see what happens to your chords. Like *Half-Open A* (#3), common partial capos have not been able to clamp XXXXOO like this. So the sounds from this are fresh even to partial capo veterans who may be familiar with a *Drop E* or *Esus* type capo.

Since the open treble strings are B and E, you get a few different options for weaving them into your music. If you play in C position, the capo will cause you to sound in D, and the open B string adds a 6th and the high E string a 9th to the D chord. If you play in D position, sounding in E, then those 2 open strings will mean that a lot of your chords won't need to be fretted on the top 2 strings. This should open up some new possibilities on the low end.

You can also play in Em position, and your regular Em chord becomes a nice-sounding F#m7 with an added 11th (Chord #42) that I have called a Fm11, though technically it should have a 9th also. For partial capo skeptics, it's a perfect example of a guitar chord that neither you nor Mel Bay ever heard before, because you can't finger 2-4-4-2-0-0 in standard tuning. It is an interesting chord, and it is as simple as playing an Em chord with the capo on. If partial capos had been around for years, someone would have probably used this in a hit song by now.

I have recorded only one song with this configuration: "*Song of the Boatman*" on the *Wind & Water* CD in 1988. I played in Am position, and took advantage of the added colors to the Am and G chords. They sounded as Bmadd11 (#17) and Aadd9 chords (#4) because of the capo. When you play F and G fingerings, you "remove" the partial capo effect, as long as you play the 4 finger G shape (chord #1).

Later in this book we will also explore some nice sounds that open up if you tune the low E string down a whole step to what is usually called "*Drop D*" tuning and still keep the capo in this position. (See configuration #29)

222200

Some Chords in the Bottom 4 Configuration p.1
TUNING: Standard

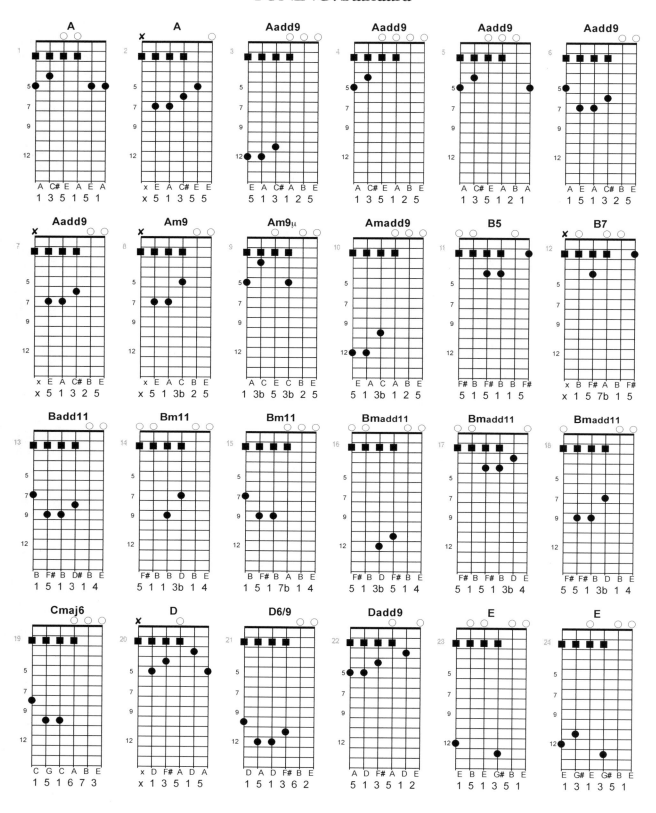

TUNING: Standard

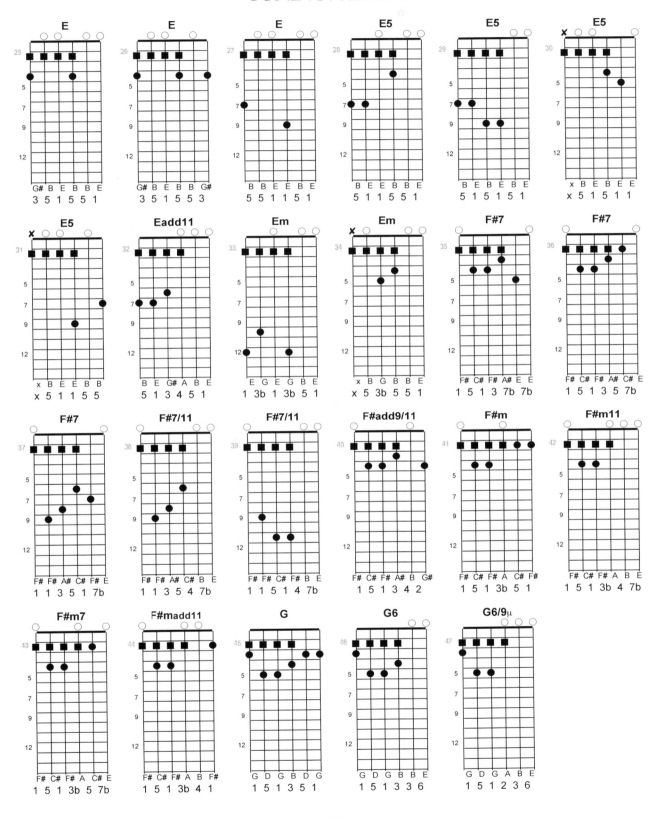

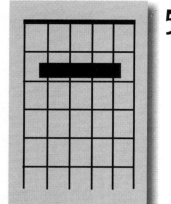

5- E-Modal "Double-Drop E" (022220)

TUNING
Standard
OPEN STRINGS
E B E A C# E

It would be reasonable to call this the *"Middle 4"* configuration also, though I named it *E-Modal* in 1982 because the tuning that this emulates, where both E strings are lowered to D, was commonly called *"D Modal"* tuning. (It is also sometimes called *"Double Drop E,"* because the tuning when you drop both E strings to D is frequently called *"Double Drop D."* It's hard to pronounce *Double Drop E* precisely.)

Mostly for playing in D, Dm or G positions, this configuration sets up the two E strings as drones. You could also play in C position, especially on songs with a strong 2 chord, which would put you in D, and take advantage of the added 9th on the top string on your 1 chord. There are some nice new chord colors, but you can still find your way around the fingerboard using familiar-shaped chords, and it is not a difficult landscape for a partial capo newcomer. When you play in C, you are used to not having open bass strings, so you play C, F and G shapes the way you always do, and new things happen.

You can really sound like you are in a full open tuning with this one, and it can be great for modal-sounding songs or instrumentals. It has a number of advantages over actually retuning the two E strings down a whole step to D. Other than specific chords, you can easily play normal chords and get out of the "drone zone" when you want to, by just playing barre chords and regular chord shapes. This is an important concept in all of partial capoing.

The E-Modal configuration.

This configuration also offers the only way I know of to play a "walking" boogie-woogie bass line (I have included the *"E-Modal Boogie"* TAB) on all 3 chords of a 12-bar blues in E, without leaving the nut position. In standard tuning with no capo this normally requires difficult left-hand stretches above a B barre chord to do even the simplest walking lines. Play in D position (use chord #9 to start,) but you get an extra spare finger on the 1 and 4 chords (play G and A shapes) to walk the bass line. It's quite surprising, especially if you have played blues guitar for a while. (New ideas are rare in blues– it's usually about old.)

0 2 2 2 2 0

Some Chords in the E-Modal Configuration p.1

TUNING: Standard

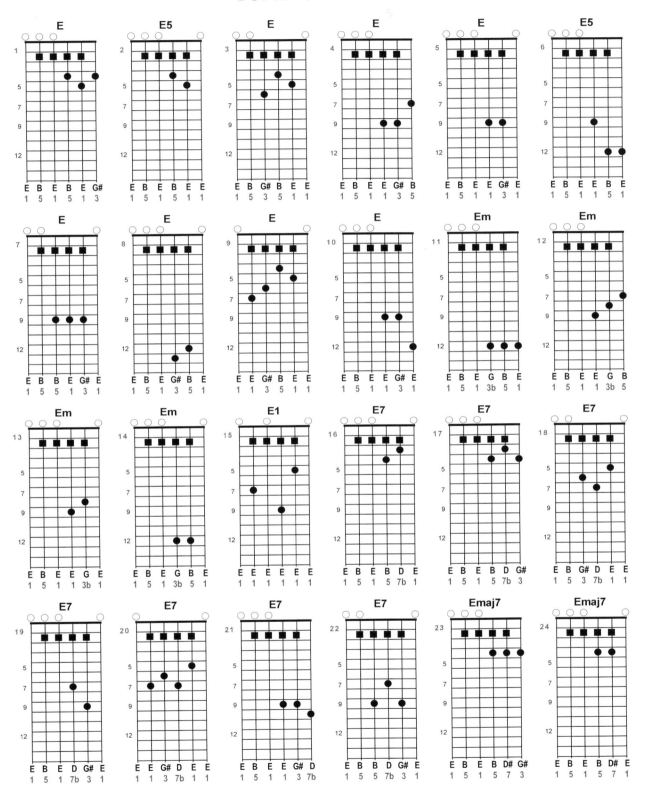

TUNING: Standard

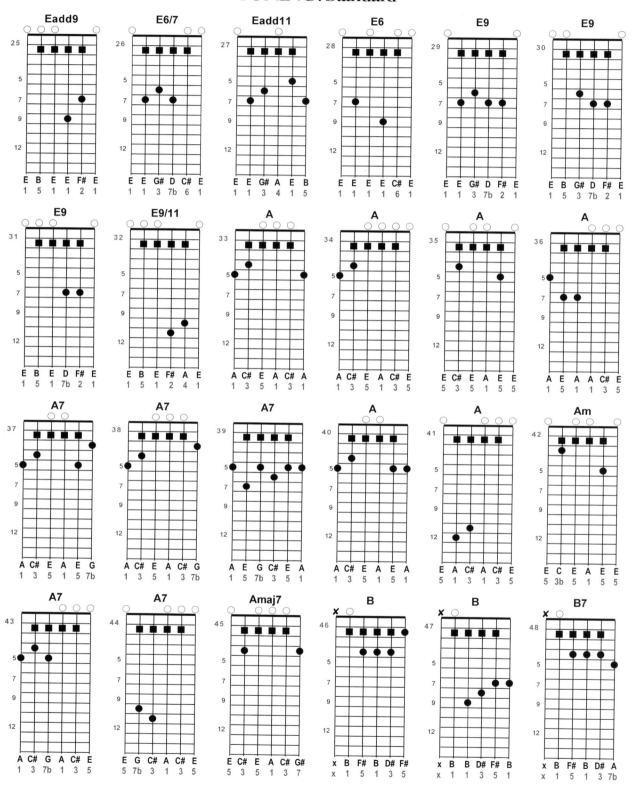

TUNING: Standard

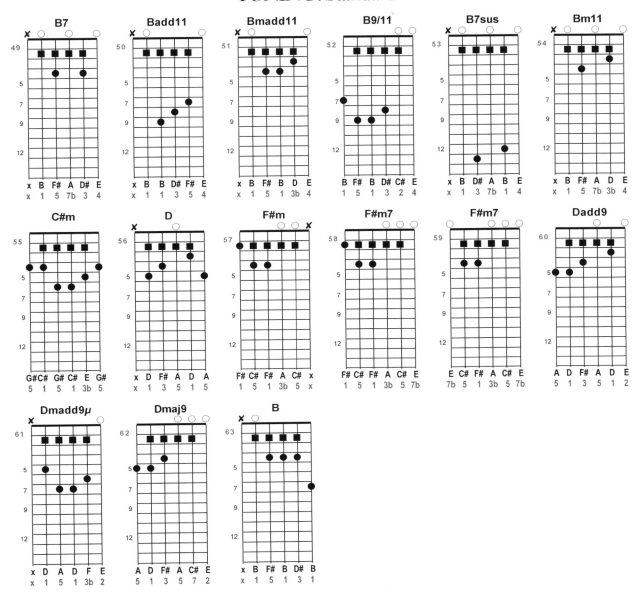

CHORD NAME CONFUSION

There is no universal chord-naming system or standard. The names *Esus* and *Esus4* for the *suspended* chord (1-4-5 scale notes) are used interchangeably. Some people (including me) call an added 9th note (scale degree 2) an "*add9*" chord, while some call the same thing an "*add2*." Technically, it has to do with which octave the added note is in, but since guitar chords are always scattered across several octaves, guitarists are often less rigorous, and may call a chord with an added 2nd a 9th. (It could be technically a 16th also, but nobody bothers to do that.)

The **slash chord** notation is sometimes used, especially in guitar books, for a "*Mr. Bojangles*" type descending bass line that is played against a chord. When you play a C chord and "walk" down a bass line underneath, it makes sense to think of the progression as C/C, C/B (C chord with a B bass note), C/A etc. rather than as a chord based on the root note B then one based on A. I support this idea, and have included a few of them in this book.

E-Modal Boogie

Harvey Reid

E-suspended (Esus) Configuration

The *Esus* (022200) configuration is the only one in my *Top 10* list that just uses a single capo in standard tuning. It is probably the most widely-used partial capo idea, and the *Liberty Model 43* does it beautifully. It's quite likely that you will spend a lot of time doing this, no matter what level player you are. Here the capo is shown attaching from the treble side.

DADGAD tuning has gained increasing popularity since it first appeared in the early 1960's. Many Celtic-style guitarists use this tuning almost exclusively, though a significant number of folk, country and pop songwriters have also discovered its charms. With an *Esus* capo to form the E suspended chord, the open string pitches are the same as if you had a capo on fret 2 in DADGAD tuning, and the "flavor" of the two are somewhat similar.

It is possible to play a few things with the capo that sound the same as their DADGAD counterparts, but only things played on strings 3-4-5 will have identical fingering. *Esus* is in no way "equivalent" to DADGAD tuning. In many ways, it is easier to play things like fiddle-tune melodies in *Esus*, since you can play standard tuning "closed-position" scales. You can generally play melodies in 2 octaves in *Esus*, and in DADGAD this is rare, since the higher octave requires extensive position-shifting, and you have to struggle to keep some bass-string support.

Esus has the disadvantage that so much music is played in the key of D. D is a crucial key for guitarists, especially those who play along with fiddles, mandolins, dulcimers and other traditional instruments. If the key of D is essential for you, try using heavier-gauge strings and tune the whole guitar down 2 frets, which will also give you the slack-string tone that is such a part of the DADGAD sound. Your other option is to get a baritone guitar, many of which have scale lengths that are exactly 2 frets longer than a regular guitar. You could then capo 2 and be at standard pitch. When you play *Esus* capo music you will then be pitched the same as DADGAD tuning.

022200

TUNING
Standard

OPEN STRINGS

E B E A B E

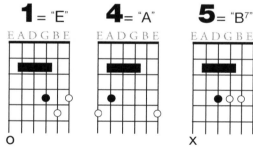

The Esus configuration.

6~ E-Suspended "Esus" (022200)

Esus (pronounced "E-suss") is short for *"E-Suspended,"* the chord formed here by the capo. It has become the most common capo configuration, and I use it extensively. Contrary to some myths, I was the first guitarist to use this, and it is a primary reason I lost interest in the *Third Hand*, since it blocks vital notes at fret 2. From 1982 until 1996 I used sawed-off standard capos to make my single-purpose *Esus* capo. *Shubb* began to make the c7b in 1995.

You most often play in D position, and you will sound in E because of the capo. *Esus* is very commonly used by serious players for writing and arranging complex music. It also has great value for beginners and everyone else in-between. It's a very accessible and "friendly" environment.

Esus is also extremely strong for playing in E minor and the various modal keys (especially *Mixolydian* & *Dorian*) associated with E. You can also cross-key and play in G position to sound in A, or even in Gm position to sound in Am. *Esus* offers a huge number of voicings for the E, A and B chords, and you can experiment with fitting them to a variety of songs. **Chords 4, 5 & 6 in the chart on the next page (plus some others later) are basically the reason why you want a 3-string capo and not just a universal model, because they have vital notes that are next to or behind the capo on the top 2 strings.**

Esus is one of the easiest and best ways to start playing guitar. Until my 2011 discovery of *"Liberty Tuning"* it was the best approach for simplified guitar. You will need to find songs you can sing in the key of E. (Or capo up to F, G or A with a full capo below the *Esus*.)

1 = "E"   **4** = "A"   **5** = "B7"

E A D G B E   E A D G B E   E A D G B E

O   X

- These fingerings allow you to make 1, 4 & 5 chords in the key of E with only one finger. The white dots show optional fingerings (that just form regular D, G and A chords).
- Only one string is muted in all three chords. (The bass E string is muted on the 5 chord)
- There are thousands of 3-chord songs you can start playing immediately.
- The "training" chords this teaches you are actually part of normal D-G-A7 chords, which is usually where beginning guitar chording starts. So the skills you learn doing this will transfer to later learning and beginners won't have to "unlearn" their finger positions as they progress.
- The chord names are shown in quotes because they are actually *E5, Aadd9* and *B7sus* chords, which function like E, A and B7 chords in most songs. The extra notes in them actually sound better than "normal" chords in a lot of songs, though in other songs they may not suit your tastes.

022200

TUNING: Standard

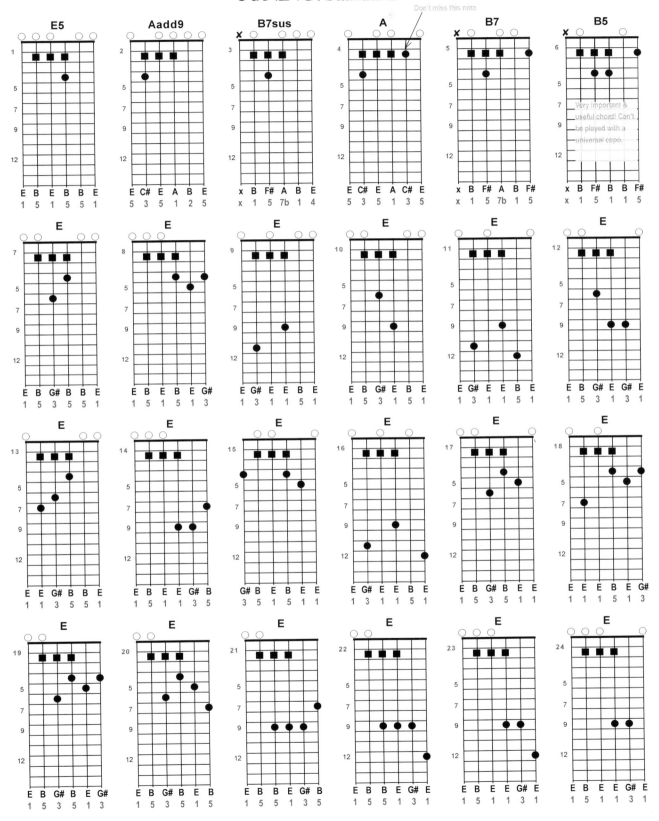

TUNING: Standard

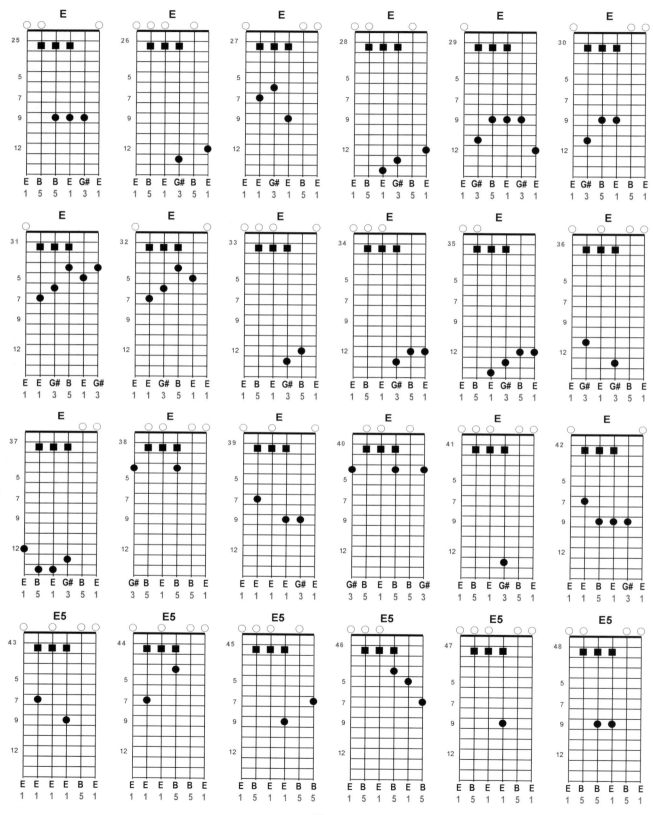

Some Chords in the Esus Configuration p.3
TUNING: Standard

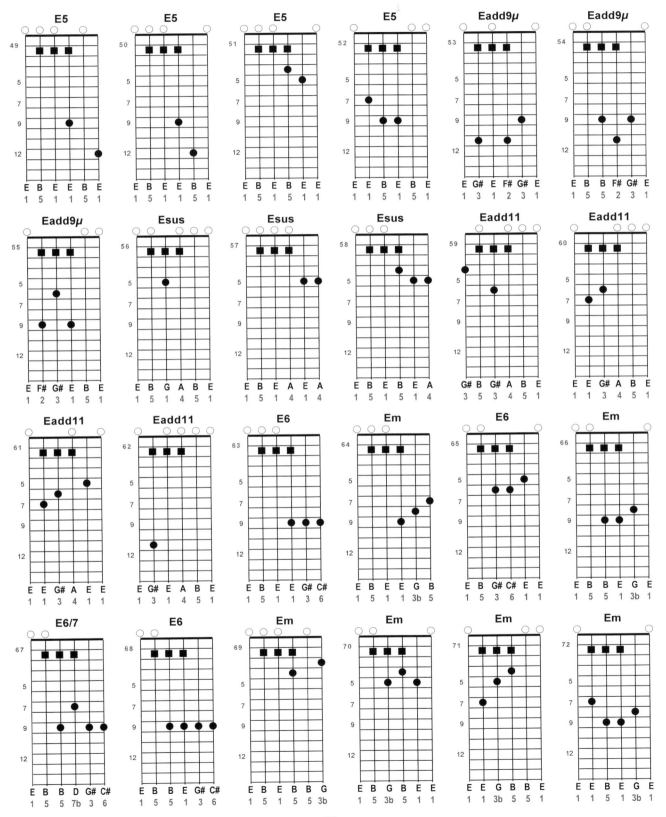

33

TUNING: Standard

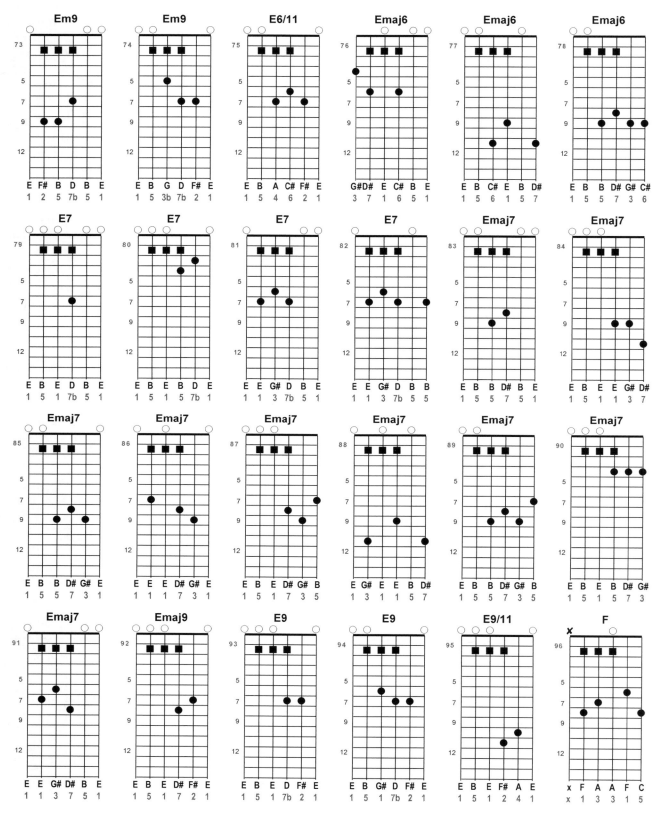

TUNING: Standard

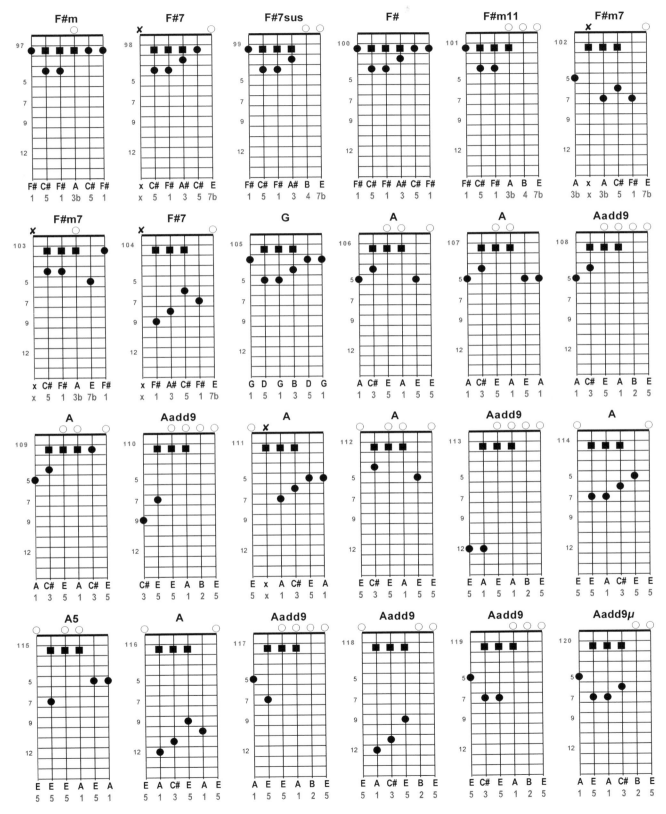

Some Chords in the Esus Configuration p.6
TUNING: Standard

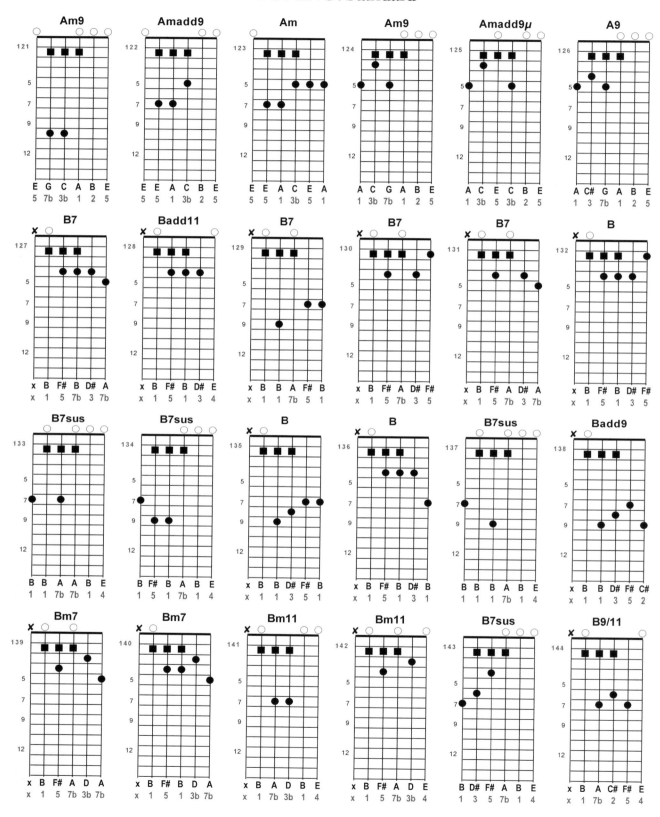

36

TUNING: Standard

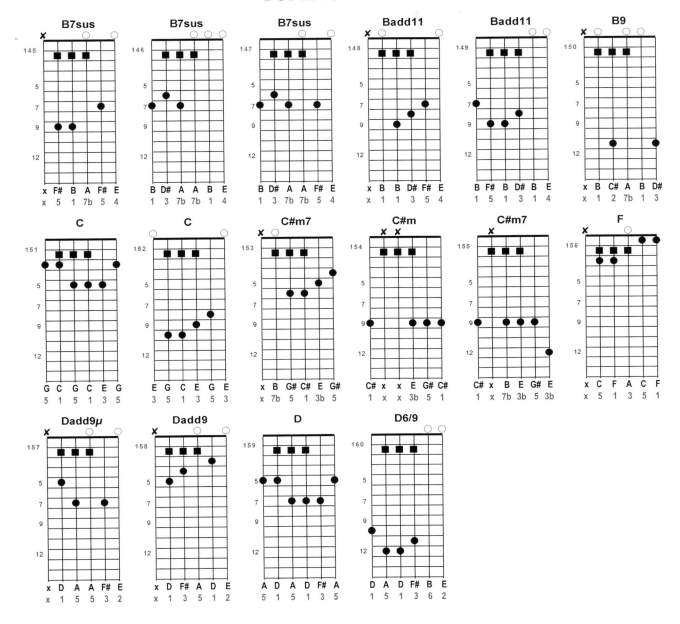

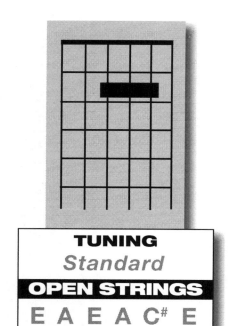

7- Open A (002220)

TUNING
Standard
OPEN STRINGS
E A E A C# E

Here the capo forms an A chord. It's one of the most obvious ways to put a partial capo on a guitar, and the first one I started with in 1976. It is pretty easy to get used to, and a good place to get oriented if you are new to the capo idea. In the early years, this was at the center of my partial capo world, though I have used it less often as I have found "deeper" configurations. I still use it a lot on 6-string banjo to create an open-tuned banjo sound that sounds a lot like a 5-string.

You can strum open-tuning-like chords, or play intricate instrumental music, and it "feels" and sounds a lot like you are playing in *Open A* (or *Open G*) tuning, though you are still in standard tuning. Just play in G position and look for what happens with the open strings. It's not great for cross-key playing. The 1 (A) and 4 (D) chords are easy in this configuration, since you just play G and C chord shapes, though it takes some skill to get a full, 6-string 5 (E) chord or to skip the 5th string with the right hand to play easier 5 chords.

This configuration is very helpful for learning right hand fingerpicking and cross-picking skills, since you can hold down a chord with the capo and not have to think about your left hand at all.

Fretting notes up and down a single string while the others drone is a great way to learn the timing you need for playing melody-style finger picking. You can also do a pretty good imitation of a dulcimer by playing melodies on just the 2nd or 3rd strings and droning the rest. I often capo my guitar up 5 frets before putting on the *Open A* capo (sounding in the key of D) and then play some "faux-frailing" techniques that sound like a banjo, especially when I add a full capo at fret 5 below the partial.

Chords with an asterisk (*) involve reaching over the capo to fret notes under or behind it.

Open A configuration. You can also attach the capo from the treble side if you need to for different access to notes near and behind the capo.

THE "E-1" UNISON CHORD

I don't like to invent notation, but could not find any name for this anywhere. There is definitely no way to do it in standard tuning without a partial capo, and not many ways to do it at all on a guitar. In chord #40 in the *Open A* configuration, the second chord diagram is not a chord at all. It is just six E's, in three octaves, and the "spelling" is 1-1-1-1-1-1. It actually sounds nice, because the timbre of each string is different, and it is useful for certain melodies. It's hard to play, but worth mentioning. You can also play it in *Esus* capo configuration and others.

0 0 2 2 2 0

TUNING: Standard

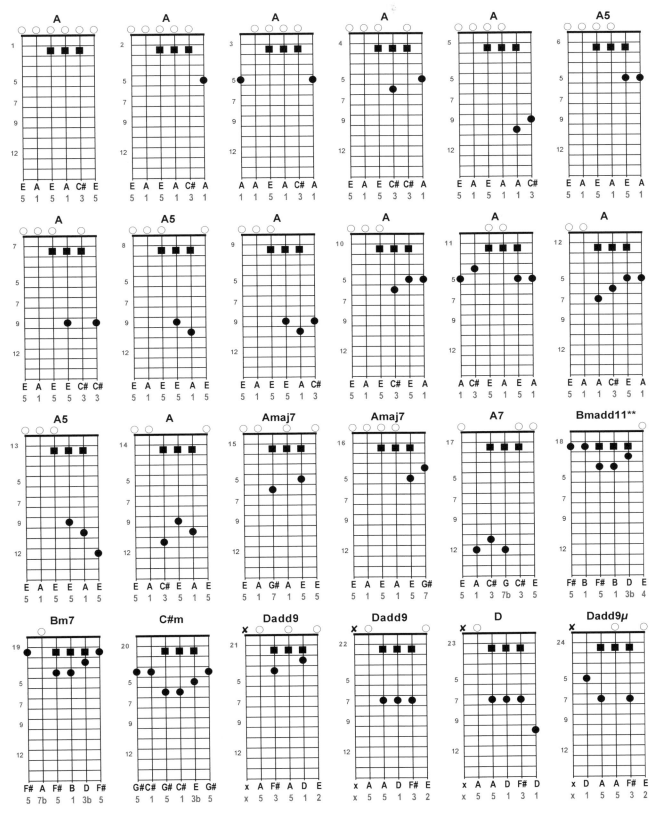

TUNING: Standard

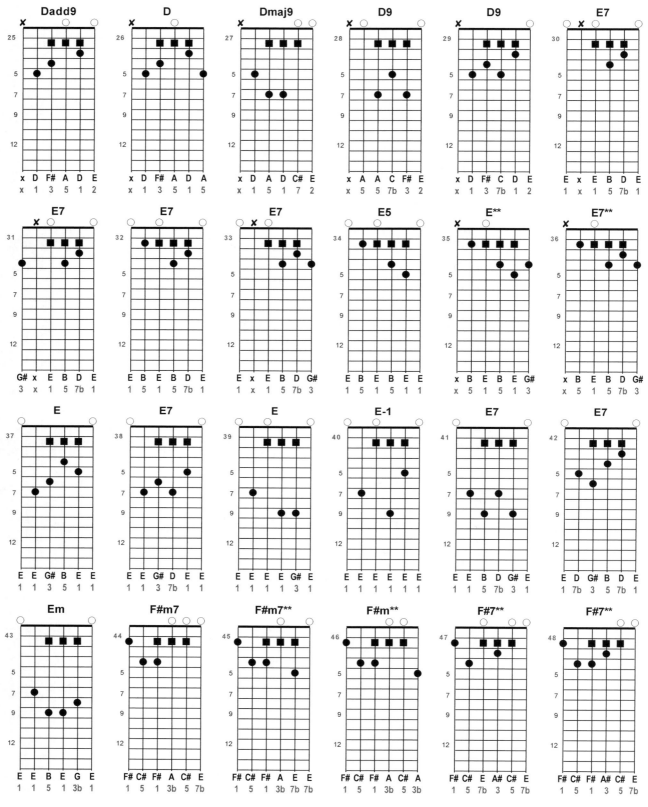

SO MANY CHOICES FOR CHORDS

It takes a while to realize how there can be so many ways to voice the same chord, and that they have different musical value. Unless you have studied the guitar somewhat, you may only be aware of a few different ways to play a chord, and not realize that there can be so many choices. This is a vital reason why we use open tunings and partial capos-- not just to get open string resonances, but to be able to get a whole new "menu" of choices for our chords, with different "flavors" and "moods."

There are some distinctive and really noticeable voicings in this book that might be just what you want for writing or arranging a song, and the ones you like will depend on the song. New voicings can add a whole new dimension to your music. It's also not intuitive that so many of the chord voicings in this book are unique, and appear only once.

The partial capo really brings this all into focus, for several reasons. When you set up a droning capo configuration, you find a large number of ways to play a few chords. You also have this same "diversity" of voicings when you use an open tuning, but since the names of the notes on the fingerboard all change whenever you change the tuning, it's not as easy to be aware of what is going on. In the chord diagrams in this book I show you where every note lies in every chord. It's a great theory lesson to study the small numbers below each chord.

ABOUT "MU" CHORDS

The legendary rock band *Steely Dan* made extensive use of an unusual type of chord that they named the "*mu*" or *μ* chord, and wrote about in their songbook. They are major chords with an added 2nd that also still have the 3rd, and there are really only three that you can play in standard tuning. When both notes are present in the same octave (it is often called an add2 when you add the 2nd in a lower octave and an add9 when the added note is an octave higher) there is a lovely effect. These chords have existed on the piano for a long time, but were never given a special name or attention on guitar.

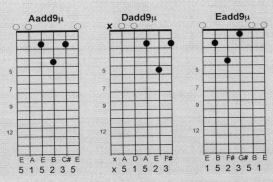

Aadd9μ	Dadd9μ	Eadd9μ
E A E B C# E	x A D A E F#	E B F# G# B E
5 1 5 2 3 5	x 5 1 5 2 3	1 5 2 3 5 1

In standard tuning, it is hard to add the 2nd without removing the 3rd. When you use a partial capo, they become a lot more common on guitar, and there are dozens of them scattered around this book (two are on the previous page) that have a 2 and a 3 next to each other. They are often but not always on adjacent strings, and some of the configurations where the capo is in the middle at the 5th or seventh fret mean that one of the treble strings played open or the capo can add this note.

I have flagged many of them with a Greek letter μ after the chord, and sometimes also "minor mu" chords. I probably should have also made up a symbol and flagged some of the other similarly interesting chord extensions that are scattered around this book, such as with added 4th and 6ths that retain the 3rds and 5ths right next to them.

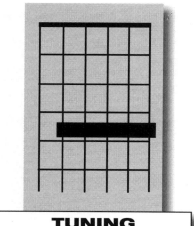

TUNING
Standard

OPEN STRINGS

E C# F# B D# G#

8- Drop C (044444)

There is no common counterpart to this in the world of open tunings, though a few players will tune the low E string down 4 frets to C. If you do that, you don't get much use out of the notes on the bass E string for chords, and its function is just as a low drone or "*bourdon*," as such a string was called long ago. I marked this as "important" because it is so easy to use, and requires very little re-thinking. There are a few songs in everyone's repertoire that benefit greatly from this idea, and you should try it.

Since lowering the E string is usually called "*Drop D*" tuning, and capoing 022222 is called "*Drop-E*" I call this "*Drop-C.*" This configuration is only really useful for playing songs in C position, which will actually sound in the key of E. You gain a low-E bass note on the C chord shape, and you can also use this low note to support the 4 chord, which is played as an F but sounds as an A chord (chord #6).

You pretty much just play C, F and G chords normally, and you get some "free" bass-string support. It makes a nice full sound that combines the low E bass note with chords fretted pretty high up the neck on the treble side. I use this heavily on my song "*From Where I Stand*" on the *Blues & Branches* album, and feature chord #11.

It is easy to get used to the *Drop C* capo position, because you just play in C normally. You can even ignore the low E string drone and play C, F and G as if you had a full capo on fret 4. (#5) The weakness is that you no longer have a root bass note when you play a 2 or 2m chord (feels like D, sounds as F#) and you also have to avoid the bass string or reach over the capo when you play 3 (feels like E, sounds as G#)or 6 chords (feels like A or Am, sounds as C# or C#m).

Model 65 forming "Drop C" partial capo configuration (044444)

"POWER CHORDS"

The "power chord," (sometimes called "*neutral,*" "*modal,*" or "*indeterminate*" chord, because it has 1's and 5's and no musical 3rd) has no official name, and it is technically not even a chord. This chord is widely used in modal music, and rock guitarists love them for crashing rhythm. Power chords offer soloists more options for playing over them, since they do not establish "tonality" the way major or minor chords do. I notate it as E5 in this book, which is the most common symbol used for it in guitar publications. There are only a few ways to play them in standard tuning, and dozens of examples in this book with only 1-5 notes.

044444

TUNING: Standard

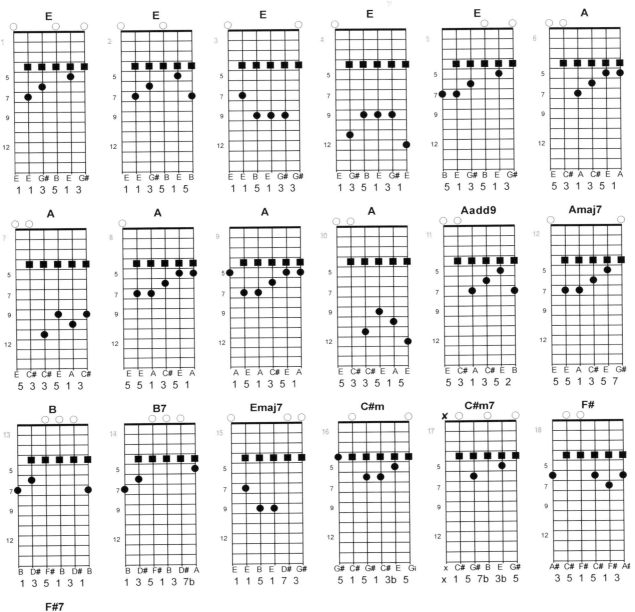

Don't forget that you can always put on a full capo
below one or more partial capos. It just raises the pitch
of everything. You'll need to do this for singing in higher
keys, playing along with other instruments, or just to get
a brighter and different timbre from your guitar.

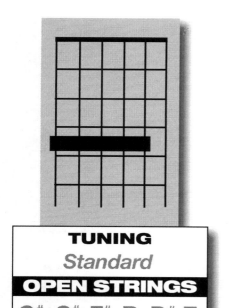

TUNING
Standard
OPEN STRINGS
G# C# F# B D# E

A Model 65 clamping the Bottom 5 @ 4 configuration from the bass side.

A Model 65 clamping the Bottom 5 @ 4 configuration from the treble side.

9- Bottom 5 @4 (444440)

This one is a surprising amount of fun, though it works best when you arpeggiate the chords or fingerpick, since there is a E^b-E dissonant interval on the treble end. It's sort of a mirror image of the previous one, and the difference between these two is a good lesson in how partial capos work. With the drone bass E string in configuration #8 (*Drop C*), you play in C position, sound in E and you have a big bass note underneath the higher-pitched treble strings. Here the idea is to use it more like a 5th string of a banjo, and interweave it with adjacent strings to add color and scale notes to the top end of a variety of chords. In the days of lute playing, a big drone bass note was called a "*bourdon*" string and a treble drone melody string was sometimes called a "*chanterelle*" string.

Your strongest option here is to play in G position, and sound in the key of B, though you can also play some nice things in C position also.

The Em chord shape (which sounds as a G#m) makes a nice minor ninth "mu" chord (p. 40). A very interesting chord is chord #4 in this chart, which I call a *9/11* chord. You'll notice that it contains the 1-2-3-4-5 scale notes, and the 1-2-3-4 are all in a row on the top four strings. If you weave this chord together with chord #9, you can arpeggiate a harp-like scale, and toss in all sorts of flowing melodic lines in an around your B chord. You could try playing a song like Bob Dylan's "*You Ain't Going Nowhere*" that uses the G-Am-C chord progression. (Lift the index finger off the B string on the Am shape and you'll get a cascading minor ninth sound.) It's not hard to embellish the chord changes with harp-like runs, and it is also not hard to just play normal G-Am-C chords also.

This is another example of how nice it is with a partial capo to be able to play some exotic voicings of things, and also to not do that and to sound just like standard tuning for other parts of the song.

The *Model 65* capo will do this from either side of the fingerboard. The only difference would be how it looks, or whether or not your fretting hand bumps into it as you play your music.

444440

TUNING: Standard

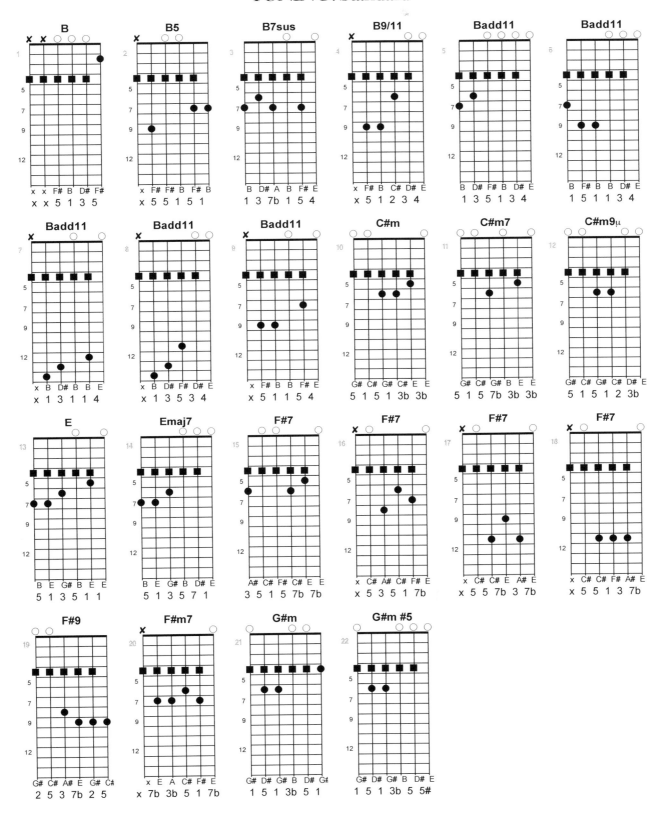

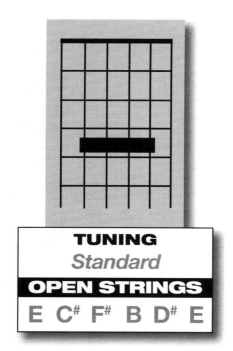

TUNING
Standard
OPEN STRINGS
E C# F# B D# E

10 - E-Modal@4 (044440)

It would also make sense to call this one "Middle 4 @4". It offers quite a number of nice chords and musical options, and it is actually easier to adapt to than either 0 4 4 4 0 0 or 0 0 4 4 4 0, which are sometimes done with an *Esus*-type capo. It's not well-known because common partial capos can't do this.

A lot of useful partial capo configurations involve shortened capos that add open strings on the bass or treble side, and there are several in this book where the capo clamps the middle 4 strings. These gives you a familiar group of strings in the middle that behave like standard tuning, and you can "spice up" your music with the extra outer strings notes.

It makes the most sense here to play in C or Am position (or related modal keys) and enjoy the extra E strings that get added to the usual chords. Since your top 2 strings sound a D# and an E, which is a dissonant interval, you will want to either take advantage of it and build it into a chord progression, or else live with the fact that you will need to fret one or both of those strings most of the time.

The 044440 configuration

Playing in Am is probably the strongest thing you can do here, since you can keep the root notes on the Am (actually C#m) and the Em (actually G#m) position chords, and the minor add 9th "mu" chord (p. 40) you get from playing an E minor chord shape is a pretty compelling sound. Try all the minor-key songs you know this way, and I bet some of them will benefit from the extra mystery of some of the added tones. There's very little you have to adapt to or look out for.

Later in the book (Configuration #43) we'll see what happens when we retune the B string slightly. It's quite startling how much it changes the set of possibilities, and yet another lesson in how hard it is to know what to do with a partial capo.

SOMETHING TO THINK ABOUT

If you play an E and an F simultaneously (or any musical *interval* of a "*minor 2nd*" -which means 2 adjacent keys on the piano) they are quite dissonant. You can hear this on a guitar with no capos at all– just play the 6th fret of the B string [F] and the open high E string at the same time.

Now try separating the notes E-F by an octave and play them again. (This time play fret 2 of the 4th string [E] and the 1st fret of the high E string [F]. The result is much less dissonant. If you play the open bass E [E] and fret 1 of the high E string [F] simultaneously and separate the E from the F by another octave, the interval of E-F is no longer dissonant.

What this means for you is that when you capo up very high on the neck, and still drone some open bass strings, the results are often less dissonant than you expect. Sometimes chords and inversions of chords sound fine if they are spread across several octaves, even though the same letter-named notes would not sound as good if they were closer together in overall pitch. For example, there are some #5 and b5 chords in this book, and those normally dissonant notes are sometimes really nice when they are played on the high strings against a root bass note.

0 4 4 4 4 0

TUNING: Standard

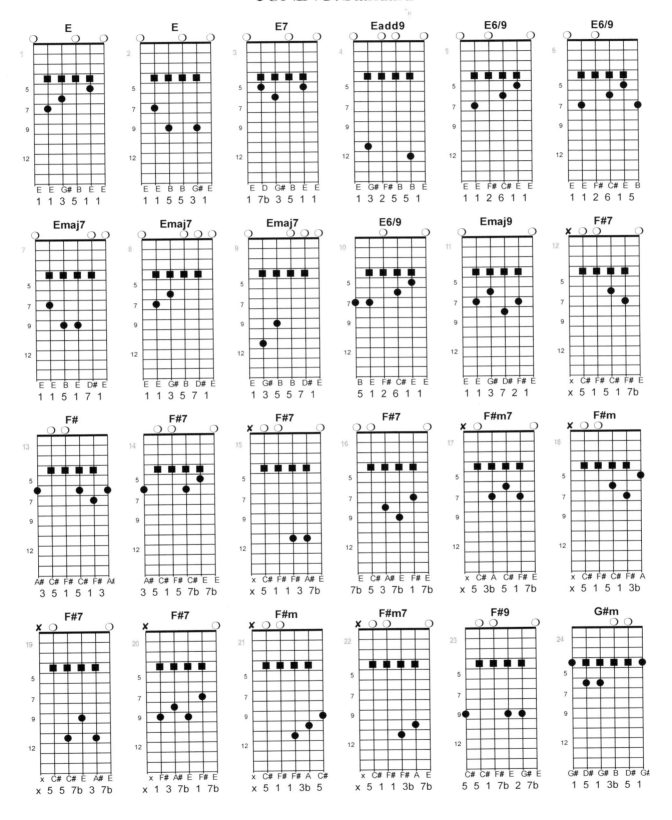

TUNING: Standard

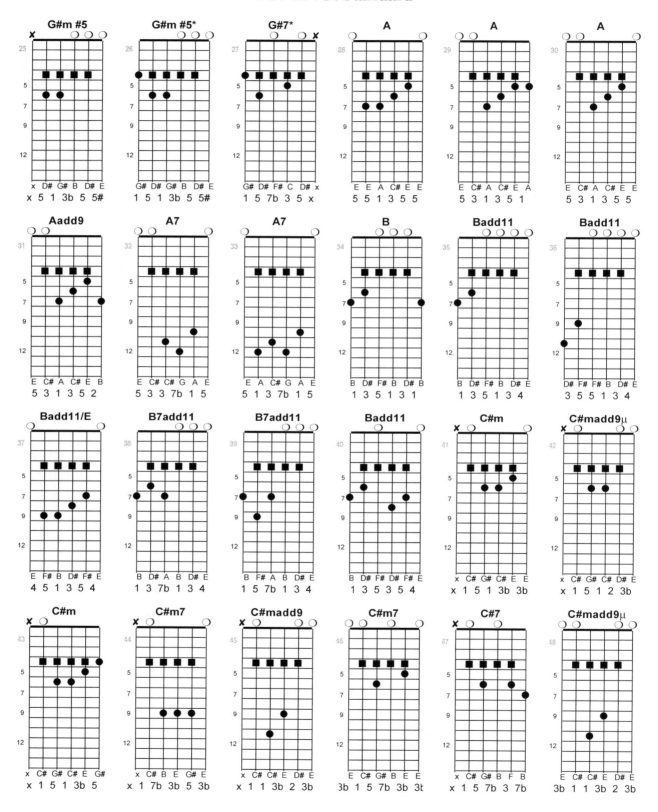

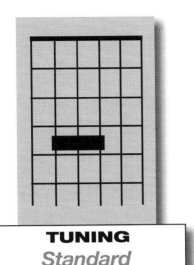

TUNING
Standard

OPEN STRINGS

E C# F# B B E

11- Esus@4 (044400)

This variant of the *Esus* is useful for singers and songwriters to achieve an "open-tuned" sound, and it offers a composer or instrumentalist some nice options. Quite a number of partial capo advocates are using this one, which is why I marked it as "important." It is best suited for songs centered around the key of E, where you are playing in C and Am positions, though you can "cross-key" and play in G position to sound in B. In *Esus* configuration, you usually play in D and sound in E, so logically here you would start by thinking like you were in C, and you would still sound in E, with some new drone strings to color things. It yields some interesting chords not available otherwise, though it is not nearly as deep and universally useful as the *Esus* configuration. It's a quick and easy way to get some very different sounds while staying in standard tuning, which is just what most people want from a partial capo.

Your 4 chord in B (E) sounds huge, and the 5 chord (F#) doesn't have a good bass root on the bottom 2 strings unless you use chords #29 or #34, play below the capo and live with a sus4 in the chord. The double B strings in the middle also grow tiresome after a while, and you may want to either use or avoid a chord like #57-58 where there are 3 unison B's in a row.

A Model 43 clamping the Esus@4 configuration

It is hard to find any "normal" sounding chords in this configuration, other than barre chords. Chords 1 (*E*), 39 (*Aadd9*) and 53 (*Badd11*) are all the same physical shape, and allow 3-chord songs to be played with one simple 2-finger chord shape, and no muted strings. The added 9ths and 11ths color the chords, and may not sound right on all songs. It is a good option if you are a beginner, have special needs, or are working with children. (Though children rarely sing in the key of E, and the usefulness of this idea is largely limited to adult men who often sing in E.)

I have only recorded one piece of music with this configuration (in 1990, "*Chanoyu*" on the CD "*Overview*," which was re-released in 1994 on "*Artistry of the 6-String Banjo*") An unusual piece (and not really typical of what this capo configuration does), it was built around an Am chord shape (sounding as C#m) with a droning low E string, and with C# pentatonic scale work played against the droning bass E string.

A Model 43 capo attaching from the other side of the fingerboard.

0 4 4 4 0 0

TUNING: Standard

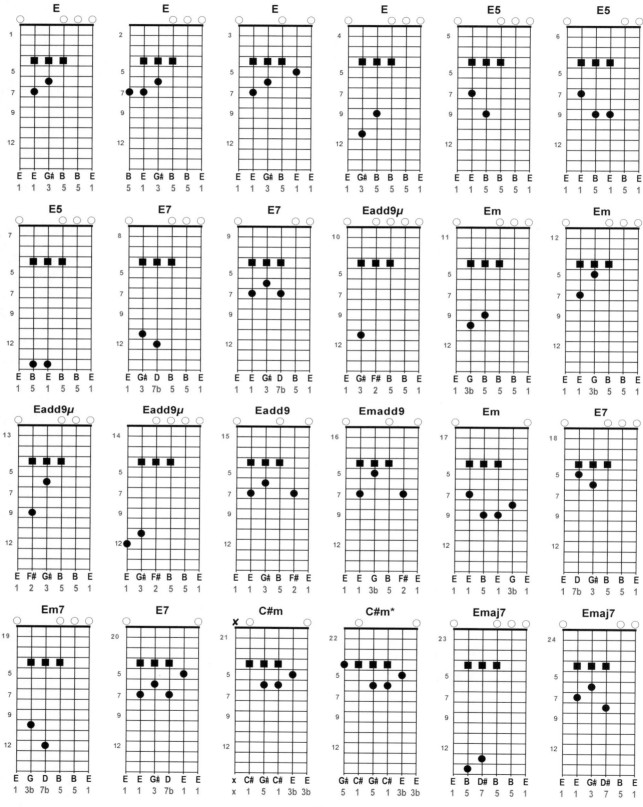

TUNING: Standard

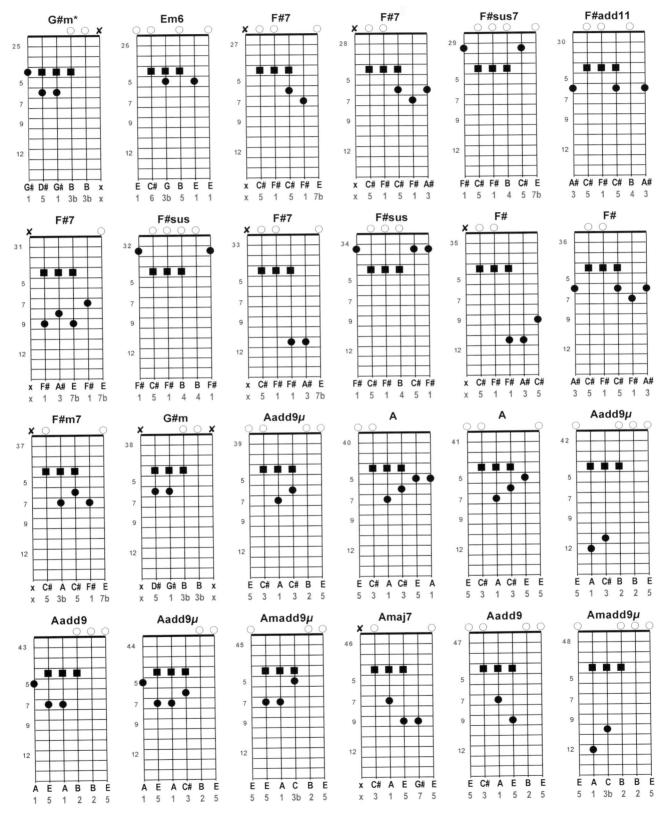

TUNING: Standard

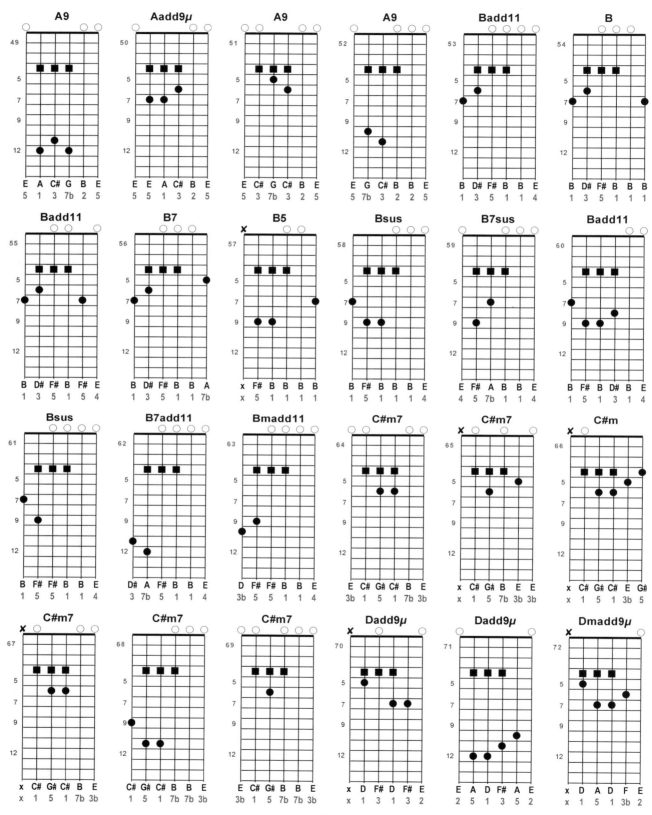

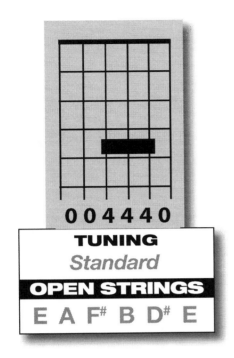

004440

TUNING
Standard

OPEN STRINGS

E A F# B D# E

12- A@4 (004440)

This one offers a few pleasant surprises, but not much of a musical world you can get lost in. The D#-E dissonance on the top 2 strings means you'll want to keep a finger on one of those strings most of the time. You can play in C position, sound in E, and get some droning, resonant chord voicings of the 1, 4 and 5 chords, plus a few flashy "below the capo" chords like #24. Or you can play in Am or G (and sound in C#m or B)and pick and choose among the various voicings that result from combining familiar chord shapes with the new landscape of open strings.

It only takes a short time to get used to it, since most of the chord shapes that work well are familiar variants of regular standard-tuning C, F and G chords. There aren't really any convenient scale patterns you can use here to play melodies, and this configuration is probably of more use for accompaniments than for pickers trying to play melodies.

There are a few nice-sounding suspensions, minor and major 7 chords that you can deploy, that come from basic chord shapes combining with the open strings. If you think one of these chords is too dissonant, try arpeggiating it rather than just strumming the whole chord. It can make a big difference.

We will see later (Configuration #42) what happens when we retune one string, which causes this slightly useful idea to become extraordinarily useful.

The A@4 configuration.

INVERSIONS & DOUBLING

I use some terms from music theory that I should define a little better. The *voicing* of a group of notes is a description of which notes appear in what order. I have never seen in a chord name mentions of notes that are *omitted*, and these affect the sound. (Jazz piano theory people are generally more strict about terminology than in guitar.) Since guitar only has a few strings, to play complex jazz chords there are usually notes omitted. With 6 guitar strings, and only three or four notes in many chords, there are always repeated or *doubled* notes. The word *inversion* is used to describe the order the notes appear in. Technically, a *1st inversion* major triad has the 3rd in the bass, and a *2nd inversion* has the 5th in the bass. It makes a huge difference in the sound of a chord which is the lowest note, and generally chords sound odd if there is anything but a 1 or 5 on the bottom. Of course, there are musical uses for the various inversions of chords, and sometimes an unusual chord voicing is at the heart of a famous version of a song. Adding 7ths 9ths, 11ths, 13th etc. onto basic chords are usually called *extensions*, and partial capos really change the opportunities of what inversions and voicings of various chords can be played on guitar.

004440

TUNING: Standard

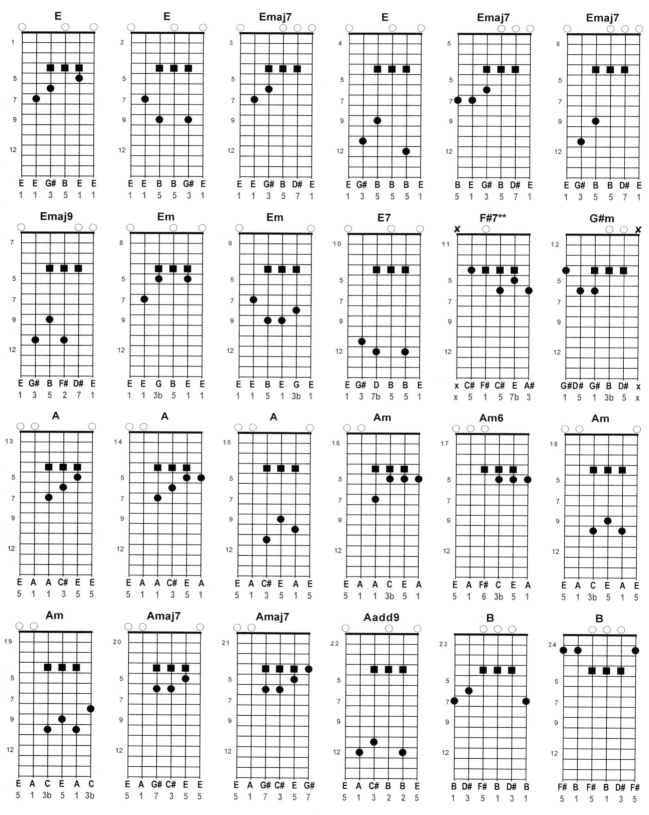

TUNING: Standard

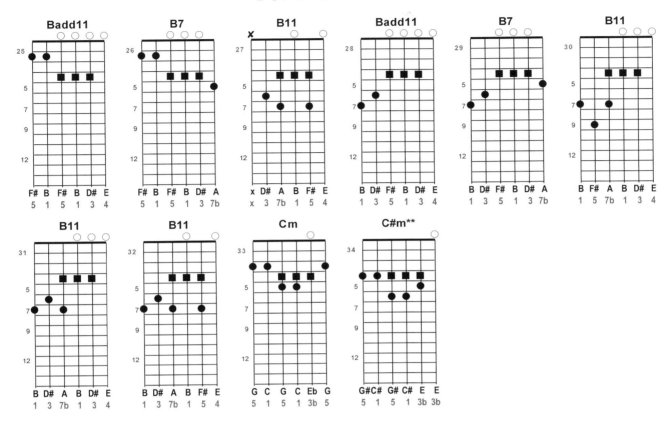

ABOUT ARPEGGIATED CHORDS

I mention often in this book that certain chords work better if you arpeggiate the notes. The word *arpeggio* is Italian for "broken chord," which means you play the note in staggered time rather than all at once. Your ear will often hear two notes played together as dissonant, while if they are separated by time they will sound much less so. Some chords in this book contain 4 or even 5 different scale notes on different strings (this sort of thing is much more common in the world of the partial capo than you usually encounter on guitar) and when arpeggiated they flow like a harp playing melodies. When strummed they can sound dreadful.

On harp or a piano, doing this is a matter of playing the notes in succession rather than all at once. On guitar, success depends on right hand skills. If you play fingerstyle, you have more options, but even with a flat pick, you can either drag down or up across a group of strings, or do some "*sweep picking*" or "*cross picking*" which involves weaving a flatpick up and down among a group of strings quickly in a way that simulates fingerpicking. The dexterity that some players develop is startling. A lot of guitarists (especially on electric guitar and with lighter string gauges) also use a flatpick and their fingers together to play a hybrid fingerpicking style. A few players even use fingerpicks and a flatpick together to solve this problem. So if a chord in this book sounds really odd or dissonant, try arpeggiating it a few different ways up and down before you decide it is not a "good chord."

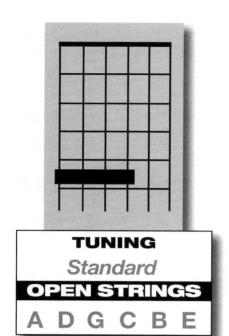

TUNING
Standard
OPEN STRINGS
A D G C B E

13~ Bottom 4 @5 (555500)

A lot of interesting music comes out of this configuration, though very few players know about it because common partial capos can't do this.

The chords seem to be jazzier and not the droning, open-tuning kinds of things that you so often get with partial capos or tunings. Like the last few ideas, it's hard to play a "normal-sounding" major or minor chord in this set-up, and it's really fun to discover how many complex extended chords come from simple and familiar left-hand shapes. There are some really nice inversions and voicings of minor 7th, maj7 and maj9 chords and a few of the "*mu*" chords (p. 40) that you might expect from a capo setup like this.

If you play in E or Em position, you will sound in A or Am, which I have shown first here. You can play in A or Am and sound in D or Dm. You can also play in G position and the open strings on the treble end put you into a Cmaj7 situation. Playing bluesy things in E7 position makes a really nice A9 chord (chord #3) and if you do some arpeggiating or fingerpicking with the E7-A7 (Dave Mason's "*Feelin' Alright*" chords) you get nice dominant 9th chords in place of the 7th you are playing that sound like Chet Atkins chords. (chords #3 and 18). In fact, you can play it in 2 keys, and start with chord #22 and then use chord #3.

You might notice that I don't include a "Top 4 @5" [0 0 5 5 5 5] configuration at this location in the book. Logically, it would be something to try, and I did. If you don't believe me, go ahead. You can play a 1-finger Em chord that makes a nice Am, but the other chords from that key, such as D major, are weak. It's a terrific example of a partial capo configuration that does not do very much– no really helpful bass notes or interesting treble notes to deploy. I may post a free chord chart on the web site as a good example of something that isn't that useful. Later in this book (#49) I use the 005555 configuration with some bass strings retuned, and it gets a lot better.

A Model 43 capo at the 5th fret making the Bottom 4 @ 5 configuration.

555500

Some Chords in Bottom 4 @ 5 p. 1
TUNING: Standard

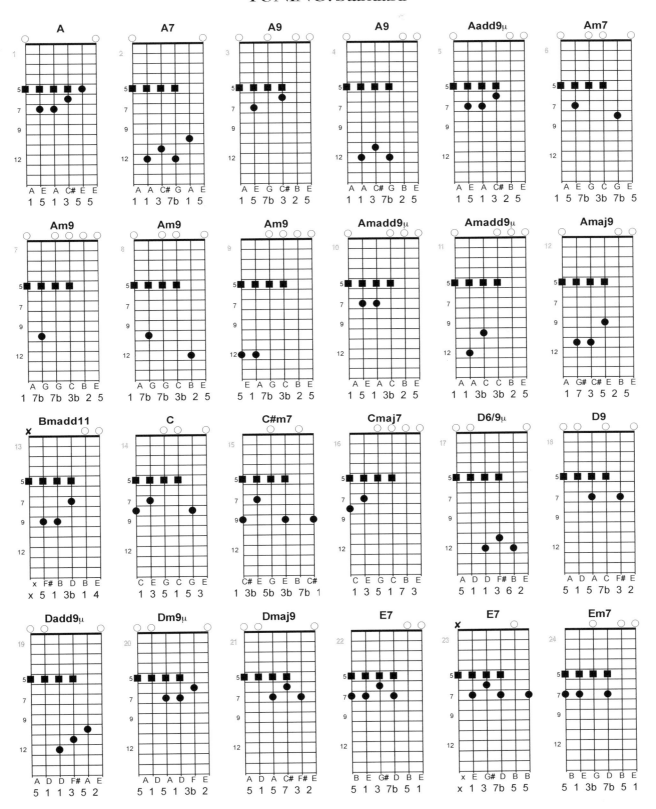

57

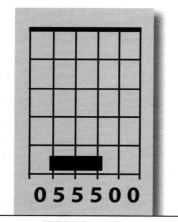

055500

TUNING
Standard

OPEN STRINGS

E D G C B E

14~ Esus@5 (055500)

If you slide the *Esus* capo up to fret 5, another new set of possibilities emerges. It is not nearly as useful for playing scales or melodic guitar as the 2nd fret *Esus* capo configuration or the 4th fret 044400, and it is probably best used as a way to get some exotic chord voicings for song accompaniments. There are a lot of *Esus* capos out there, and people are trying things with them, and this is one of the things that comes up logically, but isn't that great an environment for music. It is once again a challenge to find a way to play any ordinary-sounding chords, and you can't really stretch out and happily play a bunch of songs when you have the capo here.

It's a little unclear how to think in this situation. With the *Esus* capo at fret 2 we played in D to sound in E, and with the capo 4 we played in C and again sounded in E. Few of us play much in the key of B in standard tuning, so it's not a simple matter to "think in B" and sound in E, though that is one way to look at what is going on here. If you look at the chords on the next page, you'll see that the E and Em chords are indeed shaped like standard tuning B and Bm.

A Model 43 at the 5th fret making the Esus@5 configuration.

Likewise, playing things that feel like E position chords will cause you to sound in A. It might make more sense to try to take advantage of the fact that 4 of your open strings are in an E minor chord, and try playing in Bm above the capo to sound in Em. You could also play in G position, and sound in C, and the capo will add B's and E's to a lot of your chords. Another possible approach is to play in Am and sound in Em. Then the added open E string notes will fit, and the added B string makes a tonic minor 9th chord, which is nice.

The chords on the next page are alphabetical, and do not favor any key, because no key or tonality jumps out as the obvious best use of this slightly ambiguous capo configuration. There are some pretty interesting chords, and with some creativity you could write or arrange something that took advantage of their unusual voicings. Listen to the chords here, and see what your ear likes.

055500

TUNING: Standard

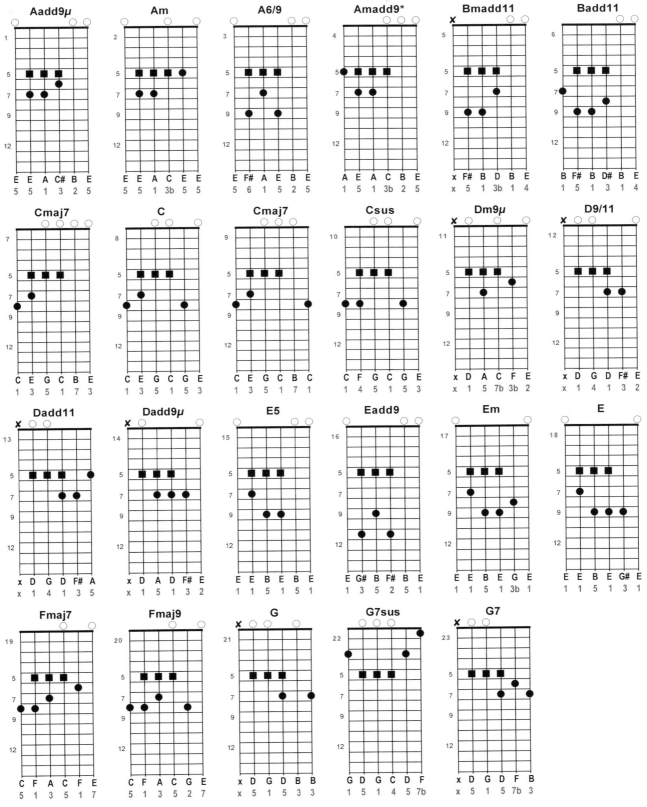

15- A@5 (005550)

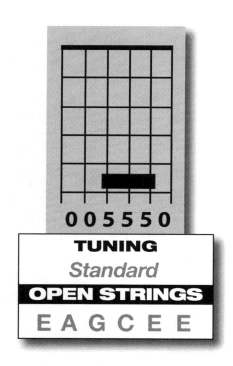

005550

TUNING
Standard
OPEN STRINGS
E A G C E E

For the sake of completeness, this one is included, though it is not as fruitful as some others. The sound of a particular chord may jump out at you and give you a great song idea, so it's worth trying. You pretty much have to think like you are in G or Em position, and sound in C or Am, and a few interesting and unusual things happen. The open strings form an Am7 chord (which is also a C6 chord in a different inversion), so it makes sense to build your musical explorations from there as a starting point. This would mean playing in Em position.

This is one of the capo configurations that leans more on the A as the root tonic note, as opposed to the considerable number of them that are based on E. You'll notice that there are some nice C, Dm and F family chords on the following page.

The A@5 configuration.

PARTIAL CAPO RECORDINGS

Ultimately, the final judgment of whether an idea like the partial capo has true musical value has to do with what music people are playing with it. I stand behind my own body of recorded work, which currently consists of over 200 songs and instrumental pieces, mostly on guitar, but a few on mando-cello, bouzouki and also quite a few on 6-string banjo. I obviously think my own music pleads the case that real music can be played with this device.

I also am trying to build a discography and a list of artists who are also using the partial capo, and since that information is so large and changing, it will probably remain on a web site and not end up in a printed book. There are now thousands of players all over the world creating real music with partial capos. If you are one of them, I'd like to know what you are doing with your capos.

www.PartialCapo.com

005550

TUNING: Standard

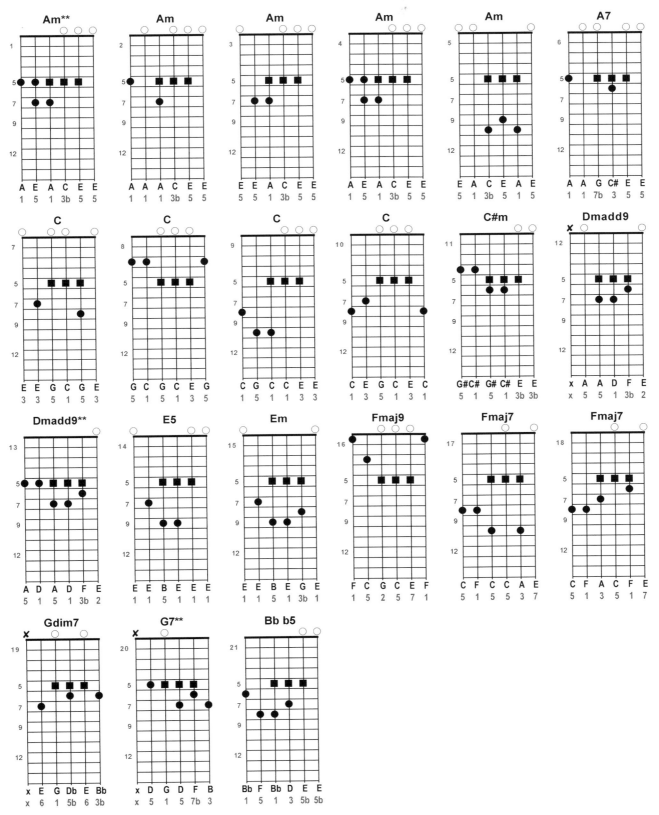

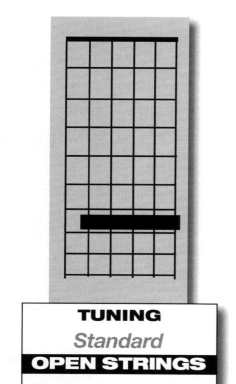

TUNING
Standard
OPEN STRINGS
E E B E F# B

16- Top 5 @7 (077777)

There are not a lot of surprises here, and you get pretty much what you would expect– a very deep bass note under a high-pitched treble. It's not a hugely exciting idea, and you might use it for a song or two.

Since the bass note is so much "bigger" than the other strings, and you have so many E's on the low end, you can't really get away with playing in anything except keys centered around E. This means you would mostly play in A or Am positions. You will need a cutaway or at least a 14-fret neck to play some of the higher-position chords shown here.

You get a much richer 1 chord in this situation, and you "trade-off" and get a weaker 5 chord, since you no longer have the open bass string when you play E or E7 shapes. The "mu" chords (μ) have a great sound, either major or minor (p. 40).

You can do this on pretty much all guitars by just offsetting a straight capo.

The "Top 5 @7" configuration.

077777

TUNING: Standard

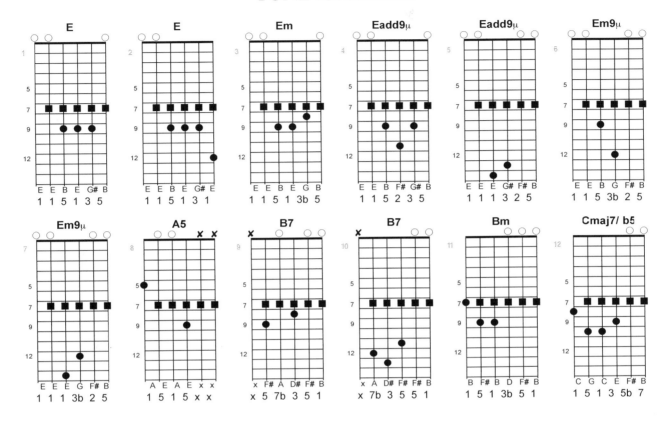

PARTIAL CAPOS, NOTATION & TRANSPOSING

For centuries, guitarists have used capos to change the key, or transpose, as well as to change the tone. This book assumes that you know how to use a regular capo, and if you are rusty, you'll get a lot of practice here. All the chords in this book are written as they sound. Even if it looks and feels exactly like a G chord, it may say A on the chord diagram, and all the notes will show at the bottom of the chord diagram the way they actually sound, with A, C# and E notes. This is not hard to keep track of things when you have a single capo at the 2nd fret in standard tuning, but when there are 2 capos at the 5th and 7th frets it's more difficult to stay oriented.

One of the most confusing things about partial capo education is that you always have to say things like "Play what feels like a G chord, and it will sound as an A." That is exactly what you do in a lot of instances, but the language gets thick when you describe things constantly this way.

The problems of partial capo notation will get thornier as more people transcribe more arrangements. Guitar music is usually written on the staff in standard notation, and when more of it gets arranged and written with partial capos, it will not be totally clear what to do. If you write the music the way it "feels" to a guitarist who knows how to sight-read music, it will not "look like it sounds." When I wrote my guitar books for partial capo, I wrote them in both TAB and standard notation, with TAB (tablature) numbers to show the notes the way they "feel" (with the capo as the 0, and occasional negative numbers for TAB below the capo.) I made the standard notation, however, look the way it sounds, so that a guitarist who knows how to sight-read would not be able to play it as it was written. Computer software for guitar notation does not know about partial capos yet, and people are using several different methods now, including counting from the capo as 0, or counting everything from the nut. It's a thorny issue that is showing no signs of fixing itself. There is a deeper discussion at the end of this book.

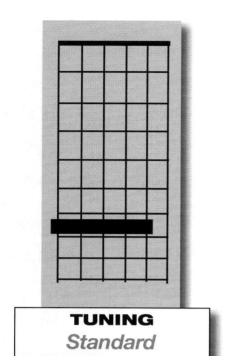

TUNING
Standard
OPEN STRINGS
B E A D F# E

17- Bottom 5 @7 (777770)

This one is more interesting than it seems at first, and the combination of the high capo (7) and the open high E string does 2 useful things.

First of all, since you most often play in G position (which sounds in D), the added open string is a 9th, which sounds great when added to many chords in that key. Since you usually have to fret the high E string when you play in G position, this means that your left hand has a lot of new freedom and is not "locked" into that familiar chord shape.

Secondly, it's nice to sound in D, since so much partial capoing ends up in E and A. The fact that the added E note on top is also the same pitch as fret 2 of your 3rd string means that you get a lot of flowing "*mu*" chords (p. 40) with different combinations of the 2nds, 3rds, 4ths and 5ths of the scale sounding in the same octave. This can add some nice extensions to your whole family of major, minor, 6th or seventh chords.

Because the high E string drones the way it does, you can use it like a 5th string on a banjo, and the musical effect this generates combined with the fact that the guitar is capoed so high gives a brightness that is surprisingly banjo-like and even harp-like, especially when you do arpeggiated picking with the right hand and "roll" the treble strings against ringing bass notes.

The "Bottom 5 @7" configuration. You could attach the capo from the treble side also if you wanted.

777770

Some Chords in Bottom 5 @ 7 p. 1
TUNING: Standard

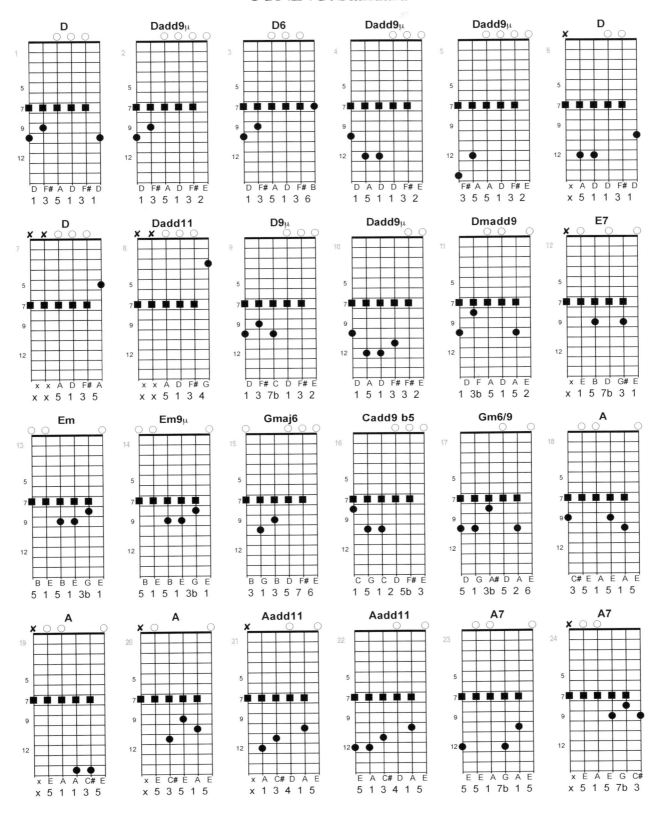

65

TUNING: Standard

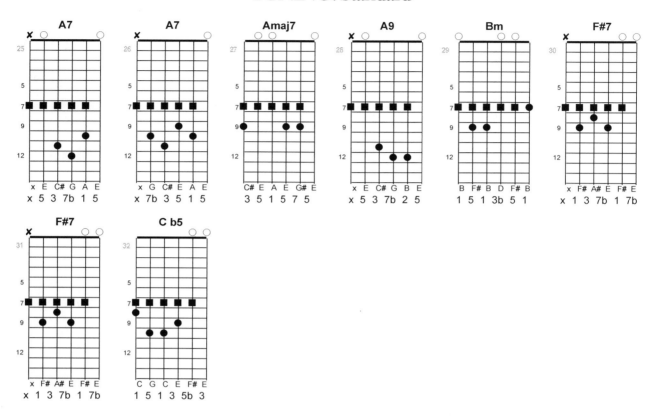

PARTIAL CAPOS & 12-STRING GUITARS

12-string players are used to having their own set of problems, and everything from strings, cases, capos, pickups are often a little different than on 6-string. The partial capo has huge value for 12-string players, especially the modern breed of them who were inspired by the roaring open-tuned sound of Leo Kottke.

You can get the same kind of huge sound with a partial capo, without all the retuning. Since the fingerboards are usually wider, you may want to shorten the long side of a *Model 43* capo to clamp 3 strings of your 12-string. You may also have trouble with the octave A string rattling, which is chronic problem with capos and 12-strings. The *Liberty* capos can apply a considerable amount of force, which can help with a rattling octave 5th string. Spring capos, which are very popular, tend to do a poor job on 12-strings, and the *SpiderCapo* does not work at all.

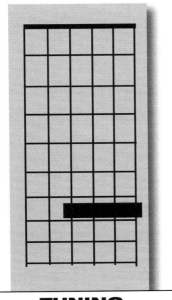

18- Top 4 @7 (007777)

The primary value of this is to play in D position, sound in A, and get a low-string drone from the bass strings that combines with the very high capo position on the treble strings.

You can also play in Dm and sound in Am and get the same advantages, and the chords associated with Dm (Gm, C F and Bb) all play normally.

If your action is really high or your guitar's intonation is not good, you may have some trouble playing in tune with this one since the capo is so high up.

This is the kind of partial capo configuration you would most likely use for a song or two in your repertoire as a "special effect." You can play in D position and do a nice version of the Beatles' *"Here Comes the Sun"* this way, and you'll get a low bass underneath the high treble melody.

TUNING
Standard

OPEN STRINGS
E A A D F# B

The Top 4 @ 7 configuration.

0 0 7 7 7 7

TUNING: Standard

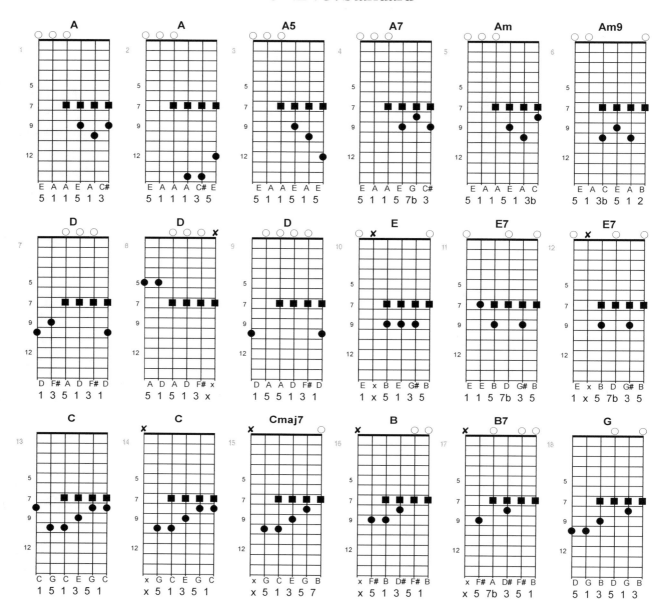

Possibly the hardest thing about the partial capo is that it behaves like a tuning but it is not. (Unless of course you are using a partial capo and a tuning at the same time.) It is helpful at first to think of many of the capo configurations as being ways to "imitate" the sound of common tunings, which sometimes can happen. But it is a different world than tunings, and only a few things can be played the same both ways.

Non-guitarists sometimes understand partial capos better than guitarists, and players who have never used tunings sometimes have an easier time with the capos than veterans of tunings. It can be confusing, but try to enjoy it. Remember Rubik's cube?

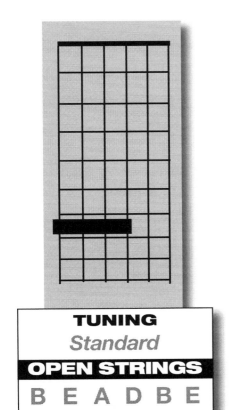

19- Bottom 4 @7 (777700)

This one has some surprisingly nice chord voicings, and it can be used to play in several keys. You might be able to work up a number of songs that take advantage of its chords. It's a bit hard to keep track of what key you are really in, since the capo is so high. You also will have trouble doing this on a 12-fret neck, and will be more successful with a 14-fret neck and/or a cutaway. Once again, because so few partial capos have been able to effectively clamp an XXXXOO configuration, this kind of idea is not well-known. Hopefully the *Liberty Model 43* will do it on your guitar neck. There are so many shapes of guitar necks there is no certainty.

You can think in G, which will cause you to sound in D, which will allow the two open treble strings to add some nice extensions to your basic chords. Or you can play in Em or Am position, which will put you in Bm or Em, respectively. The B and E drone strings will then be more consonant, and allow you to drone them in other nice ways. There are some nice bluesy sounds, and the E9 chords are especially nice inversions (chords #22 & 33). You can even play in D or Dm position, which will sound in A or Am.

I have put the chords in alphabetical order here because there is not a primary key to play in this configuration.

TUNING
Standard

OPEN STRINGS

B E A D B E

The Bottom 4 @7 configuration.

7 7 7 7 0 0

Some Chords in the Bottom 4 @ 7 Configuration p.1
TUNING: Standard

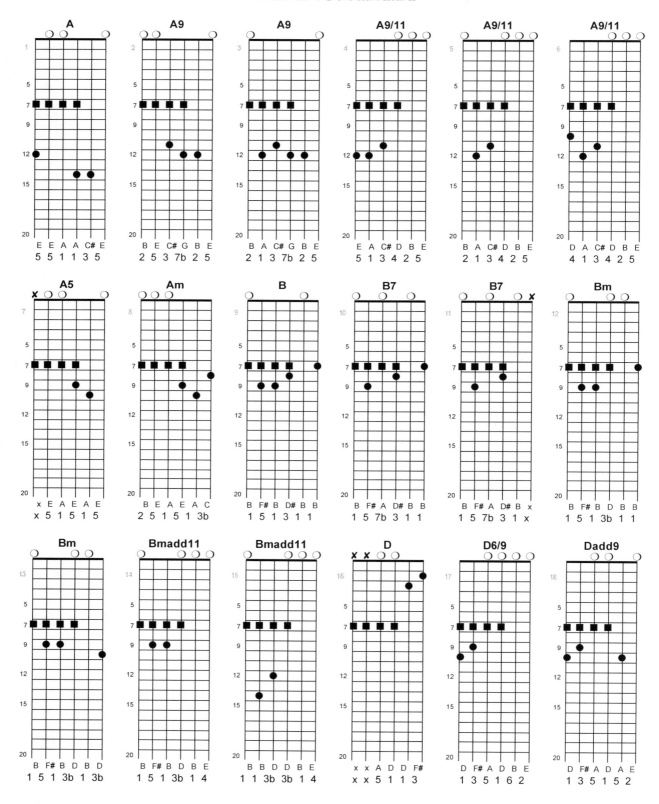

TUNING: Standard

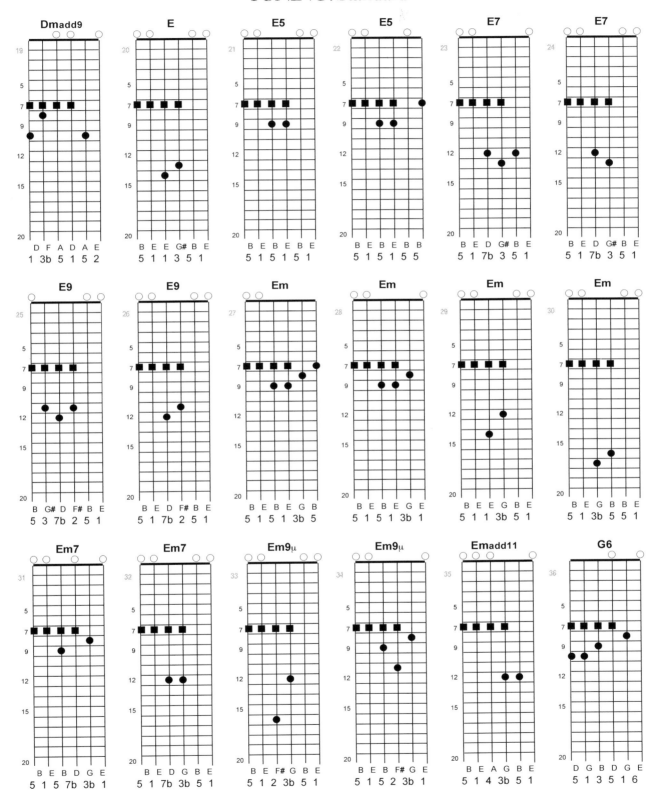

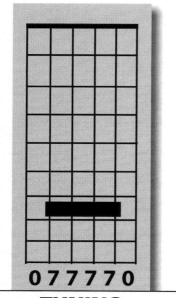

20– E-Modal @7 (077770)

With the middle 4 strings clamped like this at fret 7, a lot of nice things happen.

It makes sense to think as if you are playing in A, which means you will actually sound in E. Having both E strings droning adds to the low-end resonance and creates the open tuning sound. You will also get quite a number of the overlapping "*mu*" chords (p. 40), since you have a capo on the middle strings high up the neck. You can also work out some chromatic banjo style cascading scales that use the high E drone against fretted notes on the 3rd and 4th strings.

Having the B string sounding a musical 9th is nice, and helps get you away from the endless drone of an open-tuned chord better than having the drone string be part of the 1 chord like it would be if the capo were at fret 5. Not only does the added 9th sound good against the D chord, but the E note is part of the 5 chord (A) and also the 2 chord (E).

You can also play in minor and modal keys related to A, which basically means playing chord shapes you would associate with A minor. Playing in G position to sound in D yields some good music also.

You can also modify this one a little by dropping the bass E string to D. This would provide a nice low root, and it would musically feel like you were playing in G position in *Drop D* tuning, but you would sound in D. You could also drop the bass string to C and lower the capo to fret 5, but you would lose the *add9* on the high E string.

A Model 43 at the 7th fret making the 077770 configuration

077770

TUNING: Standard

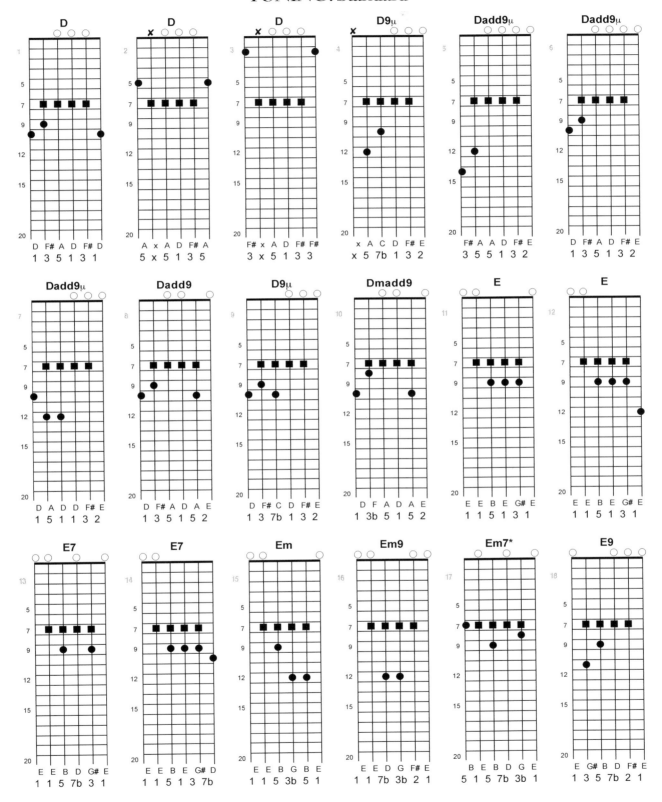

Some Chords in the E-Modal@7 Configuration p.2
TUNING: Standard

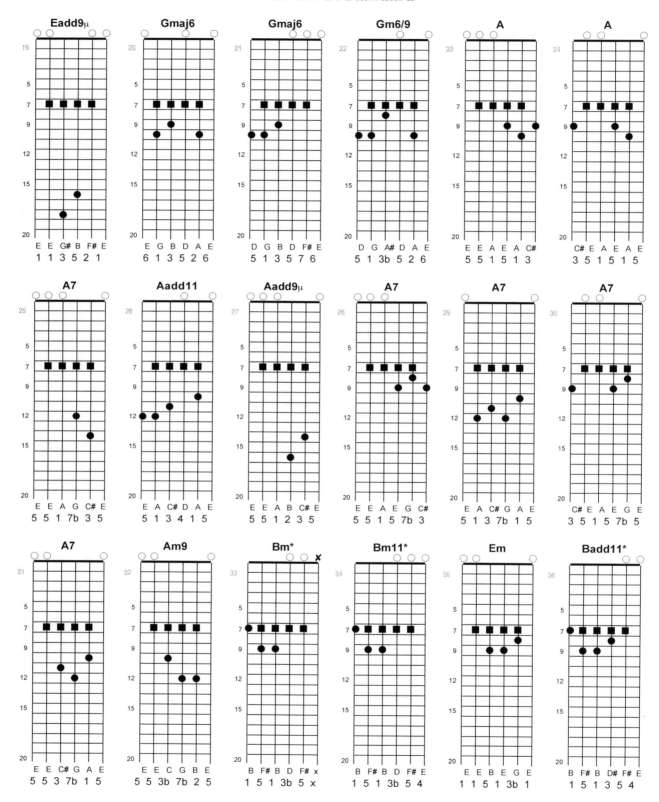

74

Some Chords in the E-Modal@7 Configuration p.3
TUNING: Standard

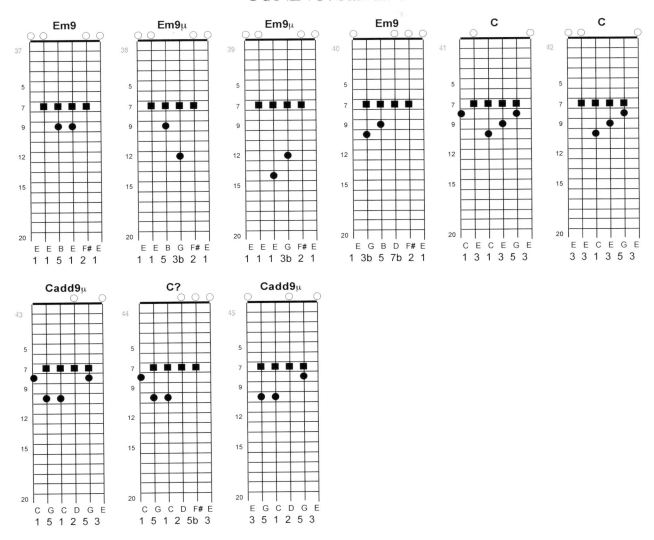

75

077700

TUNING
Standard

OPEN STRINGS
E E A D B E

A Liberty Model 43 making the Esus@7 configuration

21~ Esus@7 (077700)

This is another variant of the *Esus* idea that is done with a 3-string partial capo on fret 7. The Liberty capo does a significantly better job with this than common 3-string Esus capos from *Shubb, G7* or *Kyser*, all of which have trouble with the increased fingerboard width, string spacing and higher action you typically have at this location.

If you play in A position you can get some nice chords that sound in the key of E. Am position also works nicely; you sound in Em when you play normal-shaped chords. Just use Am, C, Dm, F and G chord shapes to start.

This configuration generates a number of lovely arpeggiated chords, including *"mu"* chords (p. 40). They work well in this type of set-up because they involve adding either a musical second (notated as a 2, which is the same note as a 9) to a chord without removing the 3. Because the capos allow adjacent musical scale notes to sometimes appear on adjacent strings, throughout this book there are also a lot of these kinds of extended chords. You'll also find added 4ths that still have the 3rds, as well as added 6ths that don't involve removing the adjacent 5th note. This kind of thing has always been rare on guitar, and partial capos generate a flood of new "overlapping" voicings like this.

The slight dissonance these kinds of chords generate can be very haunting. This is a type of chord structure that is easy on a piano or a harp, but in standard guitar there are only a few ways you can do this, and they generally require a substantial left-hand reach. Many configurations in this book, especially those with a capo at 5, 7 or 9 in the middle strings and the 1st and/or 2nd strings open generate a considerable number of new "floating" chords like this that you usually don't hear on guitar. I especially like them when there is also a low bass drone and a cross-picked or fingerpicked, arpeggiated right hand. Sometimes the notes that lie next to each other in the scale are resonating on adjacent strings, which is a lovely effect that guitars usually struggle with.

Again, this is a specialized situation, a way to get some exotic chord voicings, and to impress people by playing below the capo, where there are a few useful musical chords.

077700

TUNING: Standard

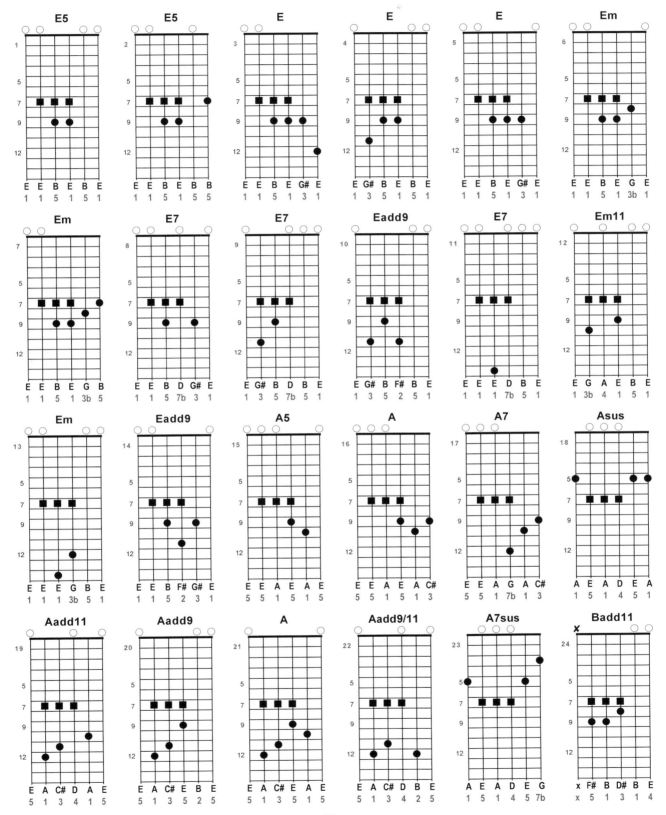

TUNING: Standard

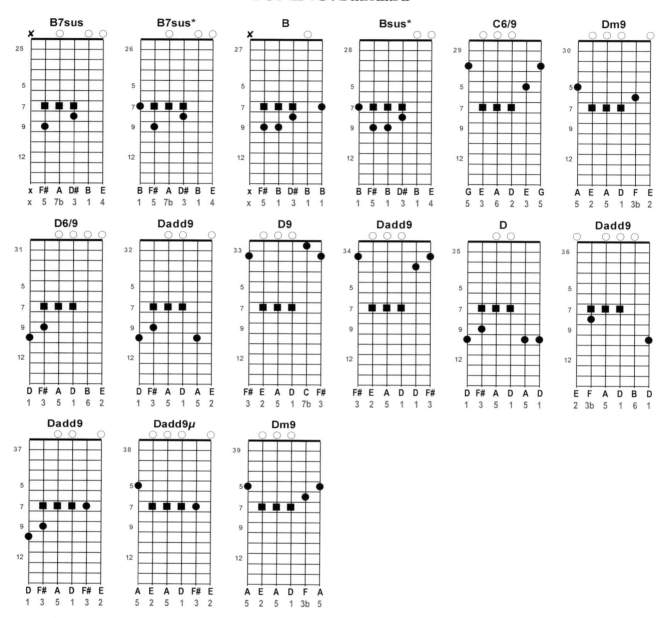

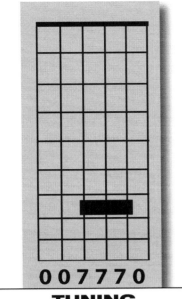

007770

TUNING
Standard

OPEN STRINGS

E A A D F# E

22- A@7 (007770)

If you play in G position above this capo, you will sound in D, and you'll notice that there are quite a number of interesting new ways to play a D major chord. Because the low A string is also open, you also get some nice A chords (which because of the capo "feel" like D chords). Because the high E string adds a 9th to the D chord and because the capo is so high, there are again an unusually large number of so-called "*mu*" chords (µ) (p. 40) with the added 2nd (same as 9th) next to the 3rd in the same octave. There are also some really hypnotic *minor add ninth* chords with a minor version of the *mu* effect. Like a lot of chords in this book, they sound better when arpeggiated rather than strummed.

There are also some surprisingly rich and normal-sounding 2 chords (E7, Em, etc) which is due to the fact that you are playing in D and have a low E bass note under it all.

The *Liberty Model 43* does this better than common 3-string capos, again because fingerboards tend to get wider and string action gets higher when you are this high on the neck. You'll need a guitar with good intonation to do this, and a really inexpensive guitar might have some tuning problems that are aggravated by having a partial capo this high.

A Liberty "Flip" Model 43 capo at the 7th fret making the Open A@7 configuration

007770

TUNING: Standard

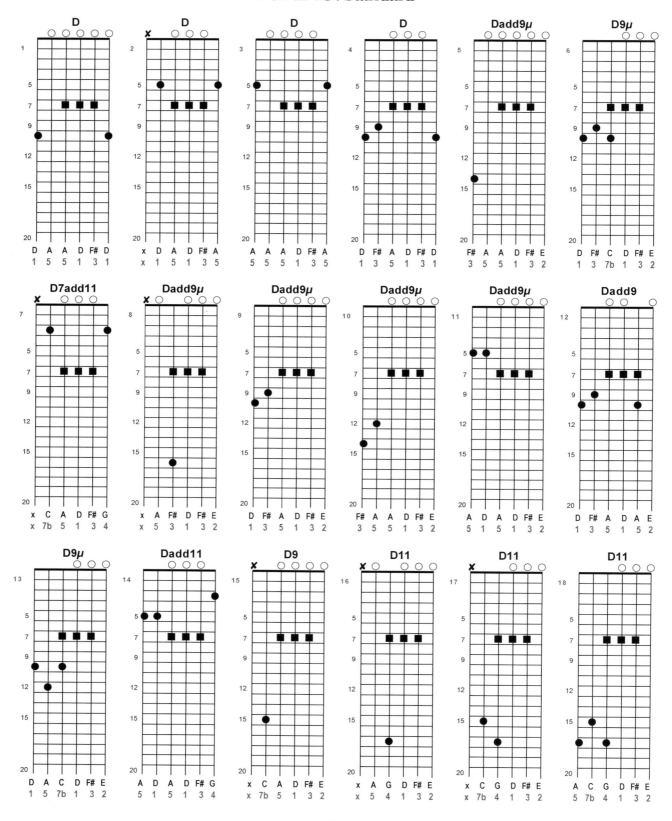

TUNING: Standard

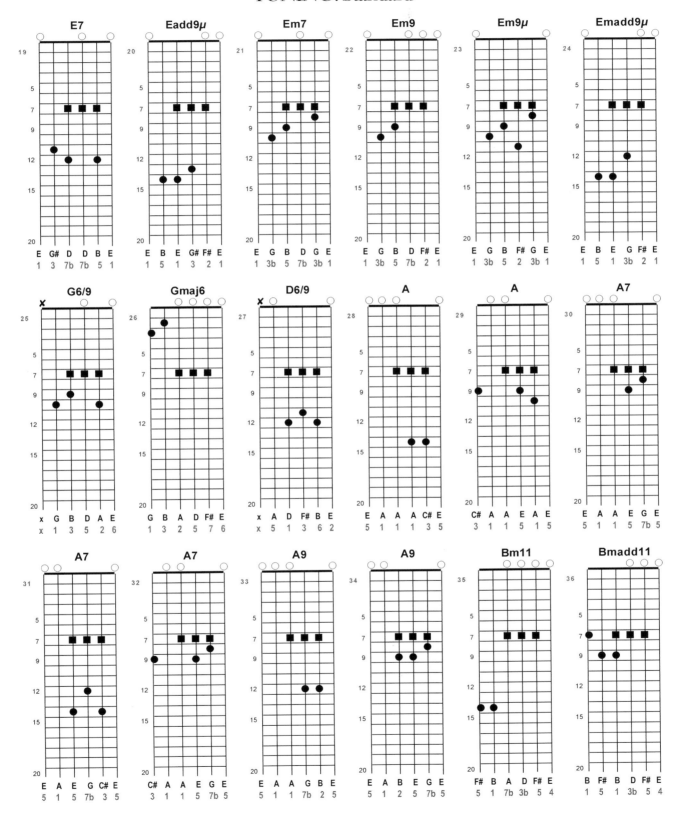

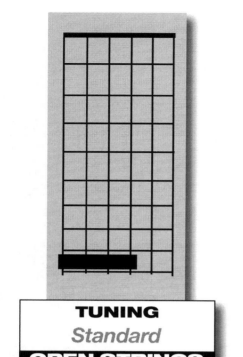

TUNING
Standard
OPEN STRINGS
C# F# B E B E

23~ Bottom 4 @9 (999900)

This is as high as a capo can realistically go on an acoustic guitar, and it offers some excellent sounds. You might have intonation problems, and you can't easily do this without a cutaway body shape, but it's worth a try.

The capo is so high that the open high E string note is the same pitch as notes on the 4th string, so the best way to use the treble open strings is really as a dulcimer-like drone. It sounds great if you do some banjo-style right-hand rolls, and play melody on the 4th and 5th strings. Even some Carter Family or Woody Guthrie style bass-string melody playing sounds great against the steady treble drone, though partial capos and cutaway guitars are not very "Woody Guthrie" or "Carter Family" fashion concepts. You'll need to be a trend-setter at an old-time music gathering to pull this out.

You're probably best off if you play in G position here, which puts you in E yet again, with some nice extensions on the Em and Am shapes. You can also play in C position, and you will sound in A.

You might logically expect that there would be a page of "Top 4 @9" chords, but I confess to deciding that there was not enough musical value to include it. Feel free to prove me wrong and use it. The term "musical value" is incredibly subjective.

A Model 43 at the 9th fret making the Bottom 4 @9 configuration.

999900

Some Chords in the Bottom 4 @9 Configuration p.1
TUNING: Standard

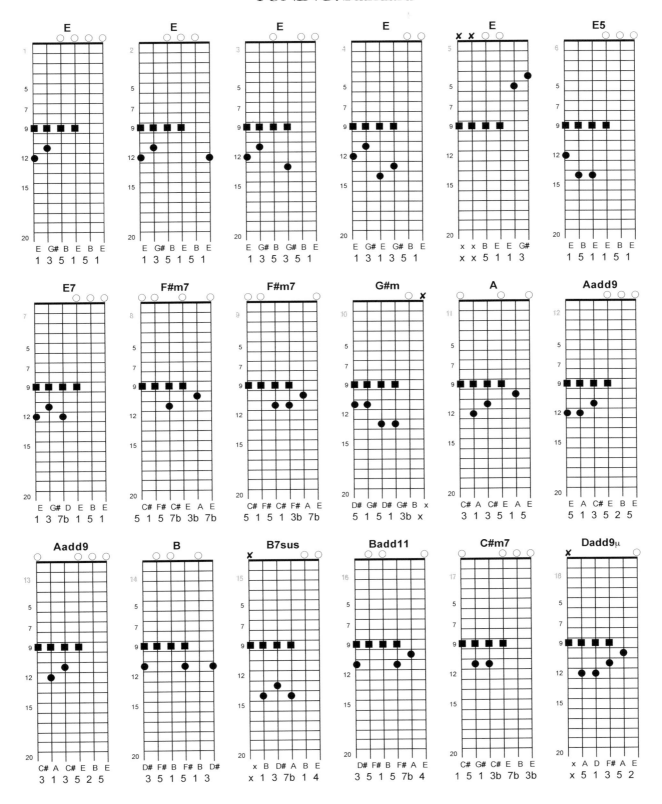

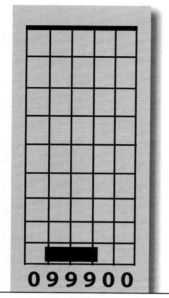

099900

TUNING
Standard
OPEN STRINGS
E F# B E B E

24~ Esus@9 (099900)

This is a final version of the common *Esus* (OXXXOO) that is done with the capo at fret 9.

The standard *Esus* capos often don't work well up this high, and the *Liberty Model 43* typically does it very well, from either side of the neck. You probably need a cutaway or electric guitar, and your guitar's intonation might not allow you to use this one, since things may be a little out of tune.

If you play in G or Gm position you can get some new sounds in the key of E or Em, and there are some sweet chords very high up the neck. The guitar has a nice and rarely-heard resonance in the higher positions, and a partial capo is one of the best ways to access that sound. When combined with open bass strings and also with the droning treble strings, there is a very nice tonal thing that happens here when you play lines on the middle strings very high on the neck.

This is one of those "less deep" capo configurations that you would use for a song or two. You would likely not want to spend several days or perform several songs in a row in this set-up.

You can orient the capo either way, and attach from bass or treble sides of the fingerboard.

At the 9th fret making the Esus@9 configuration

099900

TUNING: Standard

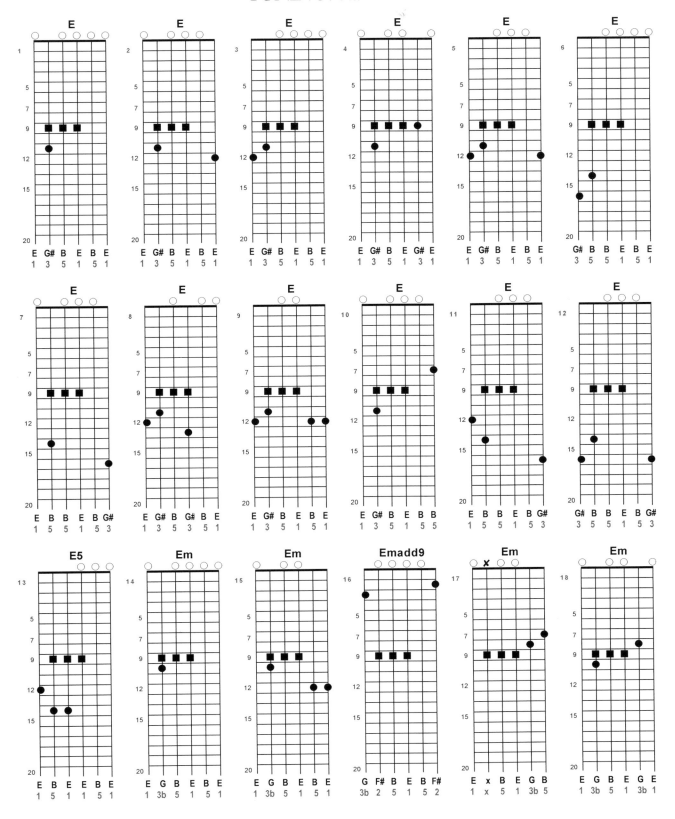

TUNING: Standard

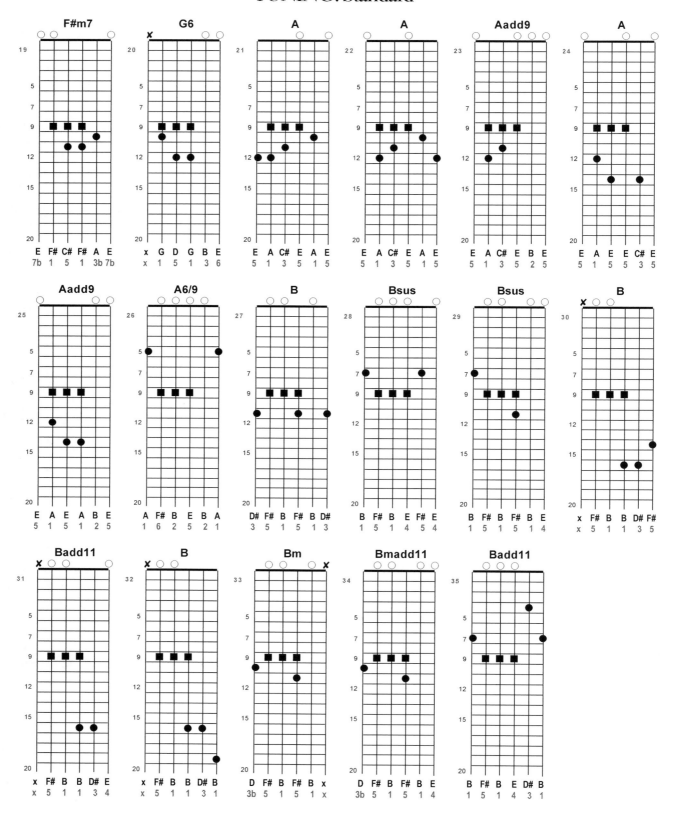

86

0 0 9 9 9 0

TUNING
Standard

OPEN STRINGS

E A B E G# E

At the 9th fret making the A@9 configuration

25- A@9 (009990)

This final variation of the *Open A* idea is done with 3-string partial capo at fret 9 on the treble side. I think it is a level more interesting and useful than the previous one.

Once again, your guitar's intonation may not allow you to use this one, since things could sound out of tune. The *Liberty Model 43* does this better than other 3-string partial capos, because fingerboards and string spacing get wider and action is higher this high up the neck.

If you play in G position you can get some new sounds in the key of E, and there are some nice inversions of the *tonic* (1) chord, plus some options to arpeggiate or drone the treble strings while playing melody on the bottom strings.

Like a number of capo configurations, this is a way to get some unusual chord voicings, and to impress your audience by playing below the capo, where there are some good chords. As with many of these more "exotic" configurations, it is a bit of a challenge to arrange a well-known song or to find any way to play familiar-sounding chords. Nonetheless, this configuration is surprisingly fun, and worth spending some time with.

You can also use it to access a sort of "tonal world" when strings 3, 4 and 5 are played very high up the neck, even above the 12th fret. If you fingerpick, play some lines with your thumb on those strings, drone the bass E and jangle the treble strings with your fingers. A number of the chords shown here sound best when a bass string is ringing and the top three strings are arpeggiated with a banjo-roll type of pattern with the fingers. If you are good with a flatpick you can also cross-pick or sweep-pick some of this stuff.

0 0 9 9 9 0

TUNING: Standard

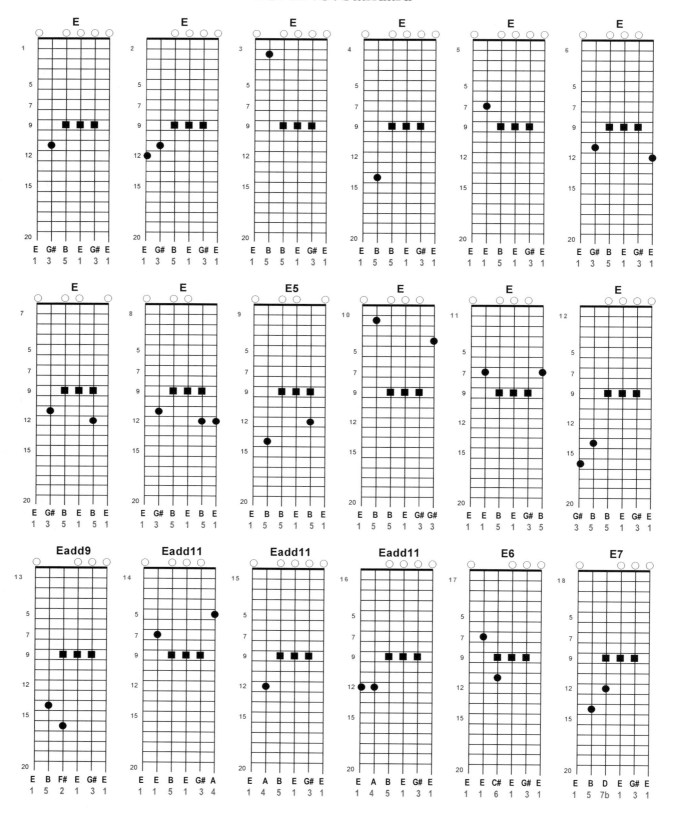

Some Chords in the A@9 Configuration p.2

TUNING: Standard

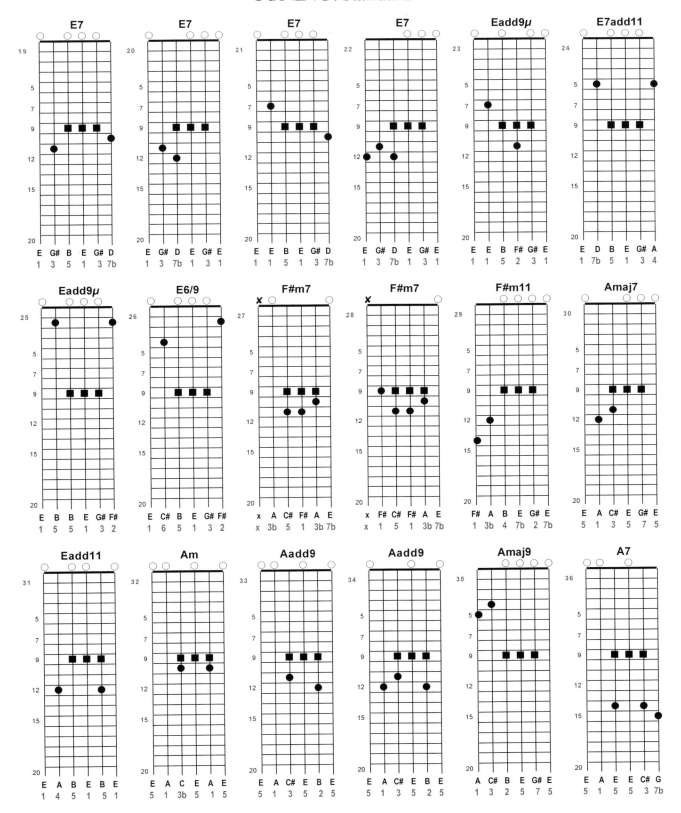

89

TUNING: Standard

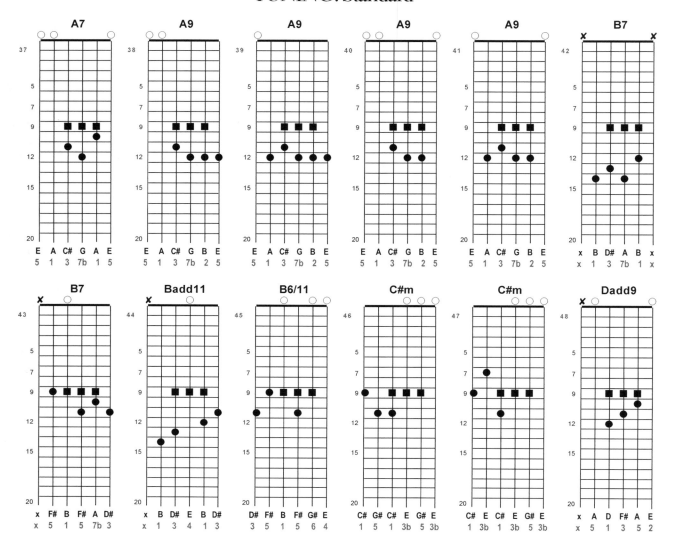

ABOUT CHORD SHAPES

Because of the nature of music and the guitar, it often turns out that a chord you find in this book (or one you find on your own) can be moved up or down the fingerboard, or even across, and generate something musical.

If you find a chord you like here, even if it has a lot of open strings and is not technically a "movable" chord, try moving it up or down 2 frets and see what it sounds like when you switch between the two similar shapes. You can often also move a shape up 4, 5 or 7 frets and find a musically compatible chord.

Especially on the bass side of the guitar, you can often move a shape "sideways" one string, either higher or lower, and find a sound that is also satisfying. Your ear is your guide. A lot of songs have been written and arranged using these kinds of "germs." Feel free to move chords shapes around like this. I have included a lot of these kinds of "matching pairs" in this book, and their names often offer no clues that they are musically related, but they often are. Look for similar shapes in these pages of chords and play them in succession and see what you can find. A lot of great songs have started this way.

SECTION

Retuning 1-2 Strings With 1 Capo

Slight variations in the tuning can produce startling results

- It is surprising how many new sounds and chord voicings you can unlock with just a string or two tuned differently.

- Some of the very best partial capo ideas do this, and they are virtually unknown, since most partial capo users stay in standard tuning or a common open tuning.

- Players who use partial capos are often trying to avoid using open tunings. So just retuning a string or two strings is a reasonable and quick option, and a lot of great music results.

- It's not as disorienting as trying to learn a whole new tuning, and even if you are not experienced with altered tunings, you can adapt to these configurations pretty quickly.

91

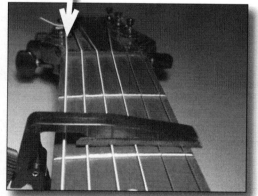

TUNING

D A D G B E

OPEN STRINGS

D B E A C# F#

Tune 6th string down 2 frets to D

The Double Drop D configuration.

26~ "Double Drop" D (022222) [Drop D]

"Drop D" or "Dropped D" tuning is the most common altered tuning, and it makes sense to begin our explorations of combining tunings and capos with it.

This looks the same as the very basic *Drop E* configuration that we looked at in the beginning of the book (#2) except that here the low E string is tuned down a whole step. This is the most common non-standard tuning combined with the most common partial capo configuration. The result is either confusing or delightful, depending on how you look at it. It's a good place to start understanding how tunings and capos can work together, since it is a simple example, and the "action" is all on the bass string, which is manageable.

Many players who use tunings think that they don't need to use partial capos, and the truth is that both are useful, and they can also be useful when done together. Some of the later examples in the book that combine a partial capo with retuning are musically deeper, though this is a good place to begin this kind of thinking.

The *Drop-E* capo configuration is almost a substitute for playing in *Drop D* tuning, and doing both at once like this allows you to play in C position, and sound in the key of D with an open bass root.

It's not a huge advantage, but it does offer some nice chords, and would be something you could easily do to play a song with a new mood if you were already playing a lot in *Drop D* tuning, which many people do. It sets a nice mood, for example, when you build a song around the Bm7 chord, for example, which is fingered as an Am7 chord.

0 2 2 2 2 2

Some Chords in the Double Drop D Configuration p.1
TUNING: Drop D (D A D G B E)

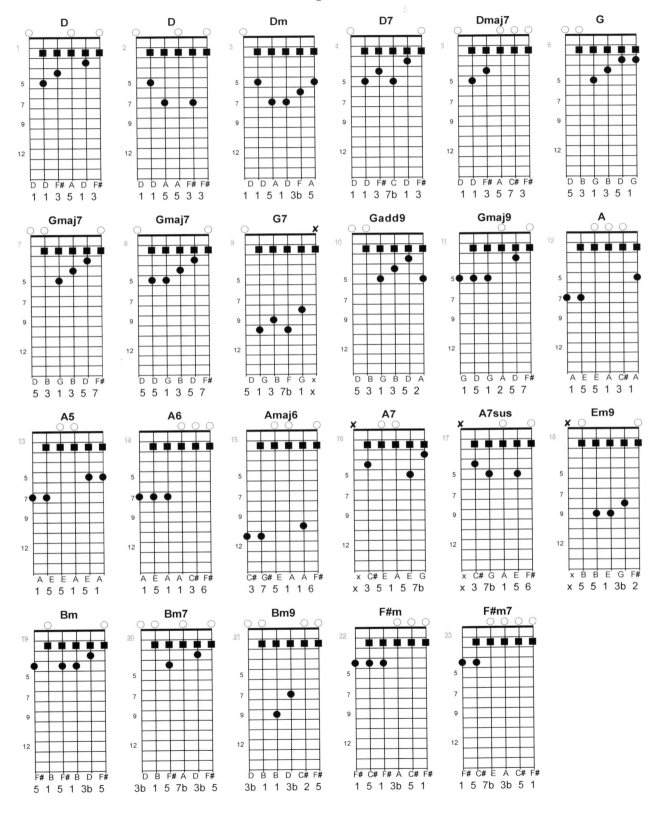

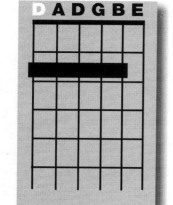

TUNING
D A D G B E
OPEN STRINGS
E B E A C# E

Tune 6th string down 2 frets to D

27~ **Drop D Bottom 5 (222220) [Drop D]**

This actually is more useful than it seems at a glance, and is a bit easier to manage than the previous one. The entire reason we use *Drop D* tuning is for the low bass note, and to use a partial capo to "undo" that like we did in the previous example, is very disorienting. Most of us who use *Drop D* spent a while getting used to it.

This way we get the familiar low end, and the capo just adds some new notes on the top end. We play in D, we sound in E, and the open high E means it takes one less finger to play D shape (1=E) chords or G shape (4=A) chords, though it adds an 11th on the 5 chord, which feels like an A when we play it. Notice that the A chord only takes 2 fingers (chord #14) which leaves a lot of room for adding melody in some fingerpicking arrangements.

There are some nice voicings, easy fingerings, and overall it's a good nice partial capo use, and one that is not obvious at all.

Moving the capo even higher does not yield much. At fret 4 you sound in F# and have a 7b on the high end, that does not add useful notes. Fret 5 adds a 6th to a G chord, though at fret 7 there is some useful stuff but the capo is pretty high and there is not much fingerboard left.

At the 2nd fret making the Bottom 5 Drop D configuration.

CAPO CONFIGURATION NAMES

I have made up some pretty good names for some of the partial capo configurations over the years, and I have to confess that some of the ones here, especially toward the end of the book, are not really very catchy and have made me wish I could find better names. The number system I use is clearly effective, but when you add the double capos and tunings things can get pretty clinical.

Maybe some day in the future someone can find a better way, and perhaps in a later edition of this book things will have descriptive and catchy names. The only way to rigorously catalog and name each capo configuration is with 6 pairs of symbols: a letter name for the pitch of the string and a number for the capo. *Esus* would then be represented by something like this: E-0, A-2, D-2, G-2, B-0, E-0.

2 2 2 2 2 0

Some Chords in the Bottom 5 Drop D Configuration p.1
TUNING: Drop D (D A D G B E)

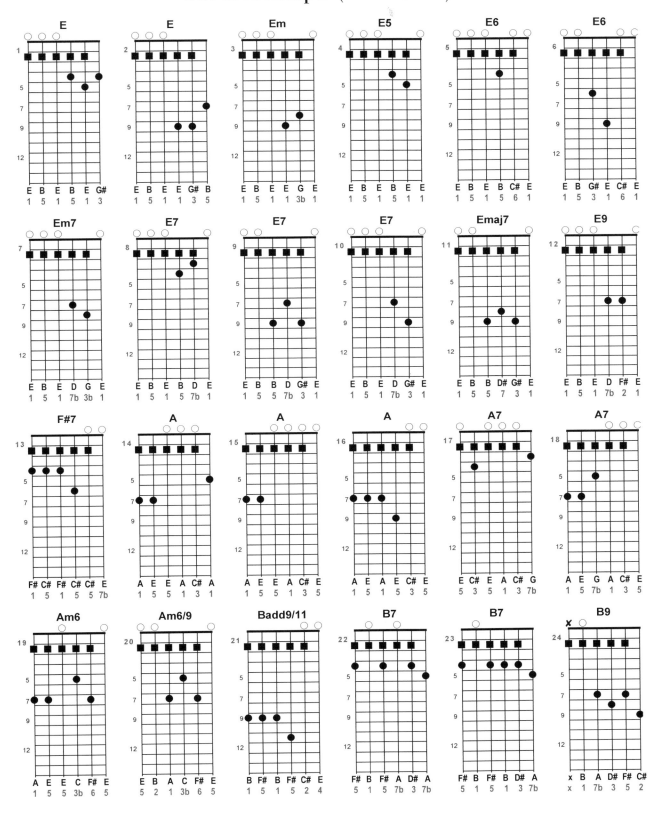

95

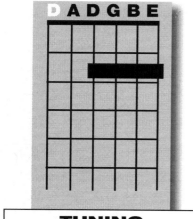

TUNING
D A D G B E
OPEN STRINGS
D A D A C# F#

Tune 6th string down 2 frets to D

At the 2nd fret leaving 2 bass strings unclamped in Drop D tuning.

28– Drop D Top 4 (002222) [Drop D]

This one is very similar to #26, and only differs in the 5th string capo position. Since the low string is tuned to D and the capo is at the 2nd fret, it makes sense to play in C position and sound in D. Your 5 chord (A) is stronger than in #26 or #27 because the open A string is now anchoring that chord.

There is not anything revolutionary about this configuration, but it has some nice chords, and if you already play in *Drop D* tuning and are looking for a quick way to get new sounds this might work for a song or two for you.

It seems to be most useful for bluesy songs, and there are some nice 7th and 9th extensions of the 1-4-5 chords that have a different flavor than if you were just playing in *Drop D* tuning without the capo. Most of the richness comes in the 1 and the 4 chord (which feel like C and G) and the 4 chord (F shape) is not ideal, as is usually the case when you try to play F chord shapes in *Drop D*. You lose the bottom end.

FAVORITE PARTIAL CAPO CHORDS

I thought long and hard about whether to flag certain chords in this book as "hot," important, or "extra-useful," since obviously some of them are going to be used a lot more than others. Likewise, I could have labeled some of them as being less important. I sort of did this by placing the chords in a kind of order. The chords at the beginning of each configuration are usually the most fundamental or important ones, or else the chords that I felt might guide you faster into the kinds of sounds or voicing choices you might be most able to use.

Obviously, this is all subjective, and we all have different tastes and may play different styles of music. I felt strongly that just an alphabetical listing of chords, or even listing majors, then minors, then sevenths etc. in some kind of order would not have allowed people to find musically useful things as quickly.

0 0 2 2 2 2

TUNING: Drop D (D A D G B E)

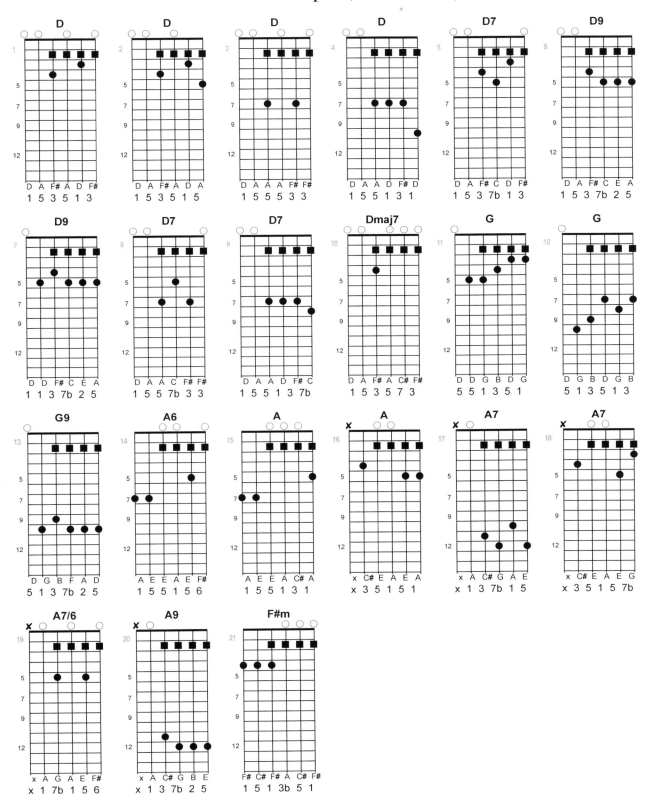

DADGBE

29- Drop D Bottom 4 (222200) [Drop D]

Here is another sneaky way to get some new open-droning sounds and extra possibilities out of the *Drop D* tuning (also called *Dropped-D*) which is the most common "non-standard" tuning. If you are at all comfortable playing in this tuning, then you can quickly change your musical landscape by adding the partial capo on the bottom 4 strings.

Some nice new voicings of the basic chords present themselves, and there is not much you have to look out for. The open strings make an E suspended (*Esus* for short) chord, which is the chord formed by the most popular 3-string partial capo, which is why I sometimes call this "*Drop Esus.*" It behaves somewhat like the common *Esus* capo configuration (0 2 2 2 0 0) in standard tuning.

This is not hugely different from normal *Esus*, but it seems to have less of the celtic & modal flavor. You can play some bass runs you can't really do in *Esus*. You also don't have to mute the bass E string on the 5 chord like you often do in *Esus*. It hardly seems like a way to play down-home acoustic blues, but it works perfectly for that genre, as well as the other kinds of songs we associate with the *Drop D* tuning. (Just pretend that Son House and Robert Johnson did this back in the 1930's.)

You will once again sound in E, but because the top two strings are B and E (part of an E chord) you can leave either of them open if you like and gain some extra fingers to play melodies and to play in new positions. And you can still keep the nice rich bass that *Drop D* tuning gives you. This is typical of the kinds of "hidden" sounds that the partial capo sometimes reveals.`

TUNING
D A D G B E
OPEN STRINGS
E B E A B E

Tune 6th string down 2 frets to D

At the 2nd fret making the Bottom 4 Drop D configuration.

MORE CHORD NAME THOUGHTS

There is no real standardization of the process of naming guitar chords, and there remain a lot of "gray areas." In classical music, there really is not a tradition of naming all chords, and only a few special ones like the *Neapolitan* or *Tristan* chord have been given names. In the worlds of folk, jazz and rock, people often do different things. I encourage everyone to relax about it all. The conventions people use are like dialects of language, and they even change with time. I speak more the folk and rock guitar here, rather than jazz or classical lingo.

Mine are the only guitar books I know of that actually shows the note names and scale positions of every note in every chord. So even if you don't like or understand the names I use, you can still study the structure.

2 2 2 2 0 0

TUNING: Drop D (D A D G B E)

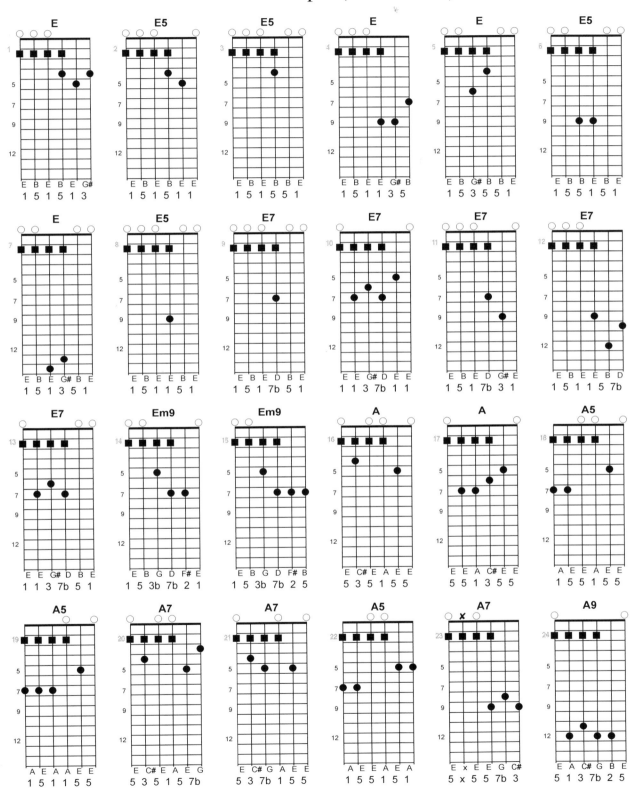

TUNING: Drop D (D A D G B E)

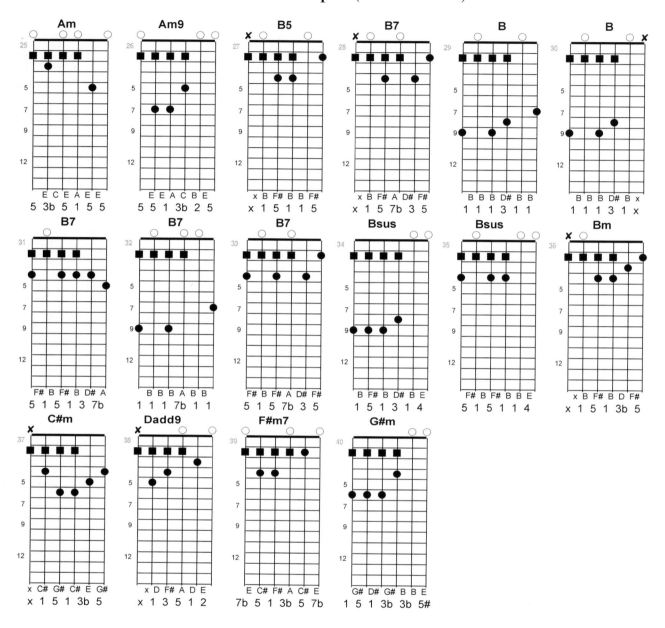

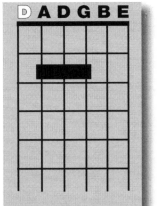

TUNING
D A D G B E
OPEN STRINGS
D B E A B E

30~ Drop D Esus (022200) [Drop D]

This is another slight modification of the common *Esus* configuration, but it yields some surprising and different sounds. If you are new at partial capoing, you again might want to save this one for later, since it is a little confusing, and some of the best sounds involve some pretty hard chords.

Since you are combining *Drop D* tuning with a capo at the 2nd fret, it makes sense to play in C position, and you will sound in D because of the capo. You can also play in A minor, which is relative to C major, and you can also build some songs out of G position, which will sound as A.

Instead of the blues, modal and celtic-flavored sounds you normally get from *Esus* and from *Drop D* tuning, you get some very extended, jazzy and new-age sounding chords, with a lot of 9ths and 11ths adding onto the chord voicings. It would be pretty easy for a good musician to write some jazz-flavored songs, with some very sophisticated-sounding chords and unusual chord changes in this configuration.

Tune 6th string down 2 frets to D

At the 2nd fret making the Esus Drop D configuration.

0 2 2 2 0 0

101

Some Chords in the Drop D Esus Configuration p.1
TUNING: Drop D (D A D G B E)

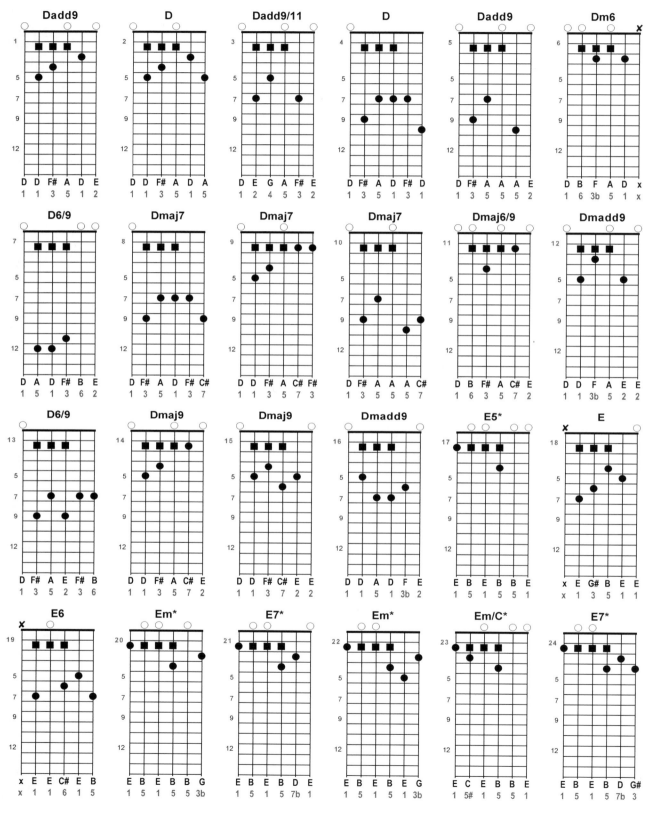

TUNING: Drop D (D A D G B E)

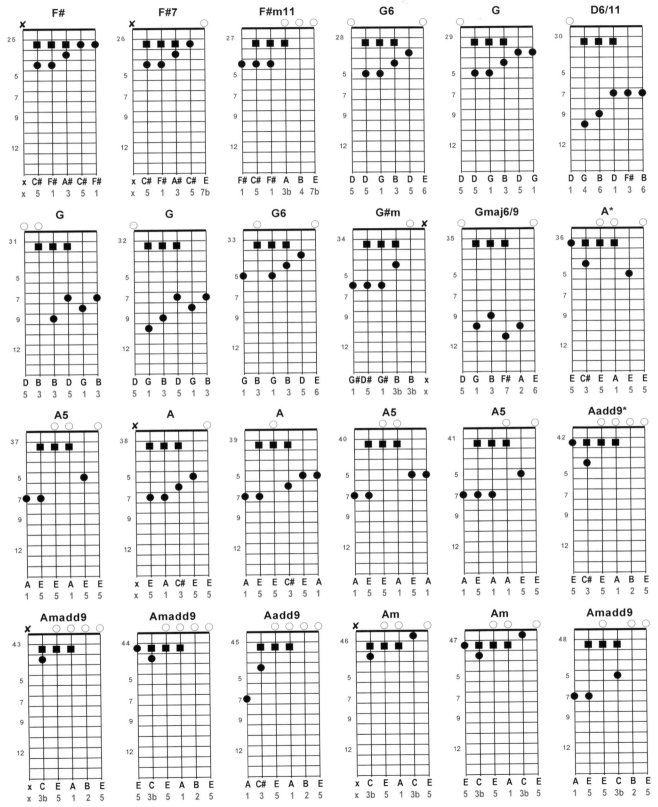

TUNING: Drop D (D A D G B E)

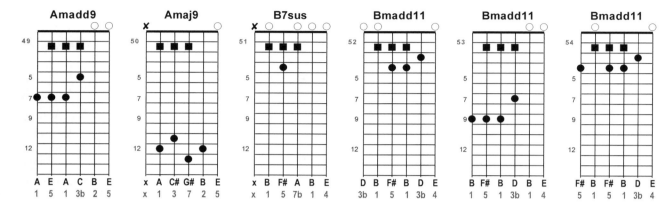

Amadd9	Amaj9	B7sus	Bmadd11	Bmadd11	Bmadd11
A E A C B E	x A C# G# B E	x B F# A B E	D B F# B D E	B F# B D B E	F# B F# B D E
1 5 1 3b 2 5	x 1 3 7 2 5	x 1 5 7b 1 4	3b 1 5 1 3b 4	1 5 1 3b 1 4	5 1 5 1 3b 4

PARTIAL CAPOS AND MODAL MUSIC

One of the most important and least-understood concepts in music is that of "modes." In standard guitar tuning, it is hard to play what are known as "modal" music chords, and the partial capo opens up a huge door to this world. Modes can be thought of as if you are playing in the "wrong key," and when you play modal scales, it feels like you are in another key, but you have a different "root" note where the music "comes to rest."

When you are playing chords in modal music, one of the things that happens often is that you need "chords" that do not have a musical 3rd in them. The most common modal song is *"Drunken Sailor"* (*"What do we do with a drunken sailor, what do we do with a drunken sailor..."*) which is basically the same melody as the old gospel song *"Sinner Man."* With E as your "key center," if you listen carefully, neither an E chord or an E minor chord sounds right, though the other chord, D major, works fine. What you need is an E5 chord, which has only 1's and 5's in it and no 3's. You will notice lots of these in this book. There are only a handful of ways to play these kinds of "modal" chords in standard tuning.

Previously the only way to get deep into modal music on guitar was to use an altered tuning. Many of the capo configurations in this book, and in particular the very important *"Esus"* make it easy to play in a number of the modes, especially those associated with the notes E and A. You will be able to play modal-flavored Celtic, blues, bluegrass and gospel songs with your partial capo with a freedom and depth that are a revelation to many players.

In classical music theory, there are seven modes, with Greek names, each based on a position in the major scale. Other musical tonalities, such as pentatonic scales, are often also called "modal" music, which basically means they are not major or minor. Music that sort of follows the do-re-mi major scale is what we usually call "major key" music, and is actually *Ionian* mode. If you play through the white keys of the piano C-D-E-F-G-A-B-C in that order, it makes a C major scale, and outlines what would be music in C major or C *Ionian* mode. If you started with the 6th note (A) and played through a C scale A-B-C-D-E-F-G-A you would be playing in A *Aeolian* mode, usually called A minor. (Technically, there are a number of minor scales, such as relative minor, melodic minor, harmonic minor but we won't go into that here.) The 12 note names (A through G with sharps/flats) each generate 7 modes.

If you started on the D or 2nd note of the C scale, that makes the D *Dorian* mode. The others are similarly generated from starting at the 3rd (*Phrygian*), 4th (*Lydian*), 5th (*Mixolydian*) and 7th scale (*Lochrian*) positions. *Phrygian* mode is the basis for flamenco and Moorish-flavored music, for example, and a lot of Celtic and bluegrass music is in Mixolydian mode. *Lydian* mode is often used in modern rock and fusion music. You can easily search on the internet and learn more about all of this.

The only mode that is easy for solo guitar in standard-tuned guitar is the Spanish-flavored *Phrygian* mode. It basically uses a C scale and the chords from the key of C: C, F, G, Dm and Am among others, but is built around the E chord and the E root note. This mode is probably why standard tuning is common, since it probably evolved in Spain and it worked for them to play their music.

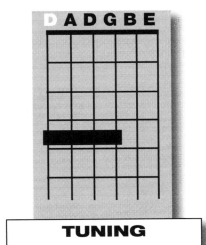

TUNING

D A D G B E

OPEN STRINGS

F# C# F# B B E

Tune 6th string down 2
frets to D

*A Model 43 at the 4th fret making the Drop
Esus configuration.*

31~ Bottom 4@4 (444400) [Drop D]

This one is a little disorienting, and it helps to be familiar with *Drop D* tuning. Most people play only in D positions (D, Dm etc.) and occasionally G position in this tuning, so here the capo puts you in F# if you play in D. This may be useful to you to break monotony or sing at this pitch, but it may be a problem if you are playing with other musicians, since F# is not a popular key. You might want to capo 1 with a full capo to put you into the key of G, though it is refreshing to play in F# if you spend a lot of your life in "normal" guitar keys.

The 1-4-5 chords in the key of F# are F#, B and C#. I find myself playing bluesy songs in F# that drone the open high E string or work it against a familiar D shape, since the high E string open is a flat 7 or *dominant 7th* note in this key. There are a few really nice F#7 chords (like chord #3) here that invite you to set up a groove, and it's not hard to riff a little on the middle strings with the drone bass under you. There are also some strong, full 4 chords, that play like G chords in *Drop D* tuning. The B5, B7 and some *add11's* have a big sound, and you can play standard 5 chords (that use A or A7 shapes,) which sound as a C# or C#7. The *Mixolydian* "drop chord" (which feel like a C) works pretty well also, and you just have to avoid the low E string when you play it.

The Dm and Dm7 chord shapes (that sound F#m and F#m7) are nice, and you could use this tuning/configuration to play songs that use a 1 minor to 4 minor progression, which would "feel" like Dm- Gm and sound as F#m to Bm.

444400

TUNING (Drop D) : D A D G B E

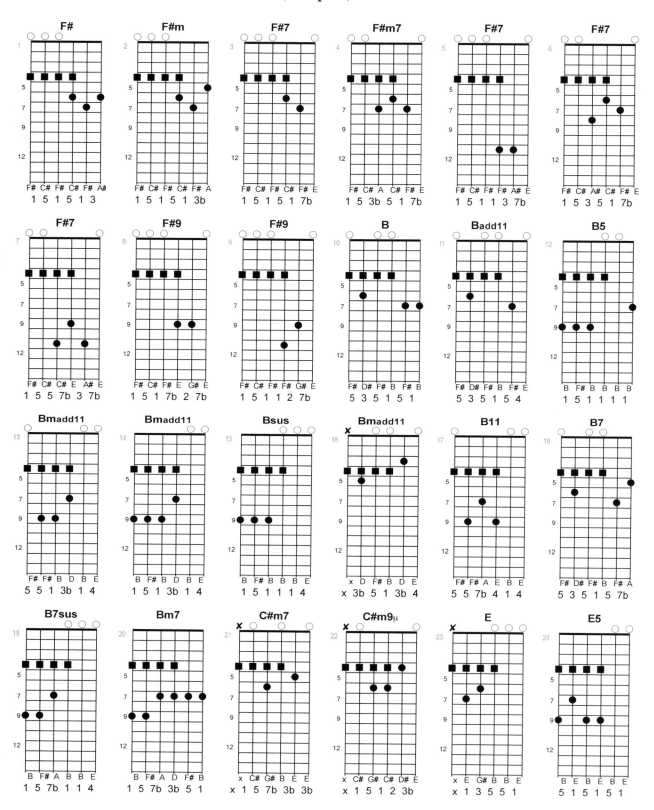

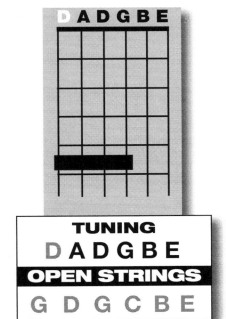

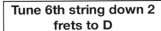

TUNING
D A D G B E
OPEN STRINGS
G D G C B E

Tune 6th string down 2
frets to D

*A Model 43 at the 5th fret making the
Bottom 4 @5 configuration.*

32- Bottom 4@5 (555500) [Drop D]

Like some previous configurations, this one capos the bottom 4 strings, but this time it is at the 5th fret. Because capos that can reliably clamp 4 outer strings are not widespread, this is a very unknown configuration.

With shortened capos, the musical "action" is always either on the bass or treble end, depending on how you attach the capo. When you leave bass strings unclamped, you are usually going after a drone bass sound, to anchor the low end of the guitar. When you leave treble strings open like this, you get treble drones, similar to the 5th string of a banjo, and you get new notes added to chords.

Not many people who play in *Drop D* tuning play in any keys other than D, or some modal or blues keys centered around D. This means that here you will end up in the key of G because of the capo. It also means that the high E string will add a 6th to your 1 (tonic) chord, and the open B string adds another 3rd. When you play a 2 chord, major or minor, you get an added "*mu*" 9th from the B string. There are some interesting chords that pop out here, and if you thump the bass in a fingerpicking style and roll some of the chords shown here in the treble end, some really nice sounds emerge.

555500

Some Chords in Bottom 4 @ 5 Drop D p.1
TUNING (Drop D) : D A D G B E

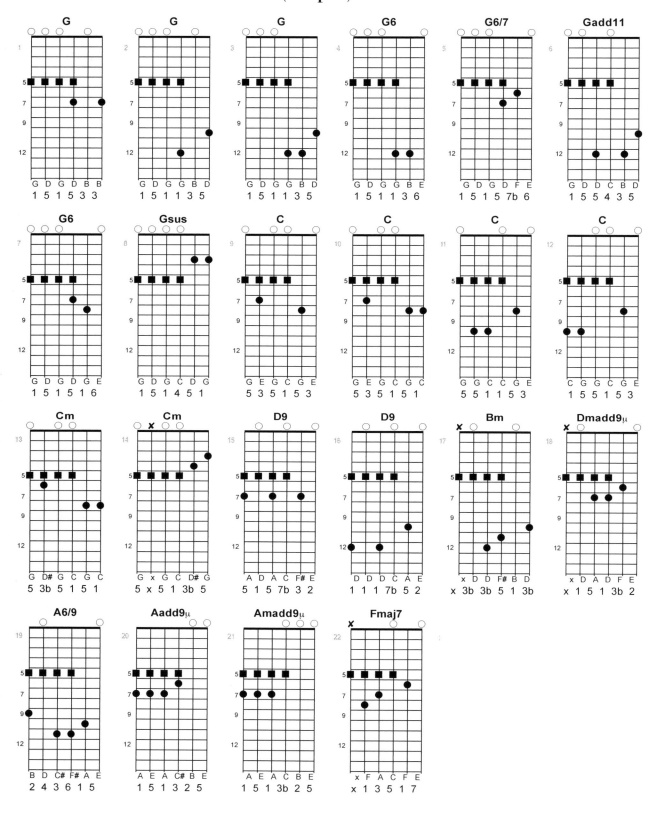

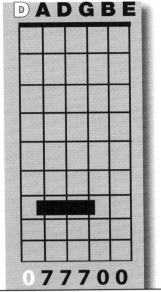

TUNING

D A D G B E

OPEN STRINGS

D E A D B E

0 7 7 7 0 0

33- Esus@7 (077700)[Drop D]

This a pretty typical partial capo environment, though I would rate it as above average. It has some wonderful and quite unique voicings and a rich sound, and it is not too hard to get to, since you just retune 1 string. It is not quite one of the deep and magical partial capo ideas, but it offers some excellent music. Chord #17 is an add9 I like a lot, for example. It is a completely unique voicing in my library of nearly 20000 chords.

With the low D in the bass, it makes sense to play in G position above the capo in order to still sound in D and use the bass root. This is a little disorienting, since most people who play in *Drop D* tuning play in D position, and not G. Luckily, we have a bass root, unlike "real *Drop D*" where playing in G gives you D-B-D on the bottom 3 strings. Now we have D-E-A. Chord #16 is thus the simplest 1 chord fingering.

The high capo means that there will be a lot of overlapping voicings, where notes fretted above the capo will land in the same octave as the open treble strings. The bottom 2 strings giving us D-E means that unless you fret one of those strings, you will get add9 voicings. The open strings make a vague chord that is somewhere between an A9/11 and a D 6/9. This kind of open-string ambiguity is sometimes good for making chords in more than one key. The most striking chords are probably #19-25. The major 6/9 chords there are pretty rare, with the 1-2-5-6-7 scale notes woven together. I have so far only found 11 of them out of 14000 chords in my library, and 2 of those live here.

**Tune 6th string
down to D**

A Model 43 capo at the 7th fret making the Esus@7 configuration in Drop D tuning.

0 7 7 7 0 0

TUNING: DADGBE

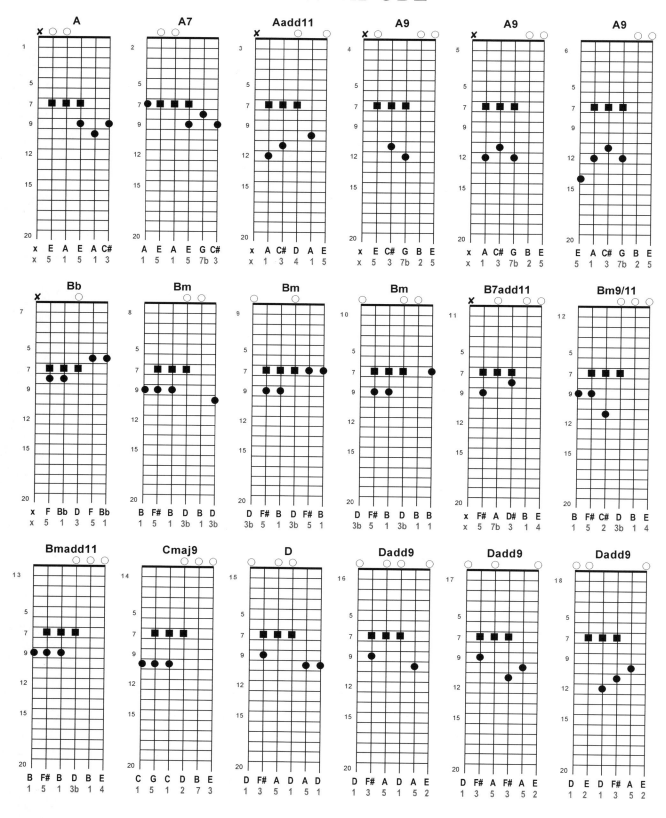

TUNING: DADGBE

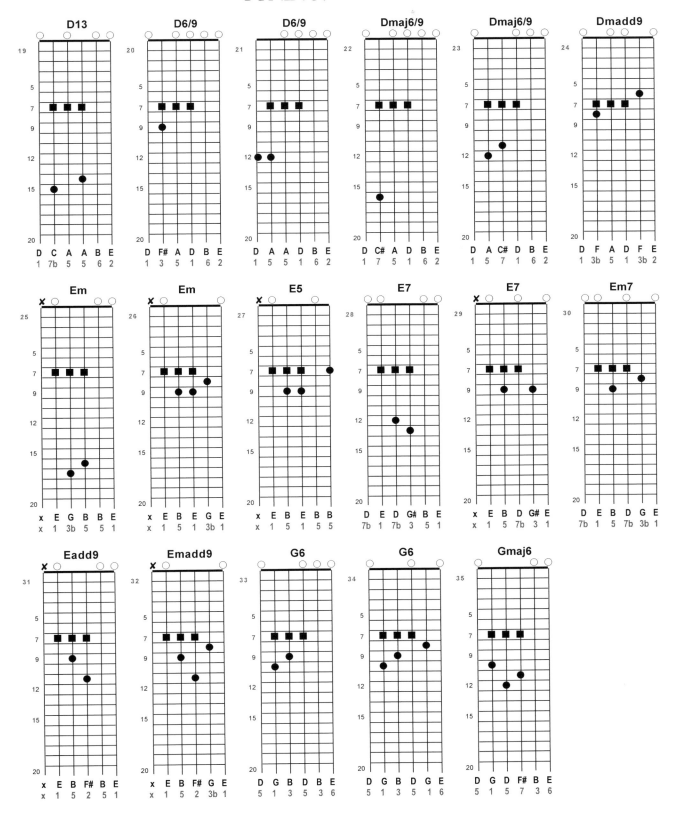

111

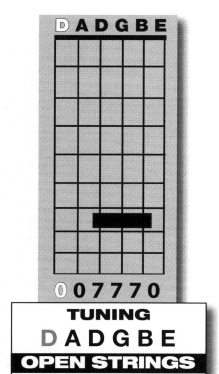

DADGBE

007770

TUNING
DADGBE
OPEN STRINGS
D A A D F# E

34~ A@7 (007770) [Drop D]

The thinking behind this configuration is that it gives the same basic sound as *Open A@9* (#25), but here you sound in D, and you only have to capo 7 instead of 9. It's nice to have the extra 2 frets of fingerboard room, and also nice to play in D instead of E. The 5th string behaves differently here than it does in that configuration.

You lower the bass E string down to D, which most guitarists are used to doing. It adds nice low-string support, and since the A string is open, it is now part of the open chord, which was not the case before. Since the high E string is still tuned to E, it rings a 2nd (or 9th) note against the D chord, which can be a nice effect.

As you might have noticed, *Open A@9* had a lot of chords shown, and had a surprising amount of depth, and this one is similar in that respect. It is also very closely related to a number of other configurations that also use a *Drop D* tuning and an *Open A* capo at the 7th fret.

Later in the book we'll add another element to this one (like I do on a number of *Open A*-based configurations) by tuning the B string up to C and making a suspension out of it. (#51) I find it to be significantly easier to manage, though you might find the extra retuned string to be confusing.

Tune 6th string down 2 frets to D

A Model 43 at fret 7 making the Drop D A@7 configuration.

007770

112

TUNING: Drop D (D A D G B E)

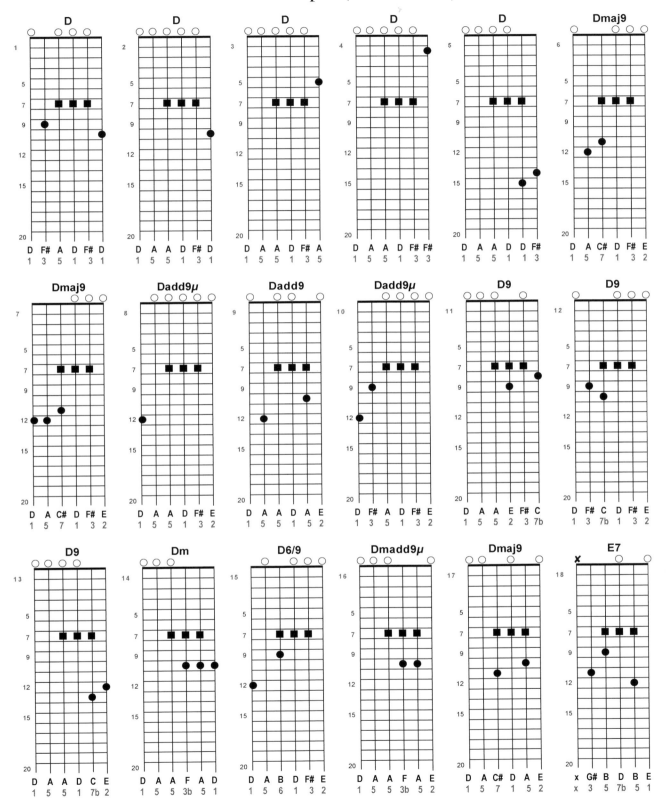

TUNING: Drop D (D A D G B E)

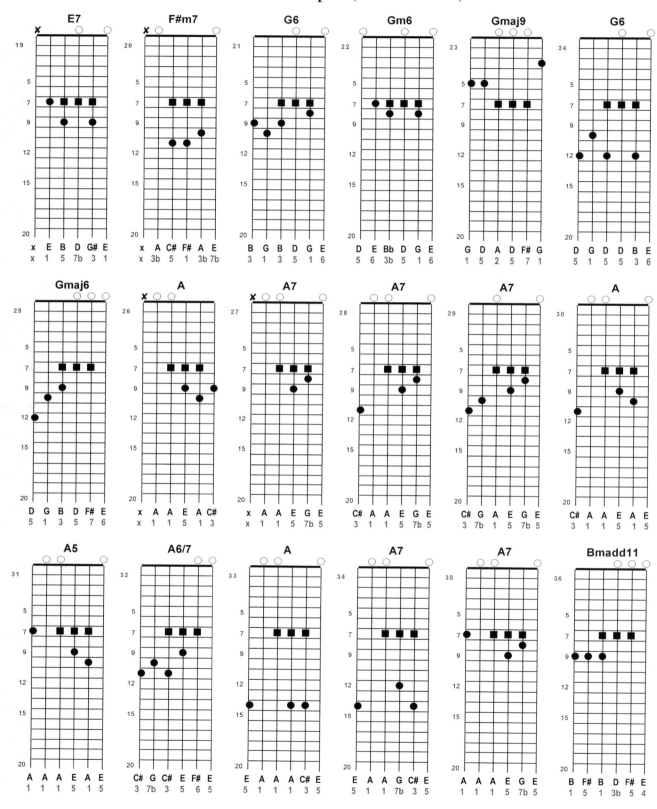

TUNING

E A D F# B E

OPEN STRINGS

E B E G# B E

Tune 3rd string down 1
fret to F#

The Easy-E configuration.

Author's Favorite

35~ Easy-E (022200) [EADF#BE]

This looks the same as the *Esus* partial capo configuration, E suspended, except you tune the G (3rd) string down one fret to F#. Interestingly, this is the tuning of the old Spanish *vihuela*, generally considered to be the historical predecessor to the modern guitar. I first used this in the early 1990's on a song called "*Maybe Someday.*" It behaves in a very different way from "regular" *Esus*, and a pretty startling number of great new chords pops out.

Instead of hearing an E suspended chord when you play all 6 strings open, you get an E chord, with the 3rd string G# providing the musical 3rd. It's a quick way to give a child or a beginner an open E chord to practice strumming or fingerpicking patterns.

Like *Esus*, it allows you to play very easy fingerings of the basic chords in the key of E, so it is also very useful for beginners and people with special learning needs.

You can also play some more sophisticated guitar in this configuration, and all sorts of new sounds emerge from just this simple retuning. A number of these more complex and difficult chords are shown here in the chord charts.

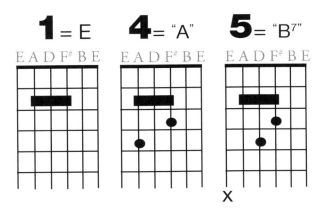

ABOUT THESE CHORDS: These 3 chords work as 1 (*tonic*), 4 (*sub-dominant*) and 5 (*dominant*) chords in the key of E, though the A (like in *Esus* configuration) is an *Aadd9* and the B7 is a B7suspended. They sound great on some songs, adequate on most, and only sometimes are inappropriate. The results are similar to *Esus*, but there is one big difference: Here the 1 chord has a 3rd and is not the "modal" 1 chord like it is in *Esus*. The 4 and 5 chords each take one more finger to play than they do in the *Esus* configuration, though they have the exact same notes.

0 2 2 2 0 0

TUNING: E A D F♯ B E

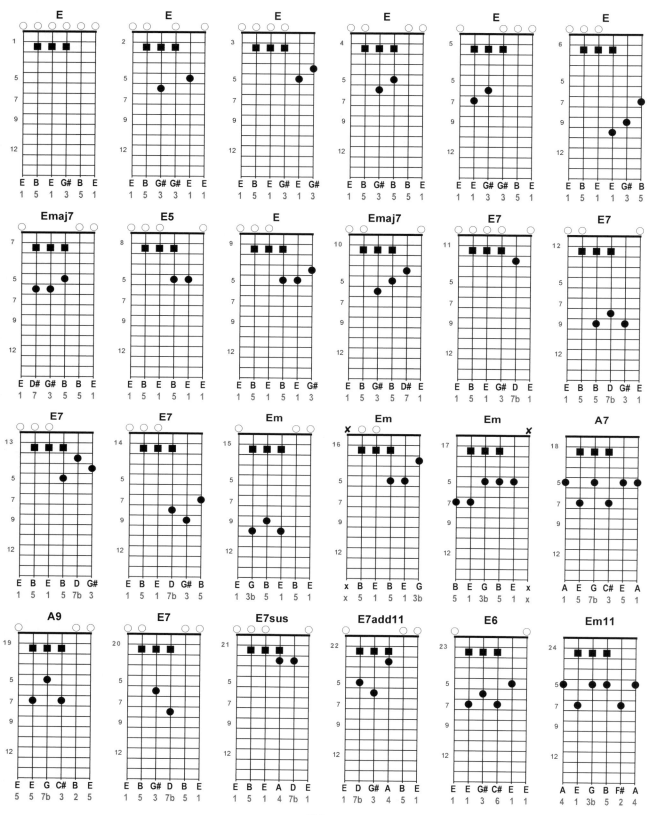

TUNING: EAD F# B E

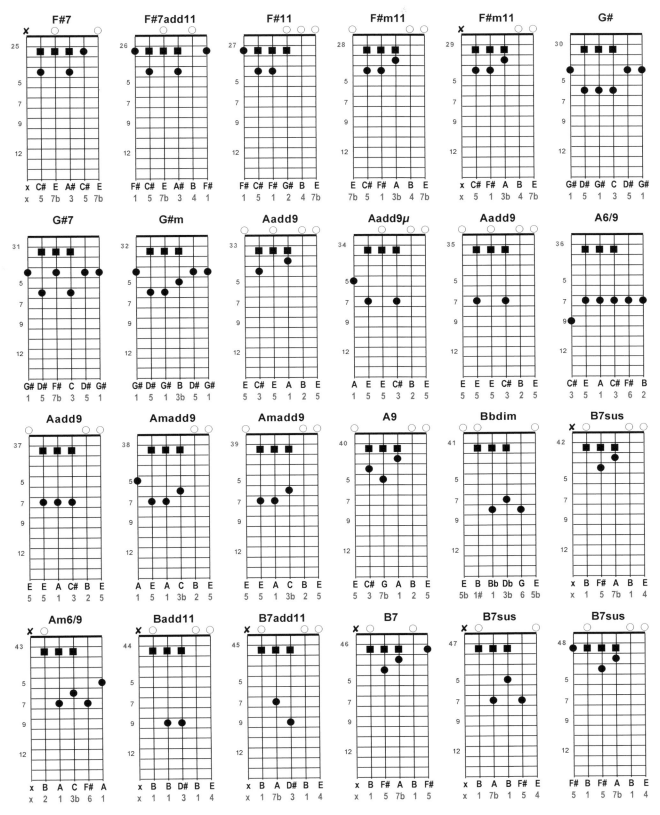

117

TUNING: E A D F# B E

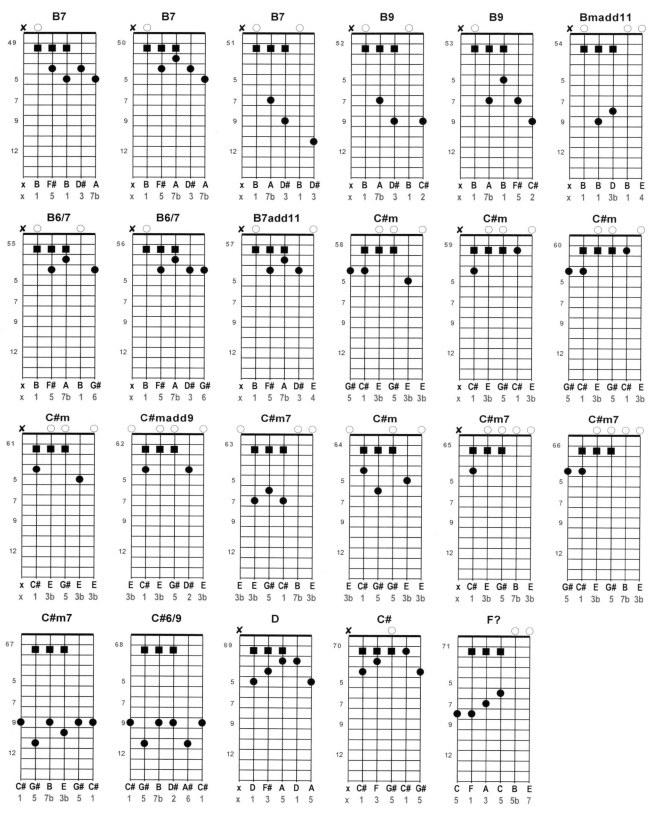

EADFBE

022200

TUNING
EADFBE
OPEN STRINGS
EBEGBE

36~ Esus Minor (022200)[EADFBE]

This also looks the same as the *Esus* partial capo configuration, and it is only slightly different than the previous *Easy-E*. Here we tune the G string down two frets to F so that the open strings form an E minor chord. As you might expect, it takes some getting used to, but it yields some great sounds.

You might think that a partial capo that formed an Em chord at the 2nd fret would be useful for playing music in E minor, but I have tried a number of times to get something out of it and not found as much as I expected. This one, for some reason, works really well for music in Em. There are a lot of nice Em chords, and also E5, E and E7 (though only the E5's in that group have much value for music in Em.) You also get, as you would expect, a considerable number of ways to extend the Em chord with 6ths, 9ths, 11ths etc.

There are also some rich chords that you wouldn't anticipate, and you can work up some satisfying and very open-tuning-flavored arrangements of well-known minor-key songs like *"Eleanor Rigby," "Paint It Black"* or *"Wayfaring Stranger."* Things you play this way have quite a different sound than minor-key music played in *Esus*, and you only need to re-tune one string to get here. The important chords like the Am and the C and G sound great, though I would have to classify this as a more "advanced" configuration, since it relies on some left-hand chords that are not easy.

If you are new to the partial capo and are just flipping through this book, you might want to save this one for later, unless you are comfortable dealing with new tunings.

The Esus Minor configuration.

Tune 3rd string down 2 frets to F

022200

119

TUNING: E A D F B E

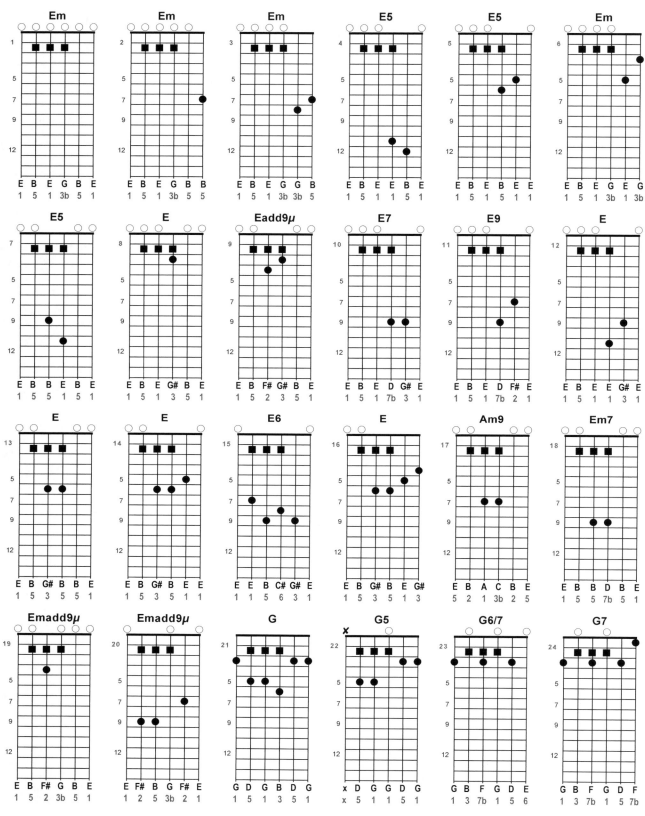

TUNING: E A D F B E

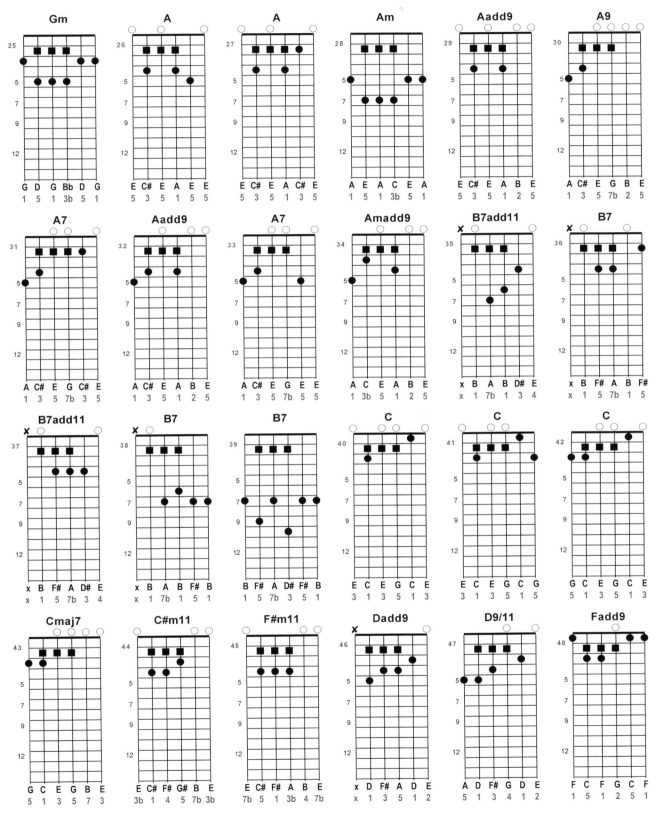

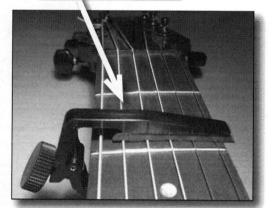

EGDGBE

TUNING
E G D G B E
OPEN STRINGS
E A E A C# F#

Tune 5th string down 2 frets to G

A Model 65 at the 2nd fret making the Drop A configuration.

37~ Drop A (022222) [EGDGBE]

Author's Favorite

This is one of the subtler and musically useful examples of a way to use a partial capo in combination with a slight retuning, and it is a personal favorite of mine, one I originated, and in my *Top 10* list. In most other cases of retuning, we changed a string to make the capo form a particular chord or else tune the guitar to a chord, but in this one we just lower the A (5th) string down a whole step to G.

The thinking behind it is that when you play in configuration #3, *"Half-Open A"* (0 0 2 2 2 2) you have to mute or avoid the 5th string when you play a D chord (which the capo makes into an E). Here we also get the same open bass strings on the G chord, a "free" open string bass note for the C chord (which sounds as D,) and we also get a full, 6-string sound from the D chord. So the 1-4-5 chords when you play in G (and sound in A) are all 6-string chords that use less fingers than standard tuning. This is vital for fingerpicking, when you need bass-string support and extra fingers to move melodies around on the treble end.

I recorded *"Camptown Races/Oh Susanna"* this way in 1991 on my '*Steel Drivin' Man*' recording. It takes a while to get used to, since you retune an unusual string, but it is a very pleasant way to play guitar. It just enhances the voicings of chords, but does not call attention to itself or feature the droning, open-tuned sound that so many partial capo configurations and tunings generate.

"Drop A" is equally useful for accompanying songs and playing instrumental music. I use it almost exclusively to play in G position and sound in the key of A but you could also play in D position and sound in E.

This is one of the only partial capo applications out there that allows a strong 2 chord (#18-21.) Usually chords with roots other than 1, 4 and 5 are weak, but not in this case. You can also play a good 6 chord (chords #58-61), which are also usually weak in partial capo configurations.

0 2 2 2 2 2

Some Chords in the Drop-A Configuration p.1
TUNING: E G D G B E

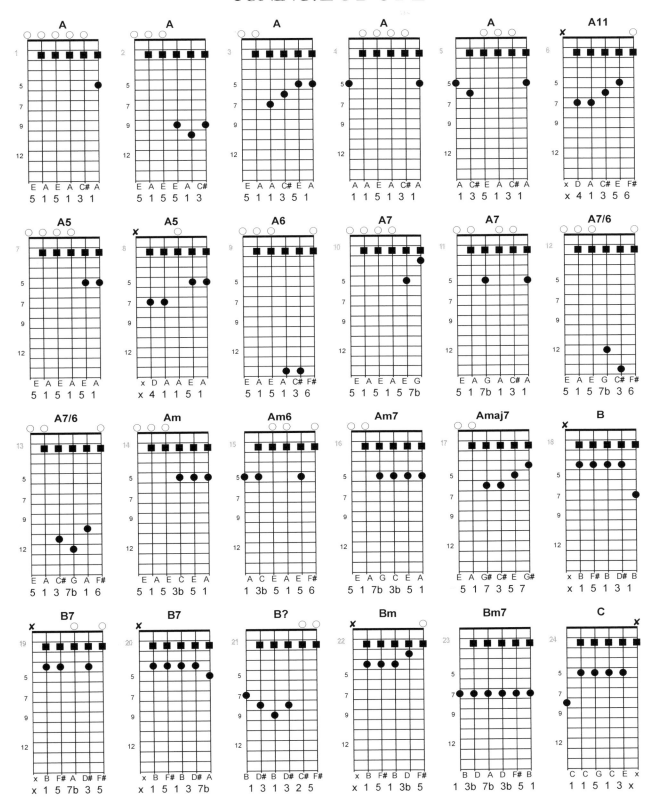

123

TUNING: E G D G B E

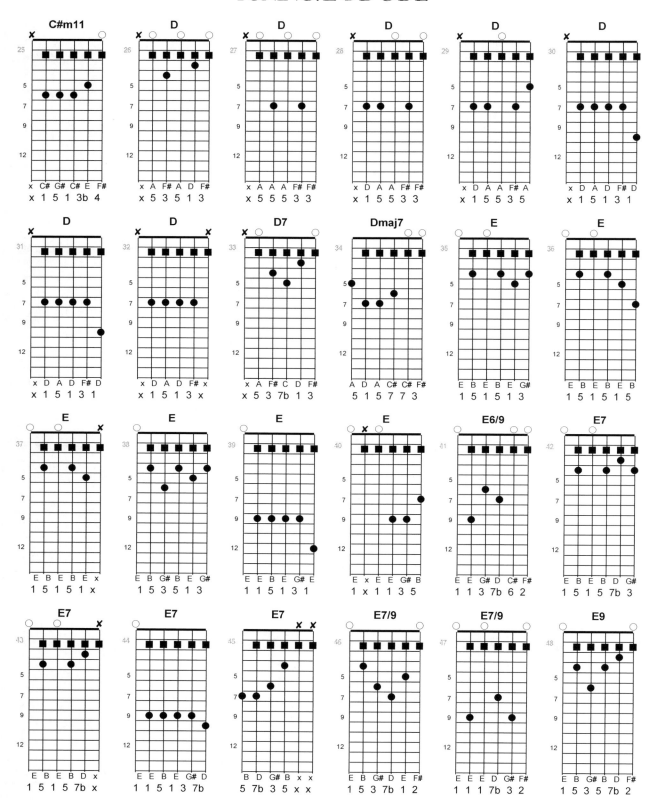

TUNING: E G D G B E

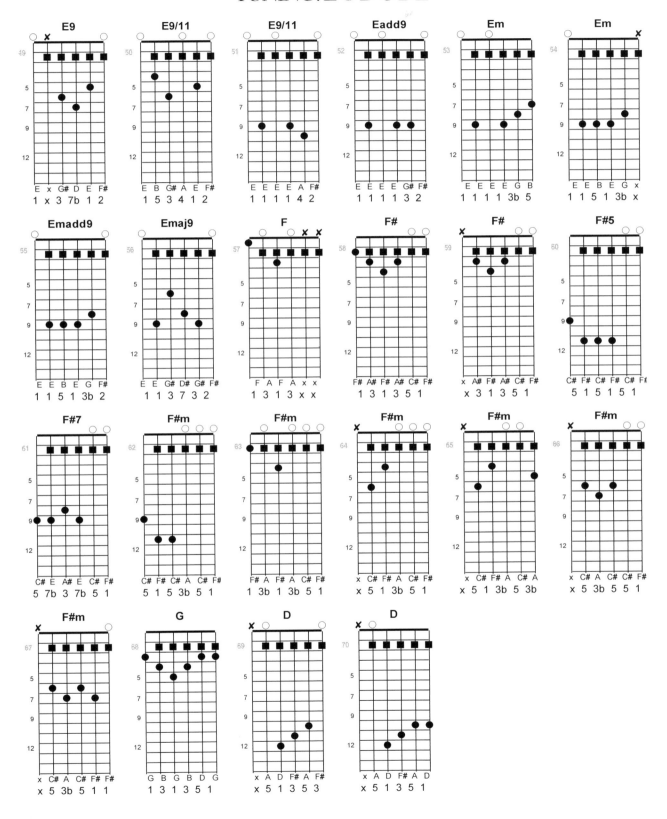

TUNING
E A D G B D
OPEN STRINGS
E A E A C# E

At the 2nd fret making the Half-Open A Slide.

Tune 1st string down 2 frets to D

38~ Half-Open A Slide (002222) [EADGBD]

There are not a lot of uses of the partial capo that directly benefit slide guitar players, and this is one of only a few in this book. It is a clever one, that allows you to get the flavor of the *Open A* (essentially the *Open G*, which is just 2 frets lower) slide guitar sound so familiar to fans of Robert Johnson and other Delta blues players. The advantage is that you only have to retune 1 string instead of the usual 3.

I first discovered this idea in the early 1990's, and used it on a tune on my *Capo Voodoo: Solo Guitar* CD called *"Johnson's Blues"* where it sounds very much like old-fashioned open-A tuned slide guitar. I don't think the idea has caught on yet, but it should, because it is very useful and not that hard to manage. Any time you just retune a single outer string it is less confusing.

The way this idea works is that if you tune the high E string down 2 frets to D, and then capo it back up by forming the *Half-Open A* configuration, the open strings sound exactly like an A chord, or an *Open A* partial capo. The key to it is that when the top 4 strings are played as a barre or with a slide at any fret, it makes a major chord. (Chords #4-5.) If you play lead guitar in a band, this would be a practical way to play open-tuned sounding leads in A with a quick retune that you could manage between songs.

Since the bottom 2 bass strings are E and A, we can thump the bass strings and slash the slide on just the 4 treble strings at fret 14 and it sounds right. Single string melody slide on the high E string, also a hallmark of the blues slide style, sounds exactly like it does in the full open tuning. Because the bass E string is an open root bass for the 5 chord, we can play slide at fret 7 (above the capo) and get a nice 5 chord, and at fret 5 with the bass A string, it is the usual Delta blues 4 chord with the 5th of the chord on the bottom.

The other nice thing is that the bottom 5 strings are tuned normally, so you can play normal barre chord shapes, familiar bass runs and rhythm chords, even with a slide on your 4th finger.

0 0 2 2 2 2

TUNING: EADGB D

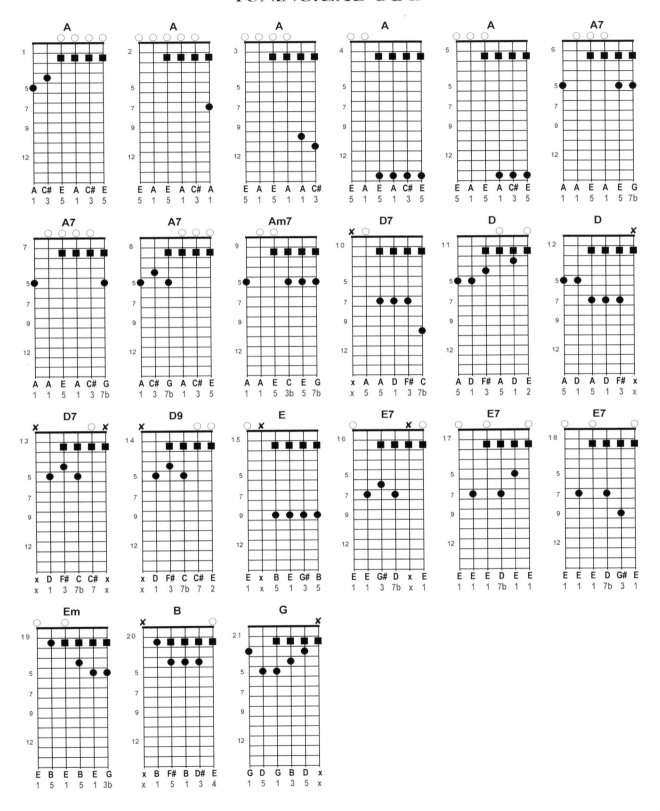

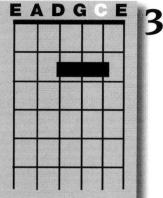

39~ A Suspended (002220)[EADGCE]

TUNING
E A D G C E
OPEN STRINGS
E A E A D E

Tune 2nd string up 1 fret

The Asus configuration.

This looks just like *Open A*, though the B string is tuned a fret sharp to C. I call it *Asus*, which is short for "A suspended," the chord that sounds when the 6 strings are played open. I found this in 1980, and it actually led me to discover *Esus*, but I did not realize its potential immediately. I first used it on a recording in 1998 on the song "*I Have Finally Found a Home*" on my CD "*Fruit on the Vine*" and I think I have used it on about 15 recorded tracks so far. I use it a lot in my concerts, and a lot on the 6-string banjo.

Like many other of the suspended-chord based tunings and configurations, this one is surprisingly fruitful and one of the most interesting and powerful of all the applications of the partial capo. It is especially useful for singers who like the partial capo idea but do not sing much in E. It offers many of the kinds of things that have made the *Esus* so popular, but it is brighter sounding, since things end up pitched a string higher than in *Esus*. With an added full capo, you can sound in keys A through D without a cutaway guitar.

Asus is more of what I might call an "advanced" configuration than some. It can be quite disorienting, probably because the B string, where it is retuned, is the "odd" string in standard tuning. *Asus* is a bit harder to adjust to than some of the other tunings in this book that only differ slightly from standard tuning.

There are fewer good 5 chord fingerings, and the best 5 chords require a pretty good left hand (see chord #101). However, it can be used to play some 1-finger modal songs and believe it or not is a wonderful way to play solo bluegrass guitar in A. It can sound very celtic, pentatonic bluesy, and can also generate a compelling mountain-modal and bluegrass flavor.

The ringing modal sound *Asus* makes evokes the sound of banjos and dulcimers, and has intrigued me for many years. It has yielded a number of complex celtic and classical-style guitar pieces, and I have used it for quite a number of blues and modal bluegrass songs. My epic 12-string piece "*Pegasus*" is played in this tuning, and got its name because of the last 4 letters of its title.

0 0 2 2 2 0

Some Chords in the Asus Configuration p.1
TUNING: E A D G C E

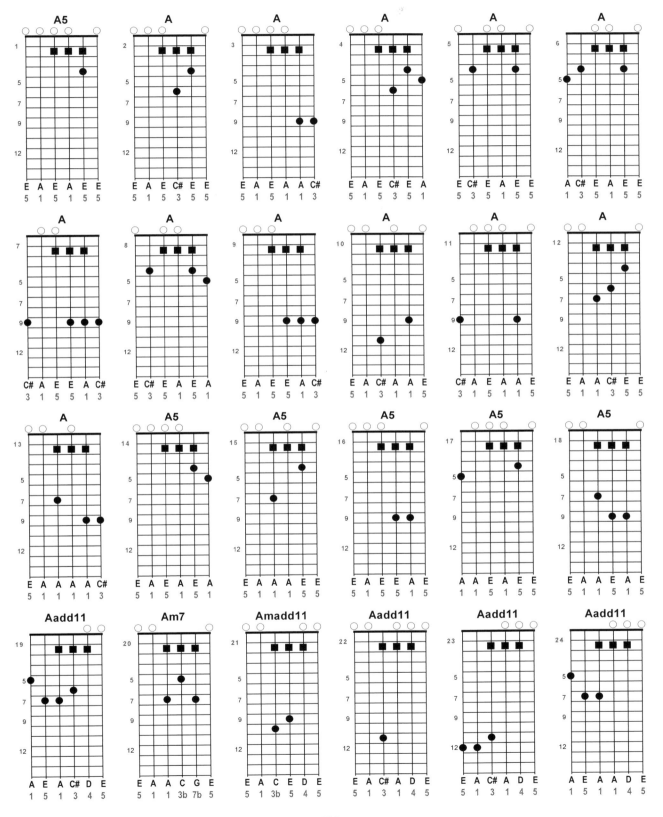

129

TUNING: E A D G C E

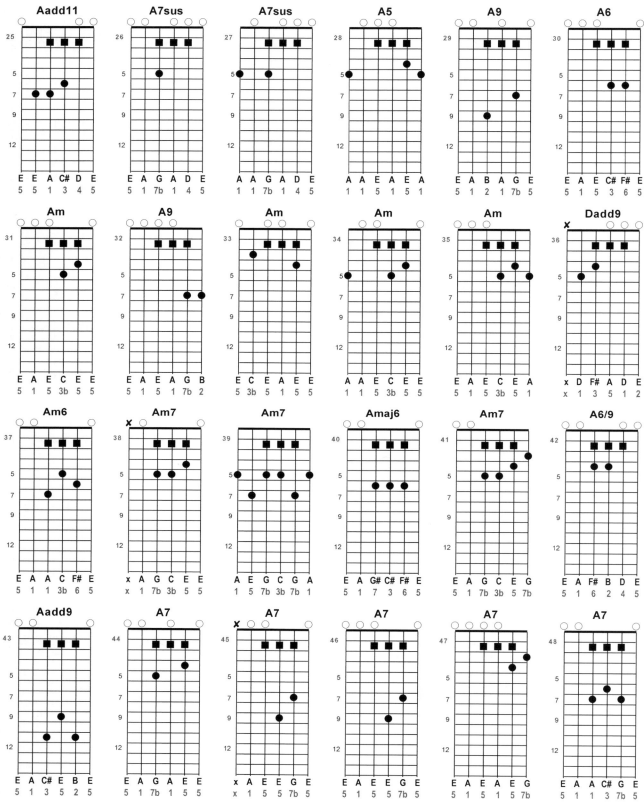

TUNING: E A D G C E

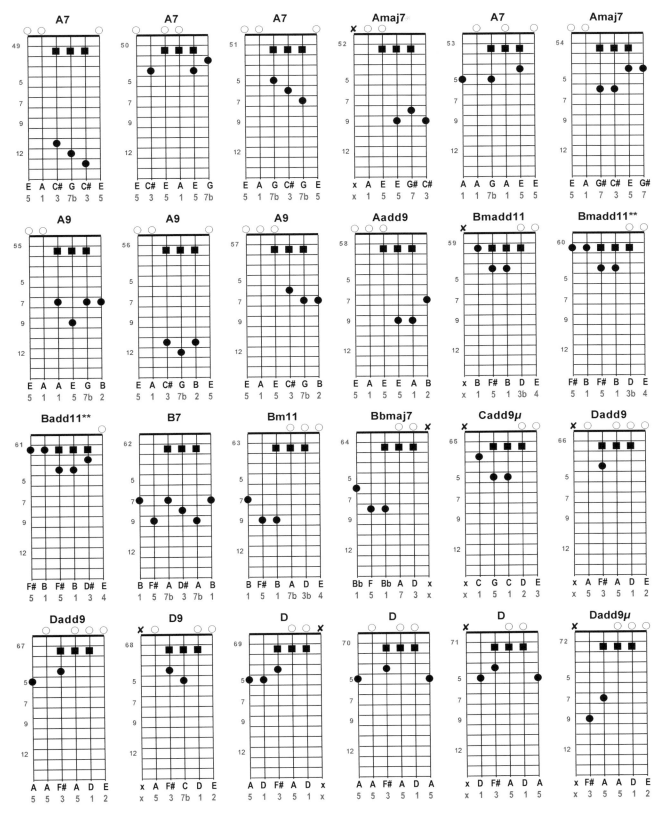

TUNING: E A D G C E

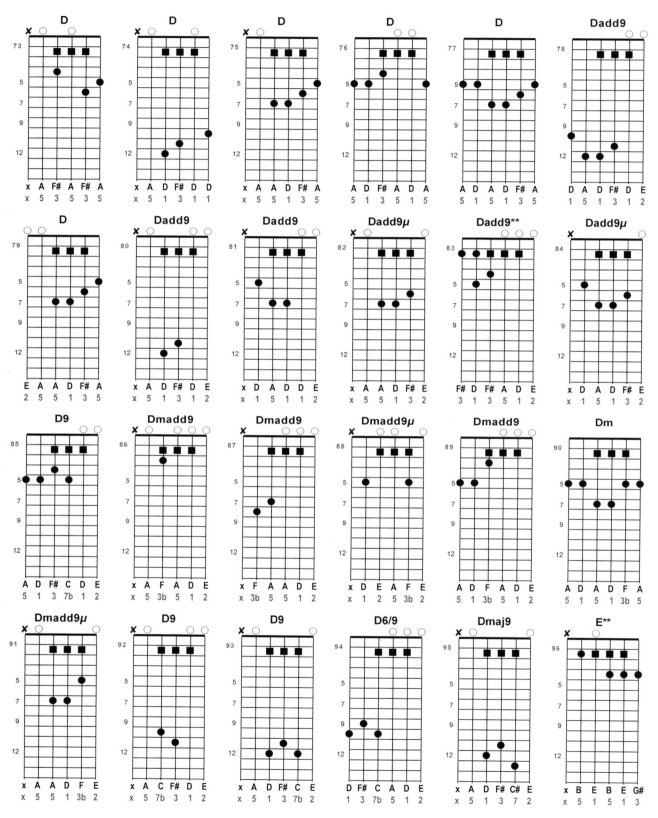

132

Some Chords in the Asus Configuration p.5
TUNING: E A D G C E

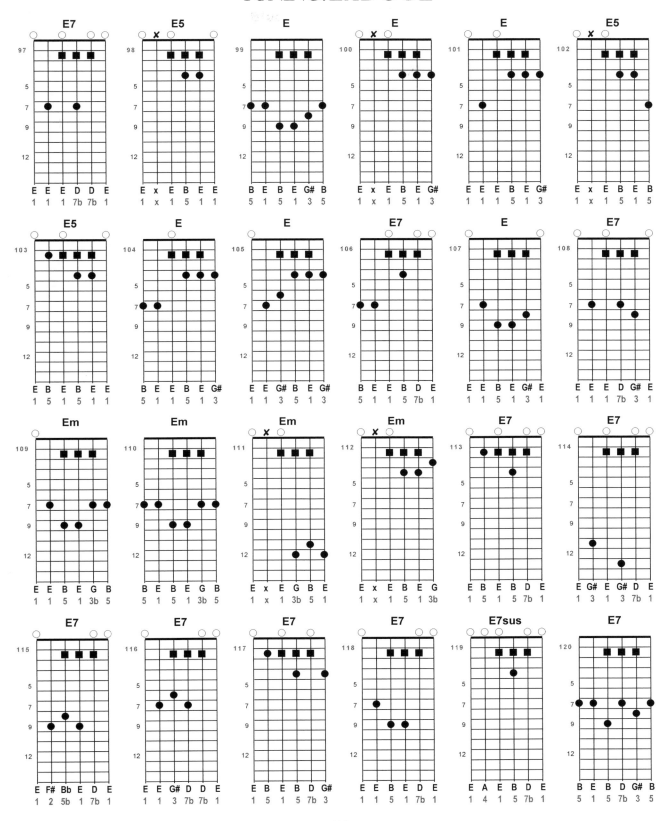

133

TUNING: E A D G C E

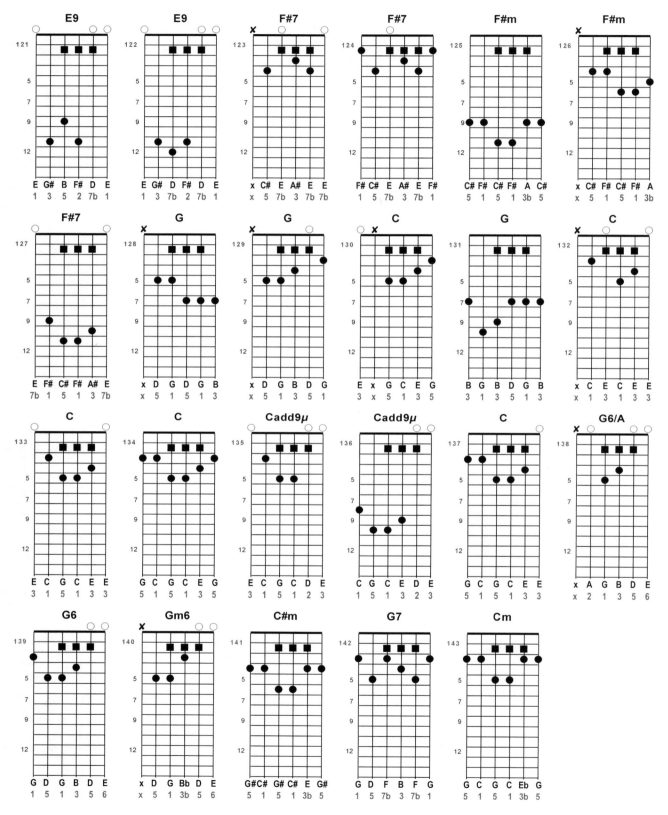

EADG B♭ E

002220

TUNING
E A D G B♭ E
OPEN STRINGS
E A E A C E

Tune 2nd string down 1 fret to B♭

The A-Drop minor configuration.

40- A Drop Minor (002220) [EADGB♭E]

It makes sense to put this one right after the *Asus* configuration, because it is a variation of the same idea of retuning the 2nd string with a capo at 002220. This one is also visually just like *Open A*, and it works pretty much the same way as the earlier (#36) "*Esus Minor*," where the capo forms an open E minor chord. Here the B string is tuned a fret flat to B♭. Like the previous *Asus* configuration, it is hard to adapt to. It does, however, make some flowing, resonant, minor-key sounds, and you could write or arrange either a song or an instrumental this way.

I would suggest that this is also more of an "advanced" than a "beginner" configuration. There are some easy A minor fingerings, but most of the other basic chords you need in this key are not simple. I have the most fun using it to play cascading minor-key scales on the middle strings, since there are not a lot of ways to do that on guitar in general, or in this book.

You could tune the B string down another notch to A, and get an *Aadd9* open chord, but I found it unproductive. If you find yourself enjoying this, you might take it another step and try capoing 057770 (like #77 in this book) and also tuning the bass E string down to D (with the B string still down to B♭). You would then sound in Dm, you would have a low D bass note underneath everything, and the guitar has a sweeter timbre. The minor-key scales you play on the middle strings would be a fourth higher, and not so dark. You would then have to fret any notes on the bass E string 2 frets higher. I could add a couple more pages to the book and map that one out for you but probably won't.

0 0 2 2 2 0

TUNING: E A D G B♭ E

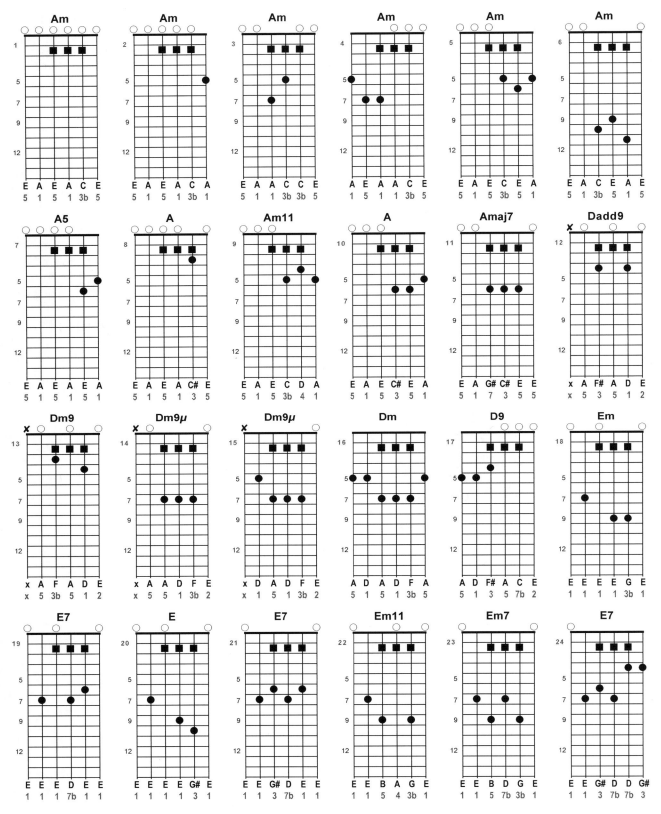

Some Chords in the A Drop Minor Configuration p.2
TUNING: E A D G B♭ E

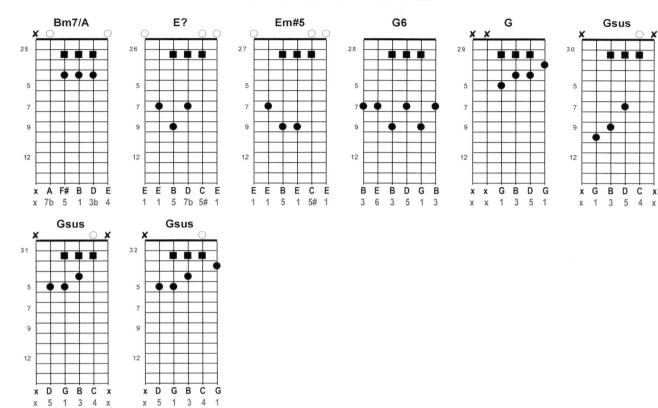

137

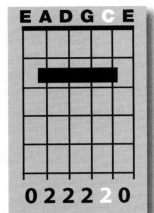

41~ "E-Modal sus" (022220)[EADGCE]

It would be reasonable to call this the "Middle 4" configuration also, though I named 022220 *E-Modal* long ago, which explains the name here.

This is an interesting tuning that offers quite a few options, once again in my favorite 1-string retuning of EADGCE. It's not hugely different from the ones that follow, though I don't think it does as much, though after you explore #42-43 you might want to revisit this one for a few songs.

If you play in E, you don't get any B or even B7 chords, and all the 5 chords have an add11. Playing in A is probably your best bet, though you only have 1 good and practical A chord. There are lots of usable 4 (D) chords, though most have add9's due to the high E string. You can also play in Em, and use Em-D or Em-B chord changes.

The 022220 capo in the E Modal sus tuning

Tune the B string up 1 fret to C

022220

Some Chords in E Modal sus p.1
TUNING: E A D G C E

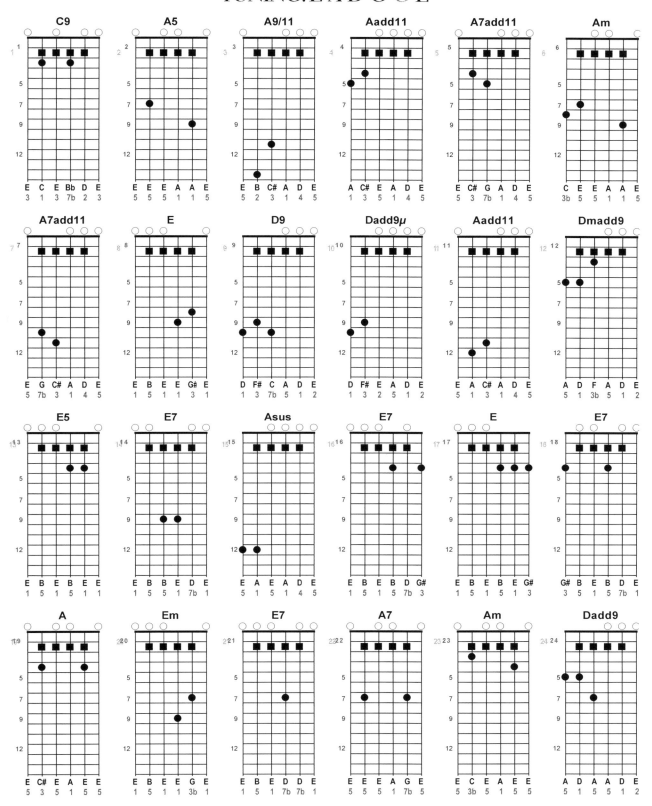

139

Some Chords in E Modal sus p.2
TUNING: E A D G C E

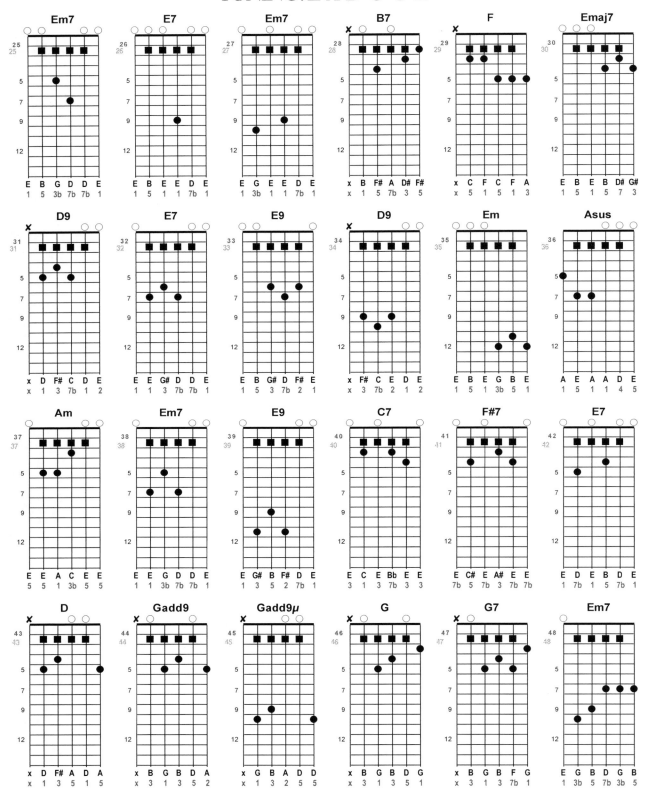

140

TUNING: E A D G C E

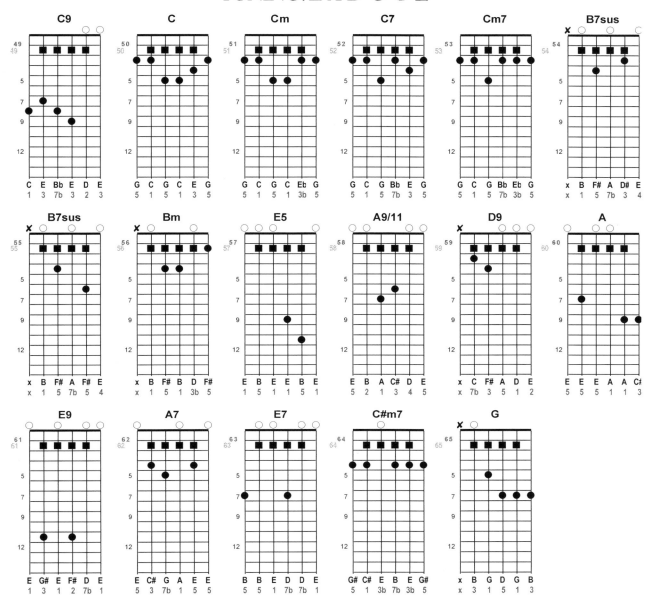

E A D G C E

0 0 4 4 4 0

TUNING

E A D G C E

OPEN STRINGS

E A F# B E E

42- "Liberty" Version 1 [EADGCE]

Author's Favorite

I have been working with partial capos for 38 years, and this game-changer was cleverly hiding right under my nose for 30 of those. I call it *"Liberty Tuning- Version 1."* It is closely related to *Liberty Version 2* (the next configuration) and these two ideas are the reason I developed the *Liberty* capo. They are extremely important musically, and I was not happy with the way other partial capo mechanisms did them. In fact, ideas like this, that combine a simple retuning and a partial capo, have been cleverly hiding in the guitar for 400 years, and they sometimes exhibit extraordinary musical power. I started tuning my B string to C as early as 1980, and you will notice that a number of ideas in this book use this tuning. It's not at all obvious or intuitive how this combination of a slight retuning and a partial capo changes the guitar so much, but it does.

This is a rather odd place to put a partial capo, and an uncommon tuning, and if you found a guitar that was set up this way, it would probably not call attention to itself. The open chord is an A with no 3rd (C#) and a 6th (F#) and a 9th (B) added in the middle. It doesn't sound like that much of a chord, nor does it beckon in the ways that tunings usually do. I have now decided that it is the most important partial capo configuration ever, and it causes a realignment and a mapping of musical ideas on the fingerboard that have had me scratching my head for over 3 years now, trying to understand how it works. It reminds me of a quote I heard about from physicist Niels Bohr– "You don't understand quantum physics- you just get used to it."

A Model 43 capo forming the 004440 capo in Liberty Tuning Version 1

Tune the B string up 1 fret to C

This tuning causes musical ideas to map onto the guitar fingerboard in an unusually orderly way, and allows an astonishing amount of good-sounding music to be played with just 2 finger chords. My book *The Liberty Guitar Method* shows how to play 16 iconic songs with just 2-finger chords. The *Liberty Guitar For Kids* shows how children as young as 4 can play full-sounding chords on adult guitars. and strum along to songs they sing in the keys of C and G. *The Liberty Tuning Chord Book* is a complete map of chords of all types in both versions of Liberty Tuning.

I have included some pages of chords from those books here to show something of the power, depth and simplicity of this tuning. First there are 2 pages of 2-finger chords, arranged in a "geometrical order," so you can see how the same simple shapes make all sorts of chords all over the neck. Then we see examples of how to play a number of A, Am and A7 chords. Then we see how to play 3-chord songs in E and A, how to easily play minor chords, blues songs, "flat 7," 2 and 6 chords.

No other simplified guitar methods offer anything even close to this many options, and if you can avoid getting too lost, you can play easy, great-sounding versions of almost every song that matters in one of the two versions of *Liberty Tuning*.

It took me a long time to uncover and sort out all the musical possibilities this tuning offers, and it's likely going to confuse you also. The more you understand the guitar, the less sense it makes.

But it works, and you can play an astounding amount of great music with easy left-hand fingerings...

0 0 4 4 4 0

2-finger chords

TUNING: E A D G C E

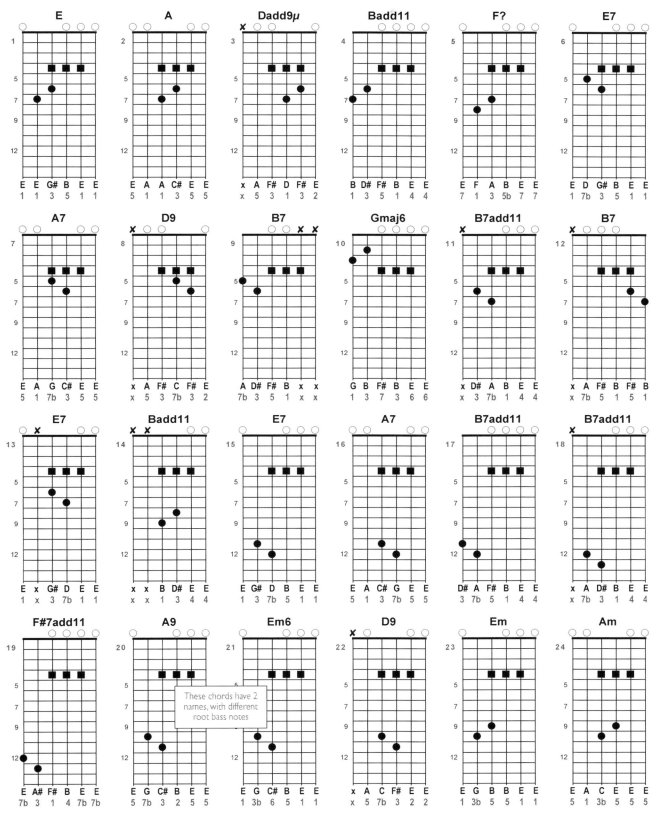

TUNING: E A D G C E

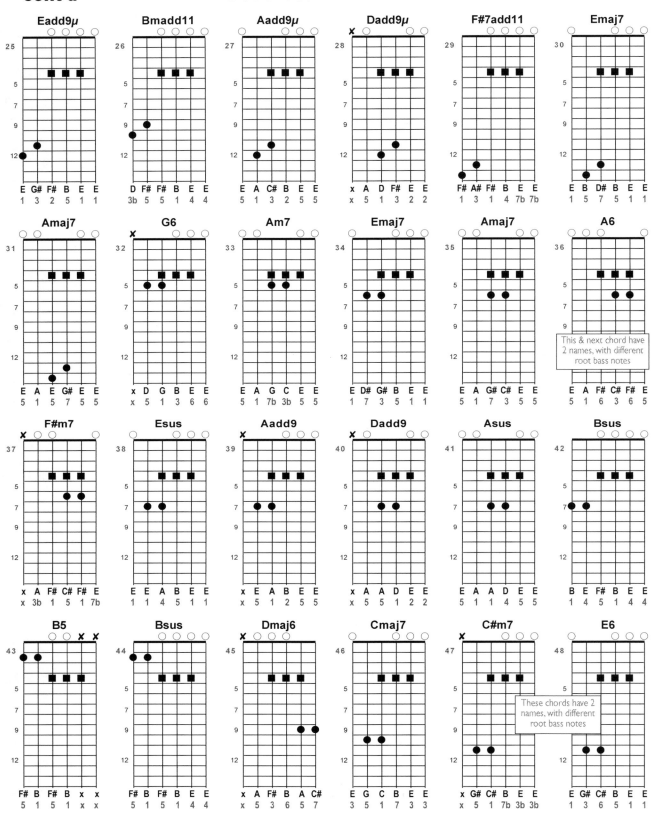

TUNING: E A D G C E

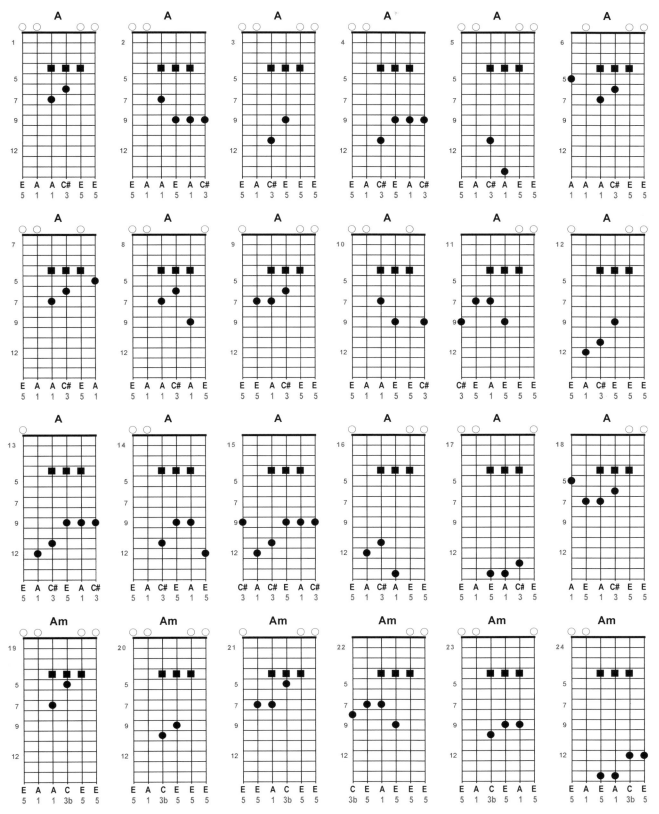

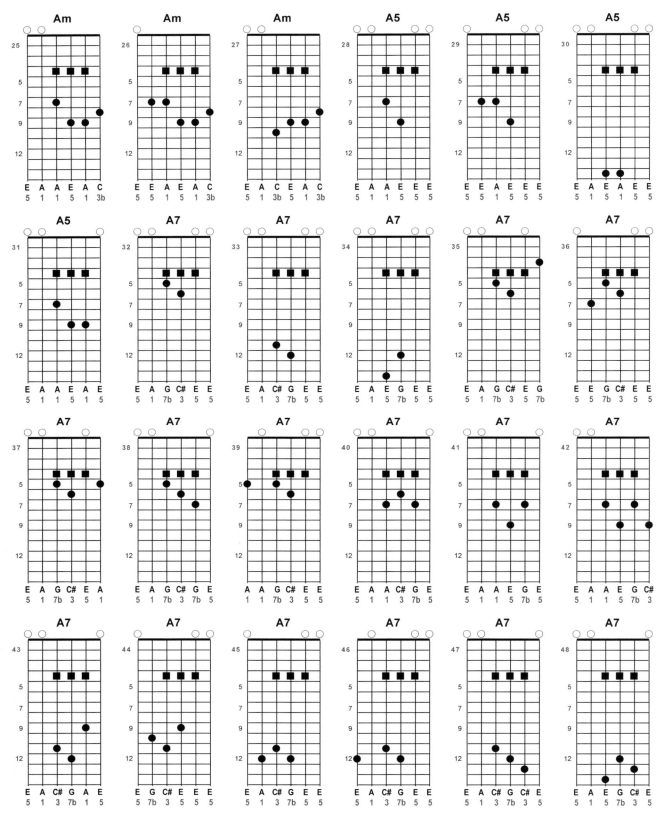

TUNING
E A D G C E
OPEN STRINGS
E C# F# B E E

43~ "Liberty Version 2" [EADGCE]

This is a "twin brother" variation of the previous one, with one string capoed differently. This slight variation makes a big difference in what music you can play. I call it *Liberty Tuning Version 2*, and I also consider it also to be vitally important in the world of partial capos. I go back and forth between thinking that Version 1 or 2 is more important.

The 5th string is clamped by the capo at fret 4 in Version 2, which seems like a small difference, but it changes a lot of the possibilities. Its especially valuable when you need to play a 2 or 6 chord. In the key of E, this means F# or C# chords. You no longer have the open A bass string, and the capo sounds a C# on that string, which is the 3rd of the A chord, so the simple A chords will work. You can't play many of the Am or D chords, but you trade that for C# and F# roots, which are incredibly useful.

Many songs can played in the key of E best with *Version 2*, and in general the same song works better with the capo in Version 1 for playing in A.

Tune the B string up 1 fret to C

Forming Liberty Tuning Version 2.

But a few songs work best in A with Version 2, and there are no hard rules. It depends on the chord changes in the song, and the melody, and always on matters of taste as to what sounds best.

You can play 2-finger versions of an even larger number of chords in *Version 2*, and the basic geometric structure is the same, though both *Liberty* versions have their advantages. *Version 1* is usually stronger with songs that just use 1-4-5 chords, and it is needed for modal songs that use a 7b drop (D) chord, since that chord does not work in *Version 2*.

Version 2's strength lies in its 2 and 6 chords, and for songs that need those chord changes it is vital. There are quite a number of ways to play an F#, F#m or F#7 chord, and since many of them are only 2-finger chords, there really is not just a single way to play that chord. The same is true of the C#m and C#m7 chords as well as the more basic E, A and B family chords.

On the next pages are some samples from the *Liberty Tuning Chord Book*. First there is a page of 2-finger chords, which you can compare to the ones we just saw in Version 1. Then I included 2 pages of 3-finger chords, to illustrate the near-mystical geometric regularity of chord fingerings in this tuning.

I then included a page of C# root chords on page 162 (The "6" chord in the key of E is C# or C#m) and then 2 pages (p. 163-164) of "2 chords" which have the root F#. After that is a "map" of how to play *Let It Be* by *The Beatles* using Version 2, from the *Liberty Guitar Method*.

0 4 4 4 4 0

TUNING: E A D G C E

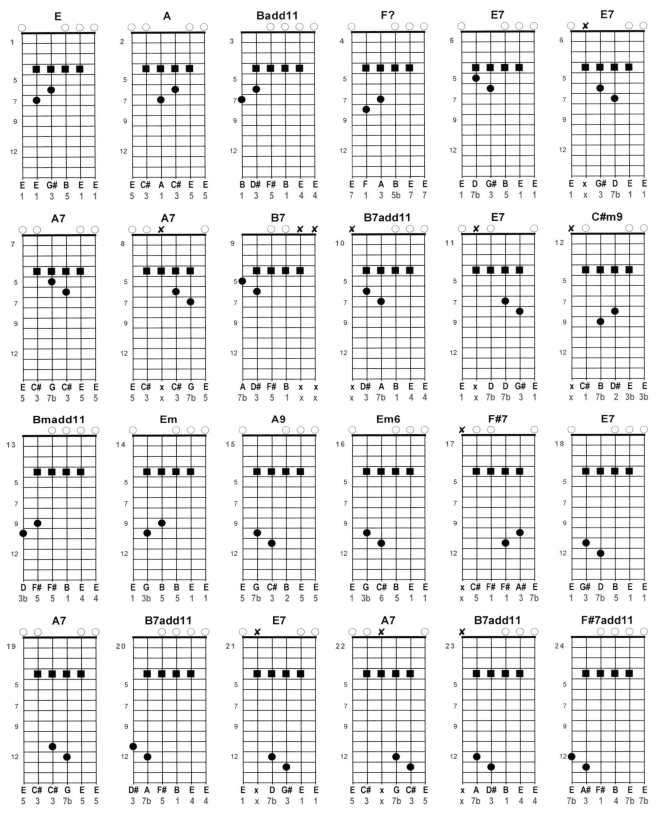

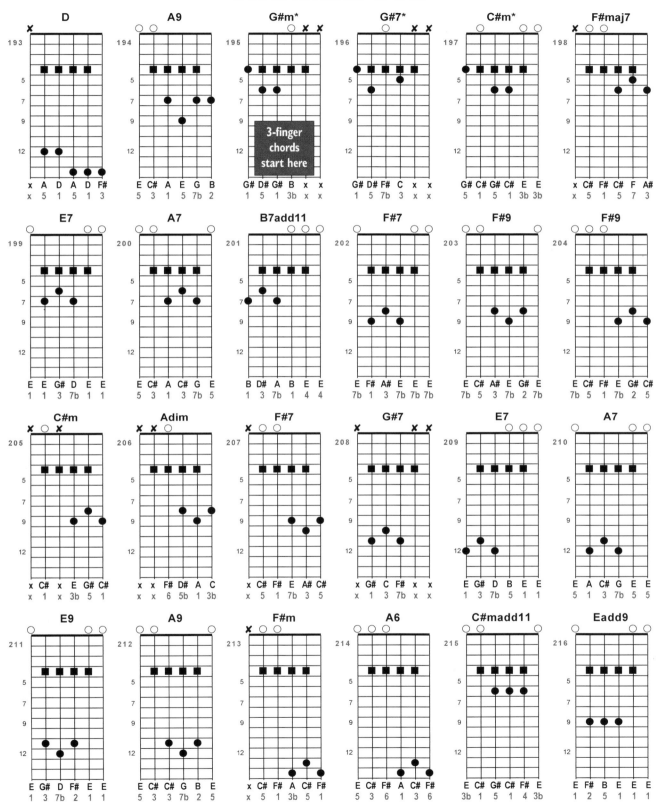

TUNING: EAD G C E

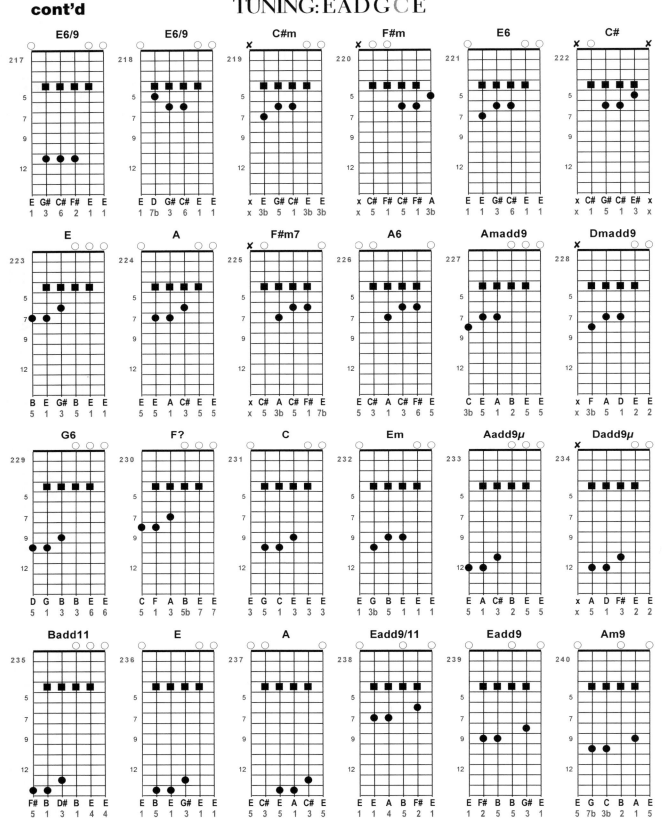

Playing Easy Two-Finger 1-4-5 "Liberty" Chords in E

Probably the most important aspect of the *Liberty Tuning* is that it lets beginners play full, nicely voiced chords in the key of both E and A with just simple 2-finger chord shapes. Here we will look at just the three basic 1-4-5 chords. You can use any 2 fingers to play the shape. It's probably best to use your 2 middle fingers if you can, since you may learn some extra things to do with the "spare" fingers later.

This is a huge advantage over all other beginning guitar methods that either have you skip strings, tune the guitar to an open chord or use other partial capo set-ups. The only "trade-off" is that your 5 chord (B⁷) has an added 4th (usually called a *suspended 4th* or sometimes an *add eleven...*) that you can either enjoy, or minimize by trying not to strum the top 2 strings which are sounding that extra E note. Whether the *add11* or *sus4* sounds good depends on the song and your taste.

We'll see later that it is just as easy to play minor, 7th, 9th, minor 7th, suspended, add9 and a lot of other chord types.

About 1-4-5 Chords

There are literally millions of songs that can be played with just 3 chords. This is a very important concept in music, especially for beginners. In music theory, they are called the *Tonic (1)*, *Dominant (5)*, and *Sub-Dominant (4)* chords. There are a vastly smaller number of 1 and 2-chord songs that are very helpful for beginners, if you can find the good ones. www.songtrain.net is a good source.

Each of the 12 musical keys has its own unique set of 3 chords, and any of the millions of 3-chord songs can be played or sung in any of the 12 keys. It will have the same structure, but in each key it will have a different overall pitch, with different letter names for the notes and chords

You should learn as many as you can of the 1-4-5 changes in the 12 major keys. There is a chart on page 9 that shows the 1-4-5 chords for all 12 keys in case you don't have them memorized.

3 Basic Chords in the Key of E

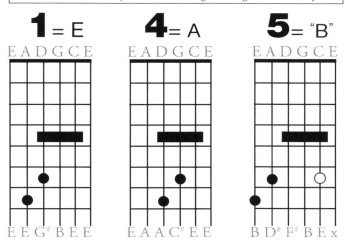

Version 1 of the Liberty Capo, clamping 3 inner strings, playing 3 basic chords in key of E with a single 2-finger chord shape.

1 = E **4** = A **5** = "B"

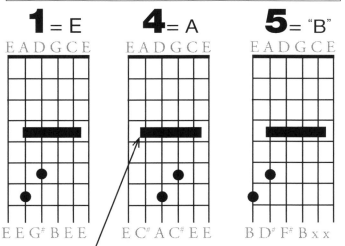

Version 2 of the Liberty Capo, clamping 4 inner strings, also playing 3 basic chords in key of E.

1 = E **4** = A **5** = "B"

The only difference in sound between Version 1 and Version 2 when you are just playing E, A and B chords is right here. Only the A chord sounds a little different, with a C♯ note instead of an A on the 5th string. When you need some types of chord changes, this difference become critical, and the value of Version 2 becomes apparent.

Playing Two-Finger 1-4-5 "Liberty" Chords in A

The same basic 2-finger chord shape we just used to play E, A and B chords lets you play 3-chord songs in A, by just moving it all over one string.

There is a little difference in sound between this and the key of E. The A chord is exactly the same, but here the 4 chord (D) has a mute string (don't play the bass E string) and an added 9th note on the high E string.

On a lot of songs, especially by more modern songwriters, this often sounds better than the "regular" D chord. You can add another finger (shown with the open circle as an optional finger) to make a pure D major chord, or just enjoy the *add9* chord for what it is.

You have to trade away a little in your 4 chord, but your 5 chord has no extra notes or muted strings, and it is a full, rich-sounding E chord. In songs that need a strong 5 chord in them, this is really helpful, especially for children's songs.

With the *Liberty Tuning*, you just learn a few simple geometric chord shapes and start strumming away. But there is a lot of other good news. You can play other simple fingerings of these 1-4-5 chords up the neck, and you will also be able to immediately play more complex chords like *minor, seventh, minor seventh, sixth, add9* and even jazzy *ninth* chords with similar simple geometric, 2-finger chord fingerings. It's bewildering.

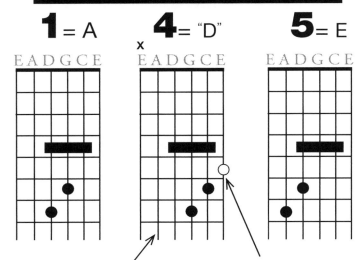

3 Basic Chords in the Key of A

1 = A   **4** = "D"   **5** = E

Version 1 of the *Liberty Capo* leaves the 5th string open (unclamped) while *Version 2* clamps the 5th string at the 4th fret. This puts a C# bass note in play which clashes with the D chord. Thus *Version 2* is generally not used to play 2-finger songs in the key of A, unless the song has no D or 4 chord.

Optional added finger makes a "pure" D chord without the added 9th. This is not hard to do.

You can play 2-chord songs in D using these D and A chords. There is only one easy G chord: it works poorly as a G chord in D, but well as a "drop" chord for modal songs in A.

It is hard to get a big sound in *Liberty Tuning* in the key of D, since you have to capo 5 and then add the *Liberty* capo. Men and women often sing in D. Consider tuning your whole guitar down 2 frets and playing as if you were in E, or using a baritone guitar that is designed to be tuned low.

Once you learn these most basic chords, you might want to find some alternate versions of them and start using them too. There are quite a number of E, A, B, B⁷, D and E⁷ chords that are not much harder than these. They all have different sounds and "flavors."

There are all sorts of alternate chords that often sound as good or better than a basic major chord. On some songs, An E⁵ or Eadd9 might sound better than an E chord. Often a B⁷sus or B⁷add11 sounds better than a B⁷.

There is no "correct" chord, and if you like the way it sounds, use it.

An Example of Why Liberty Tuning is Mysterious

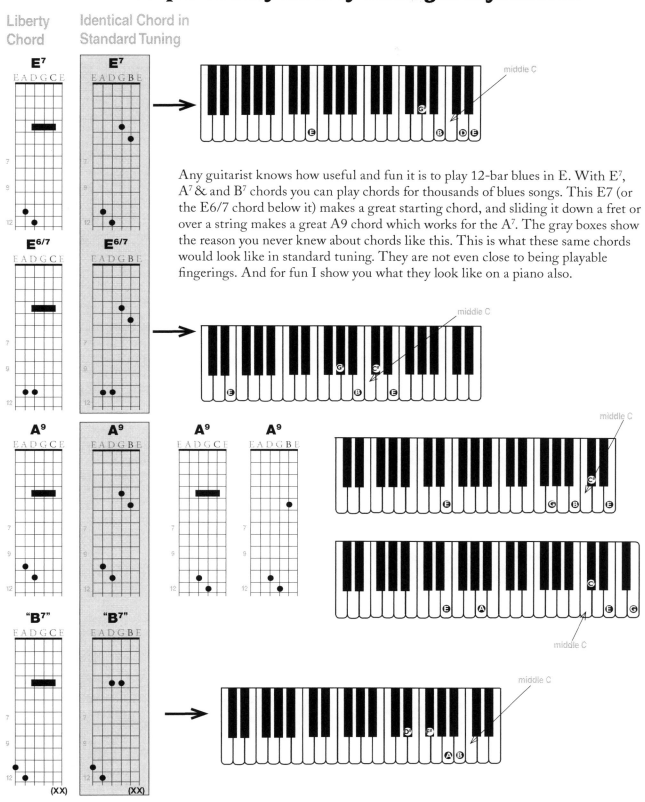

Any guitarist knows how useful and fun it is to play 12-bar blues in E. With E⁷, A⁷ & and B⁷ chords you can play chords for thousands of blues songs. This E7 (or the E6/7 chord below it) makes a great starting chord, and sliding it down a fret or over a string makes a great A9 chord which works for the A⁷. The gray boxes show the reason you never knew about chords like this. This is what these same chords would look like in standard tuning. They are not even close to being playable fingerings. And for fun I show you what they look like on a piano also.

153

Playing 2 & 6 Chords

After the 1-4-5 chords (and their related seventh chords,) probably the next most common chord changes are usually called the "two" and the "six" chords, often written 2 and 6 or sometimes as II and VI. The 2 chord is also sometimes called the "5 of 5" because it is the 5 chord of the 5 chord. It is very common in hymns.

Because the *Liberty Tuning* gives you 2-finger versions of 2 and 6 chords in addition to 1-4-5 chords, for the first time beginners can play beloved songs like the *Tennessee Waltz, Mr. Bojangles, My Girl, Under the Boardwalk* or *Brown-Eyed Girl* with only 2 fingers. There are actually multiple ways to play easy versions of those chords in *Liberty Tuning.*

In the key of C, the 2 chord has the root note of D, which would mean a *D major, D minor, D7 or D minor 7 etc.*

In this key, the 6 chord has the root of A, which includes *A, Am, A7 or Am7* etc. You basically just count letters A through G. You don't need to "understand" the reasons for the sharps and flats notation system to use it to describe what you are doing. There are only 12 major keys, and campfire guitarists usually only play in about 5 of them (E, A, D, G, C.)

In the 2 keys we are playing in most often with a *Liberty* capo: Key of E, the 2 is F# and the 6 is C#. In the key of A, a chord with a root of B is a 2 chord, and the 6 chord has an F# root.

The 6 is often followed by the 2 chord, which is in turn often followed by the 5 chord. 2 or 6 chord changes can be major or minor, or even a minor seventh or more complex.

> In addition to 1-4-5 chords, *Liberty Tuning* gives you a number of easy ways to play 2-finger versions of 2 and 6 chords. This is a very important feature of this tuning.
>
> *Liberty Tuning Version 2*, playing in E, generally does gives better results with these changes than *Version 1*, though there are some usable 2 (B) and 6 (F#) chords available in the key of A.

There are not nearly as many 2 or 6 chords with *Liberty Tuning Version 1*, and you'll have to try and see if the fingering or the sound of these chords here work for the song you are playing, and switch to Version 2 unless you have to sing or play in a key inaccessible with Version 2.

On the next 2 pages there is a large number (but not all) of all the ways to play F#, F#m, F#7 and F#m7 chords in *Liberty Tuning Version 1*, in order of complexity of the fingerings.

There are a startling number of good choices for these chords with easy fingerings, especially in Version 2.

Beginners have never been able to play songs with 2 and 6 chords, and there is a vast repertoire of well-known songs that use them.

More experienced players will appreciate how many voicings of these chords can be easily played, and it is a bit of a challenge to pick through them and find the ones that sound best on each of the songs you are playing.

> **There are so many alternate ways to play simple 2-finger versions of many chords in *Liberty Tuning* that it is actually disorienting.**
>
> **Beginning guitarists often don't even realize there is more than one way to play an E or an A chord.**

> It's tough to get any good two-finger C# rooted chords in *Liberty Tuning Version 1*. If the song needs one of these chords, you might want to use *Liberty Version 2*, unless there is some other reason you can't do that.
>
> If the song needs a 7b "drop" chord then you have to use *Version 1* and live with the weak C# chord or skip the song.

C#
root chords

TUNING: E A D G C E

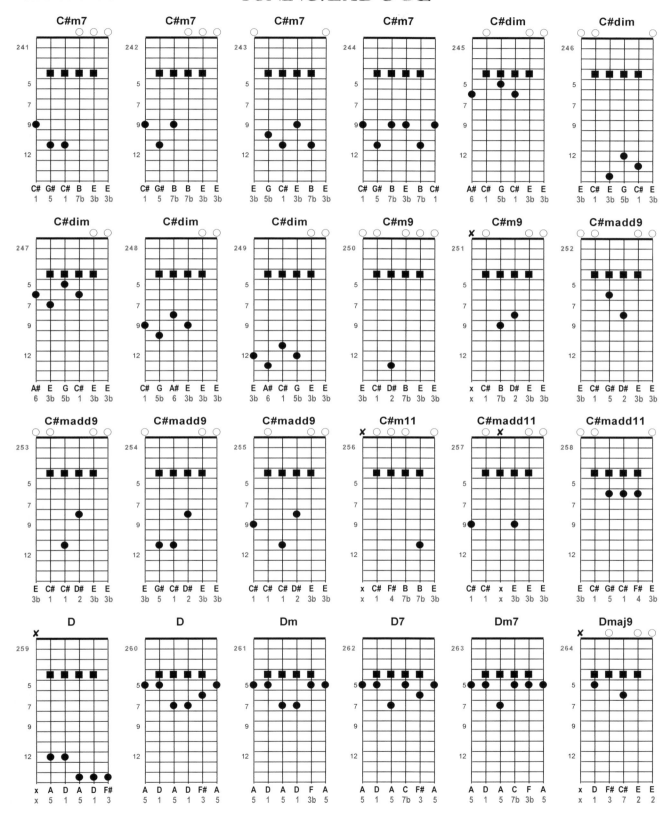

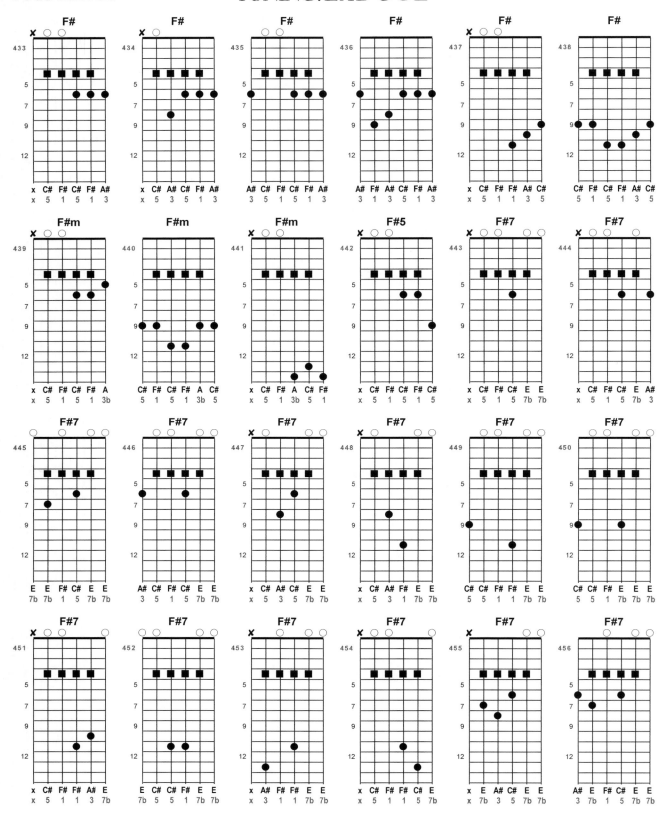

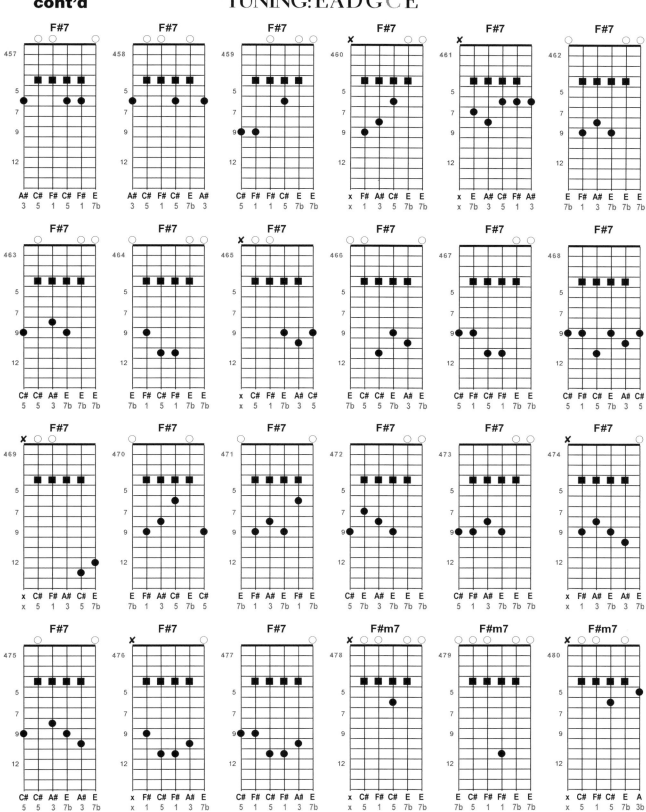

157

Playing Minor Chords

Open-tuning and other partial capo simplified fingering methods allow almost no common minor-chord options. *Liberty Tuning* lets you play rich-sounding minor chords easily, and many of the chords you need to play minor-key songs can also be played with two fingers. You can easily play a lot of major-key songs that have some minor chords in them, and we can also play a lot of good-sounding minor-key songs.

Minor-key songs commonly use a basic chord change such as Am to G, or from Am to E or E⁷. Am-E is easy in this tuning, but the 2-finger Am-G change is not great, and you really need a 2-finger barre chord in this tuning. So we need to put songs that use that chord change into E minor or B minor to play them with just 2 fingers. The Am-G and Am-E chord changes become Em-D or Em-B in the key of Em, and in Bm they are Bm-A and Bm-F♯. (Pages 76 and 125 have many more usable F♯ chords.)

Depending on the song and the key you need to play it in, you may need to use either *Liberty* capo *Version 1* or *2*. You can play in Em in both versions; in Version 2 you can't play a good Am, though in Version 2 the F♯ chords are much stronger. You can play in Bm in both capo versions.

You can get a nice Celtic-flavored Bm-A chord change by moving just one finger as shown with chords 1 and 3 in the bottom row at right.

The pages of chord charts later in the book show many other ways to play all of these chords. You can explore them to see if their sound is better for the songs you are playing.

Part of the explanation of how *Liberty Tuning* simplifies the guitar is that it focuses on the middle 4 strings, and the outer 2 strings are often (but not always) muted or played as open strings.

You'll find yourself adjusting your chording, right hand strumming and picking to concentrate on the middle of the fingerboard.

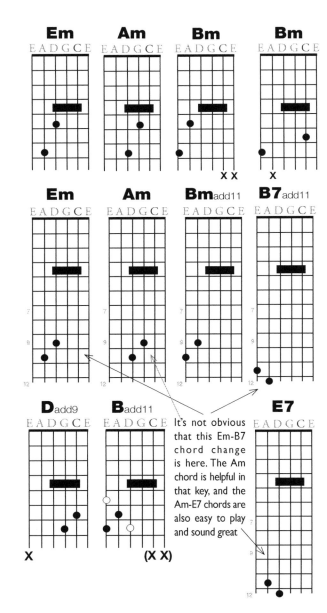

It's not obvious that this Em-B7 chord change is here. The Am chord is helpful in that key, and the Am-E7 chords are also easy to play and sound great

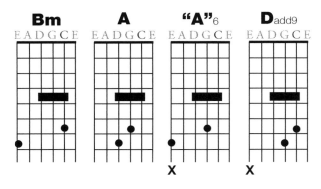

158

Playing Modal 7ᵇ "Drop Chords"

A lot of well-known songs use a "*flat 7*" or 7ᵇ chord, often called a "*drop chord*" and *Liberty Tuning* allows even total beginners to play easy, 2-finger versions of the "*drop*" chord. (*Norwegian Wood* by the Beatles is a well-known example. It uses E, D, Em, A and B7 chords.) The 7ᵇ chord is usually a sign that the song is "*modal*," which means it is not in either a major or minor key. The "*drop chord*" is one whole step (2 frets) lower than the root chord in each key, which means that the drop chord in E is a D, and the drop chord in A is a G chord.

In standard tuning, once you finally master the regular basic guitar chords, then you can play these kinds of songs using the A-G, E-D or D-C chord changes. In the various tunings and other partial capo configurations, there are usually no easy ways to play this chord change, and beginners have never had a way to play good-sounding modal songs before. This is yet another valuable feature of *Liberty Tuning*.

In *Liberty Tuning* we actually have four options for the modal songs that use the "drop" or 7ᵇ chord: E, A and sometimes B and F♯.

The key of E, using *Liberty Capo Version 1*, is the strongest one for modal songs, though the drop chord (D) has an added 9th on the open high E string. The A to G chord change in Version 1 also does not sound right for all songs.

In B, our 1 chord (B) has an added 11th (E) note in the treble. The two B chords shown have an added 11th that often sounds fine, and they can also be avoided if you are careful with the strumming hand. The drop chord (A) is a perfect voicing. Playing in the modal key of B is nice for celtic-flavored songs, especially for *Dorian* mode that is close to a minor-key flavor. The F♯-E chord change in Version 2 sounds great, and you usually also need a B chord in that key.

Before *Liberty Tuning*, there was no easy way to play the basic modal chord changes with tunings or capos. A lot of great songs are newly accessible to beginners.

2 ways to play a 1-7ᵇ modal chord change in the key of E

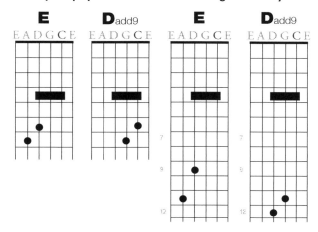

2 ways to play a 1-7ᵇ modal chord change in the key of B. The "B" chord sounds great with the 5th string muted. It is actually easy to do this because when you play the second of these 2- finger B chords, you commonly "bump" the A string enough to mute it. Capo *Version 1* is generally better in B because of the A note that sounds on the 5th string

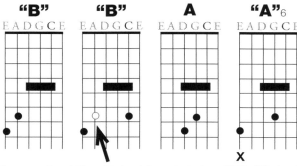

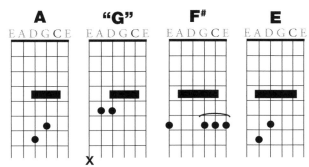

Playing a 1-7b modal chord change in the key of A. You could use *Liberty Version 2*, but the A chord is much better in Version 1, with an A bass note instead of the C♯ that Version 2 gives you. Add the D chord for most songs.

Playing a 1-7b modal chord change in the key of F♯. You need to use *Liberty Version 2*. The 3rd basic chord in this key is B, and several versions work.

159

Playing Blues in E

It's just as easy with the *Liberty Tuning* to play the 7th and dominant 9th chords that are common in blues as it is to play major or minor chords. Simple, movable geometric fingerings instantly give you beautifully-voiced blues chords in the keys of E and A. The fingerings are easier and the chords even sound better than regular standard tuning! Standard 12-bar blues songs most often use E⁷-A⁷ and B⁷ chords in the key of E, and A⁷-D⁷-E⁷ in the key of A. The B7 chord here is not great, and we'll learn some better ways to play it.

Let's look first at the key of E with the capo in *Version 1*. We'll line up several sets of 1-4-5 chords that occur at different places on the fingerboard. The results are remarkable. They sound good, they are easy to play, and are easy shapes to remember.

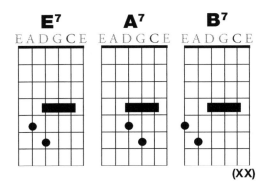

It's pretty astounding to play good-sounding blues songs with just these simple movable chord shapes. The blues chords sound right, and because so many of them can be played with just 2 fingers it's easy for non-beginners to add melody notes and embellishments around the chord positions. (You can just play different 2-finger combinations of the larger chords if you want to stay strictly 2-finger.) It's quite amazing that you can play the 1-4-5 blues chords this easily, and yet you actually have numerous choices for all the chords. Here are a few of the many options...

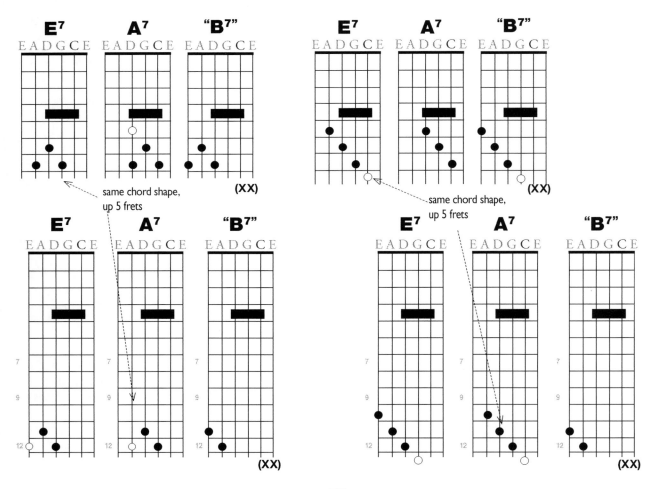

160

Notice the amazing geometric similarity of these chords, and also notice how good they sound.

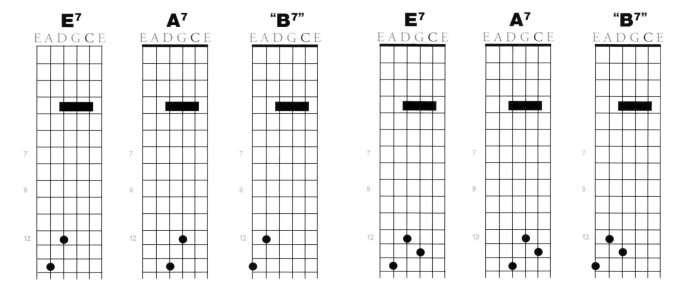

Substitute Ninth chords for Blues in E

It is common to substitute 9th chords (not what we call "add9" but the "real" 9th chord that has the 7th also) in blues songs, especially on the 4 chord (A9 in this case.) They are also geometrically consistent, good-sounding, and in some cases easier than the 7th chords...

There are actually 7 different places you can move this 2-finger shape that all work as an E7 chord: 4 up here and 3 more down by the capo. And each one can be slid either over or down 1 fret to become a 2-finger A7 or A9! It's crazy...

These 4-finger chords are hard to play, but you can play any 2-finger subset of them. You have open E and A bass strings, so you get 3 or 4 different 2-finger E7, A7 or B7 chords out of this one linear pattern.

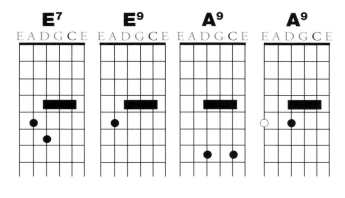

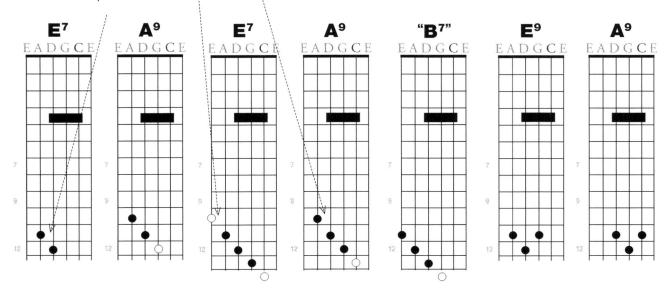

Playing Blues in A

The *Liberty Tuning* (especially Version 1) also lets you easily play blues songs in the key of A, with nearly the same geometric shapes used in E. The chord patterns are so consistent it actually gets confusing, because so many of them look and feel the same. This will have you scratching your head, and is one of the most impressive features of the *Liberty Tuning*.

You can play 2-finger blues songs that sound fine, but adding a 3rd finger makes them sound significantly better. These chords are a great incentive to explore more than just the 2-finger chords in this tuning. More experienced players have access to some great chords and riffs, since 2 fingers can establish the chords and the others can embellish the song.

When you play major key songs in A, your 4 chord (D) has an added 9th note (E) unless you add the 3rd finger on string 1. For blues in A, this is almost an advantage, because when the 9th note is added to a A^7 chord, you get a bluesy *dominant 9th* chord. In this key we also get a very nice 5 chord (E or E^7) without the add11 (E) that is hard to avoid on the B^7 chords in the key of E. Even the muted bass E string on the D chords is no big deal, and doesn't sound that bad if you don't mute it properly.

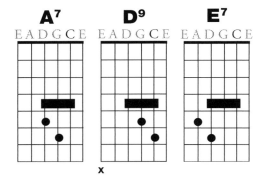

It's almost unbelievable how easy it is to play blues chords in the two most common blues keys of E and A.

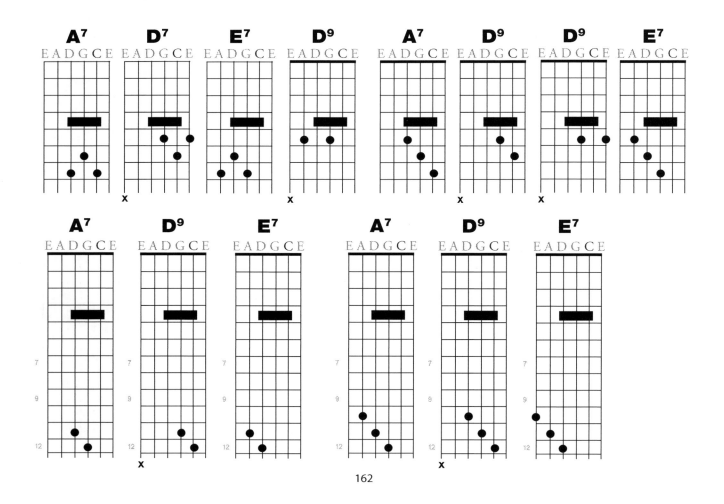

162

Once again you see the amazing geometric similarity of these chords, and also notice how good they sound. The D chords have a "built-in" 9th, and it's actually hard to play a pure D^7.

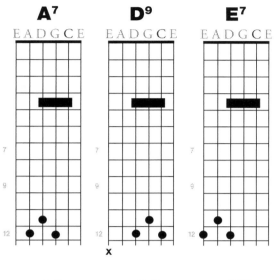

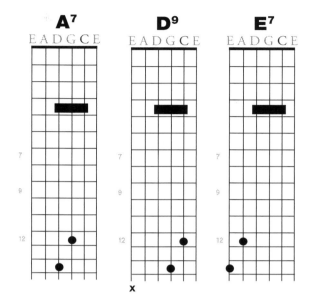

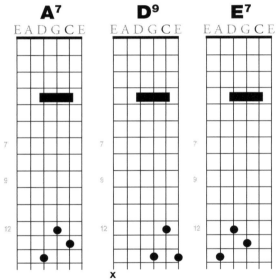

Playing 2 chords in the Key of A

The observant reader will notice that the B^7 family of chords that we used as the 5 chords in the key of E function as II (2) chords in the key of A. We'll look more at these chords a little later, but since many of them are the same geometric shapes as all the other blues chords we have been playing it's not any more work to add them to our repertoire of chord changes. 2 chords are most often followed by a 5 chord, and the progression 1-2-5-1 is very common.

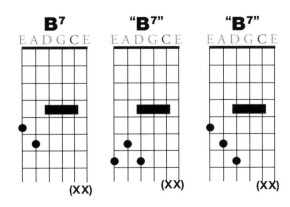

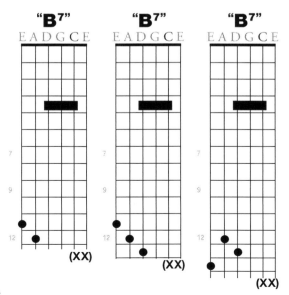

Example: House of the Rising Sun

This is a dramatic example of a more complex song that is typically played on guitar in A minor, with these chords, that are not at all beginner level chords. If you capo 4 frets it sounds in C#m, where I sing it.

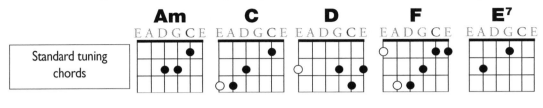

Standard tuning chords: **Am** **C** **D** **F** **E⁷**

Am   C   D   F   Am   C   E⁷

There is a house down in New Orleans they call the Rising Sun

Am   C   D   F   Am   E⁷   Am

And it's been the ruin of many a poor boy and God I know I'm one

Play it with just your 2 middle fingers in *Liberty Tuning Version 2*. If you use a *K-Lever RED* capo, you can avoid the muted bass E string on the E⁷ (G#⁷) chord and also on the C#m (Am) and the F# chord is probably best done with the thumb on the bass string and the middle finger clamping across all 3 treble strings as a partial barre chord. It's not easy, but it works, and if you only had two functioning fingers you could play a great and classic song with chords that sound right. This would be impossible without *Liberty Tuning*.

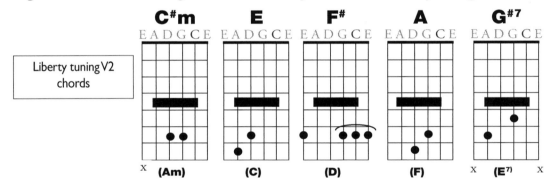

Liberty tuning V2 chords: **C#m** (Am), **E** (C), **F#** (D), **A** (F), **G#⁷** (E⁷)

Liberty Tuning On the 6-String Banjo

A Model 65 capo paired with a Model 43 3-string partial capo to make Liberty Version 1 on a 6-string banjo

The *Liberty Tuning* also lets you make a 6-string banjo (tuned like a guitar) sound amazingly like a 5-string, with simple chords. Put a full capo on fret 3, the *Liberty* capo on fret 7, and you sound in G and C, keys that people most expect to hear a banjo playing in. Cuts on the CD that come with this book illustrate this sound. I use a reverse "faux" frailing that drones the high strings.

The 6-string banjo sounds very natural capoed up this high, and there is plenty of neck for double capoing. You even have 2 ringing drone high G strings, much like a 5-string. Put a full capo on fret 5 to play in A and D, the other most common banjo keys.

164

Let It Be *(Lennon/McCartney)*

Due to copyright restrictions we cannot print the song lyrics here, so you'll need to do it yourself. Write them down while listening to our recording, or find them somewhere else.

VERSE 1:

1   **5**

_____ _ ____ _____ in _____ of _____

6m   **4**

_____ ____ _____ to __

1   **5**   **4**   **1**

_____ ____ of _____ , ___ __ __

1   **5**

In __ ____ of _____

6m   **4**

___ __ ____ __ in _____ __ __

1   **5**   **4**   **1**

_____ _____ of _____ , ___ __ __

CHORUS:

        6m   **5**   **4**   **1**

___ it __ , ___ __ __ , ___ __ __ , ___ __ __

1   **5**   **4**   **1**

_____ _____ of _____ , ___ __ __

VERSE 2:

```
              1                              5
___  ___  ___  the  ___  ___  ___  ___  ___   ___  ___  ___  ___  ___
   6ᵐ                            4
___  ___  __  the  ___  __  ___  ___  ___
   6ᵐ                      5                              4              1
___  ___  __  an  ___  ___  __  ___  __  ___  ,  ___  ___  __  ___  __  ___
  1                         5
___  ___  ___  __  may  __  ___  ___  ___
                6ᵐ                                        4
___  ___  is  ___  ___  __  ___  ___  that  ___  ___  ___  ___  ___
   6ᵐ                       5                              4              1
___  ___  __  an  ___  ___  __  ___  __  ___  ,  ___  ___  __  ___  __  ___
```

VERSE 3:

```
  1                              5
___  ___  the  ___  ___  __  ___  ___  ___  ___
             6ᵐ                                    4
___  __  ___  ___  ___  __  ___  that  ___  ___  ___  ___  ___
   6ᵐ                        5                        4              1
___  __  ___  ___  ___  ___  ___  ___  ,  ___  ___  __  __
  1                          5
___  __  ___  ___  the  ___  ___  ___  ___
   6ᵐ                4
___  ___  ___  ___  __  ___  ___  ___  me
   6ᵐ                        5                        4              1
___  ___  of  ___  ___  ___  ___  ___  ,  ___  ___  __  __
   6ᵐ                        5                        4              1
___  ___  ___  ___  ___  ___  ___  ___  ,  ___  ___  __
```

This is about as simple a chord progression as *The Beatles* ever used. It's great to be able to play one of their most beloved songs with just 2 fingers and easy chord shapes.

Because of the 6 minor (Dm) chord, it only really works with the capo in *Liberty Version 2*, playing in E position. Add a full capo to sing in the keys of F, F♯ or G. Here it is shown in F, where I sing it. The chords you are playing are E, A, B and C♯m, and the full capo pushes you up from E to F. I like it in F or F♯ and Joyce likes to sing it in E. *The Beatles* did it in C, which is high for men.

The 2 high strings on the 5 chord sound an F note against a C chord, which is known as a *"suspended 4"* chord, but the song sounds better if you just hit the bass end of the guitar. Bumping those two strings a little is OK. On the other chords you can strum all 6 strings, though you may want to avoid the bass E string note (F) on the Dm chord.

This is a four-chord song, with a 6 minor (Dm) chord along with the basic 1-4-5's.

Avoid these two strings if you can

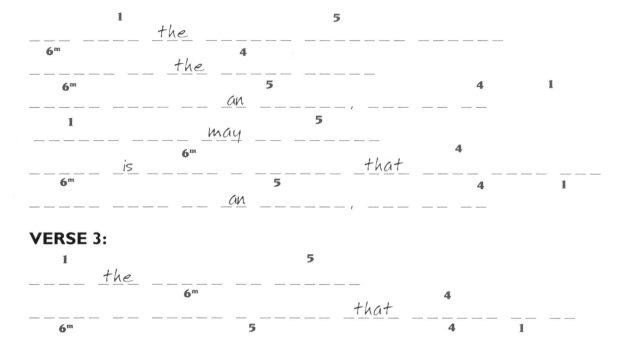

Key of F

1	4	5	6ᵐ
F	**B♭**	**"C"**	**Dm**
E A D G C E	E A D G C E	E A D G C E	E A D G C E
full capo fret I	full capo fret I	full capo fret I	full capo fret I
F F A C F F	F D B♭ D F F	C E G C x x	F D A D F F

Singing pitch of 3rd word of song: "f _ _ _" = C

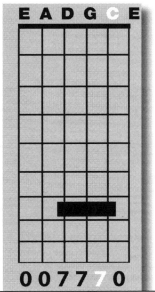

TUNING

E A D G C E

OPEN STRINGS

E A A D G E

44~ Asus @7 (007770) [EADGCE]

If you are going to tune the 2nd string sharp and use a 3-string capo to make the *Asus* configuration, *Asus @4* or one of the *Liberty* tunings, you might as well move the capo up higher because some nice things happen at a few places. You may need a 14-fret neck and/or a cutaway, and the *Liberty FLIP Model 43* capo does this much better than conventional 3-string capos.

You can play in either a "G" position, which then sounds in D, or you can play a 4th higher in what feels like C, and this will put you in the key of A. There are some really striking voicings, with some low notes against very high treble, and also a large number of the overlapping "*mu*" chords (p. 40), and some of the mysterious 9/11 chords like #11-14. If you fingerpick or arpeggiate those they are amazing, especially with some low bass strings still ringing.

In Config. #51 we will look at what happens when you also drop the 6th string to D.

Tune 2nd string up 1 fret to C

The Model 43 capo making Asus @7.

0 0 7 7 7 0

TUNING: E A D G C E

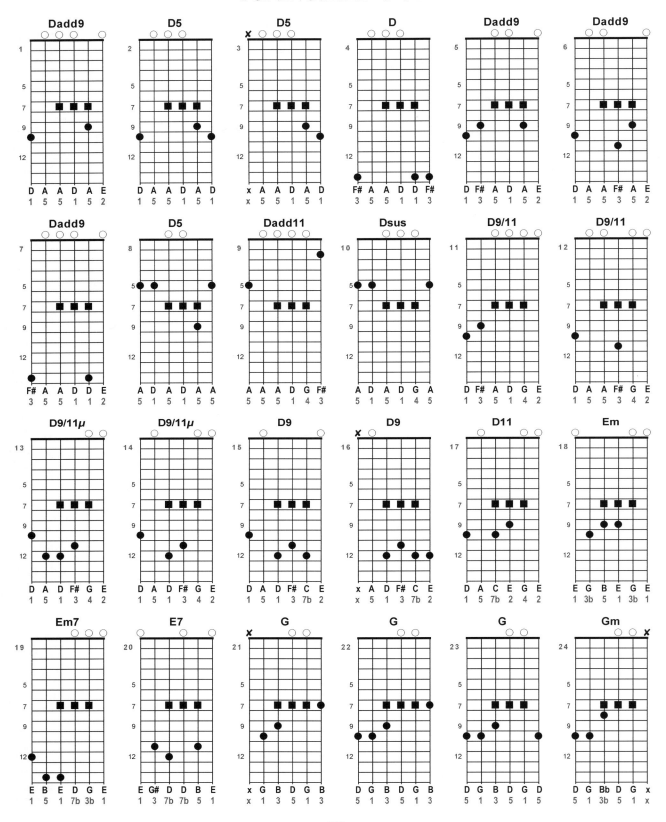

TUNING: E A D G C E

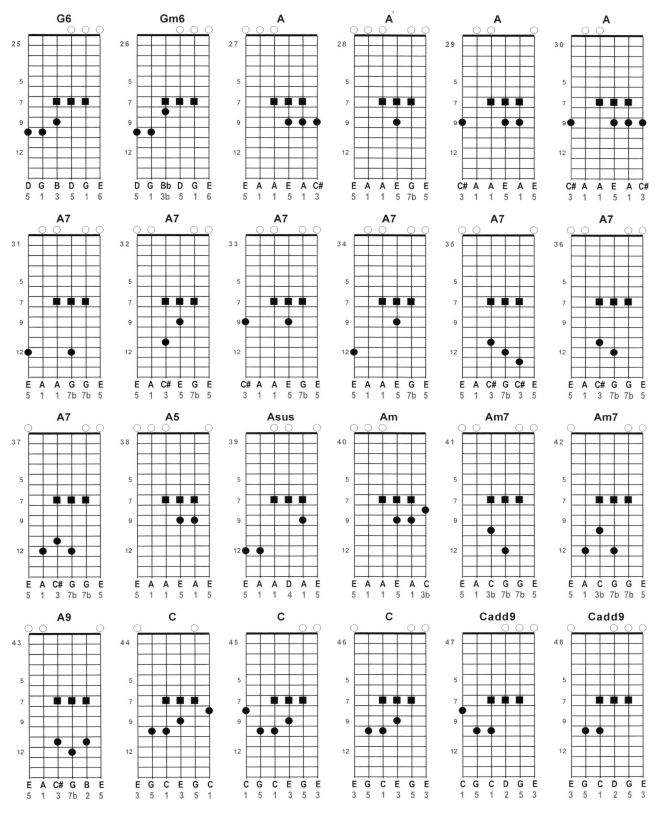

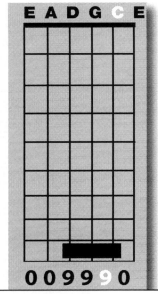

009990

TUNING
E A D G C E
OPEN STRINGS
E A B E A E

45~ Asus @9 (009990) [EADGCE]

If your guitar and your capo can handle it, it's fun to move the capo up one more notch to fret 9. Now when you think in "C" position (which is kind of hard to do unless you are used to having the 2nd string retuned,) you sound in A, and you pick up some "free" open notes on the 1st, 5th and 6th strings.

There are some great chords here with very easy fingerings, and the sound is somewhat exotic. The guitar has a really interesting timbre in this situation, and the voicings are so unusual that even strumming simple songs sounds great.

For starters, try to play a 3-chord song in A with chords #4, #1 and #6.

Tune 2nd string up
1 fret to C

Making Asus @9.

009990

TUNING: E A D G C E

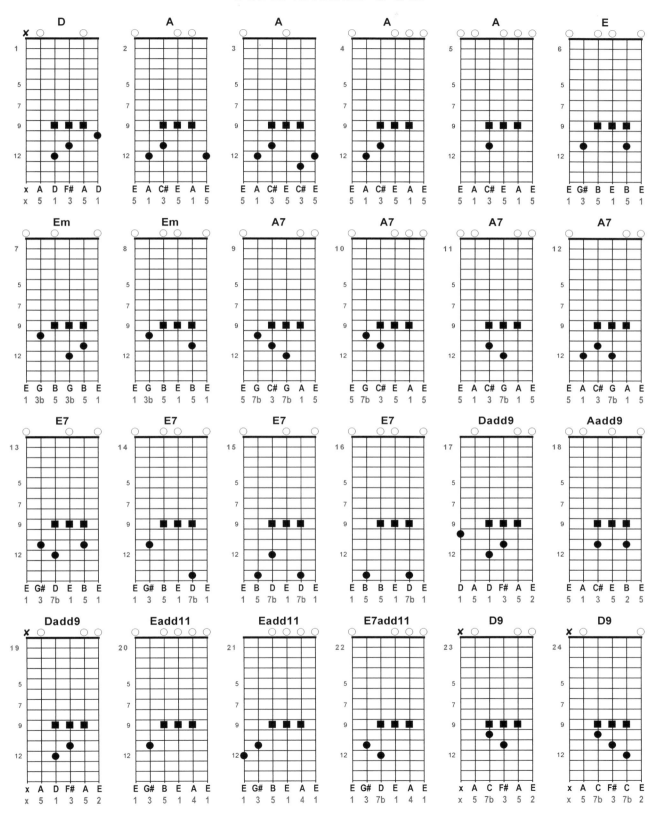

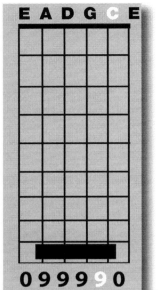

TUNING

E A D G C E

OPEN STRINGS

E F# B E A E

46- Middle 4 @9 sus (099990) [EADGCE]

I didn't bother to include what you might call *"Middle 4 at 9"* in standard tuning, because it just didn't seem to yield much that I thought was interesting. Sharping the B string (yet again) seems to "wake it up" and it allows some good things to happen.

You may not have enough fingerboard to do this, and you'll need a guitar with good intonation to make it work.

With the open strings giving us an F# in the bass, we are not going to get the huge open-chord drone sound that tunings and capos sometimes gives us, and you'll see that a lot of the chords here have a finger fretting the 5th string. (The D, F# and B root chords all make use of that low F#.) Playing in E or A lets you enjoy the open bass string, and if you play in E minor, you're able to play B7 or D chords.

Trading away the open 5th string A note, and replacing it with the F# makes the minor chord (#31-32) really easy, and you don't have to reach around the capo for the F# note.

The Middle 4 @9.

Tune 2nd string
up 1 fret to C

099990

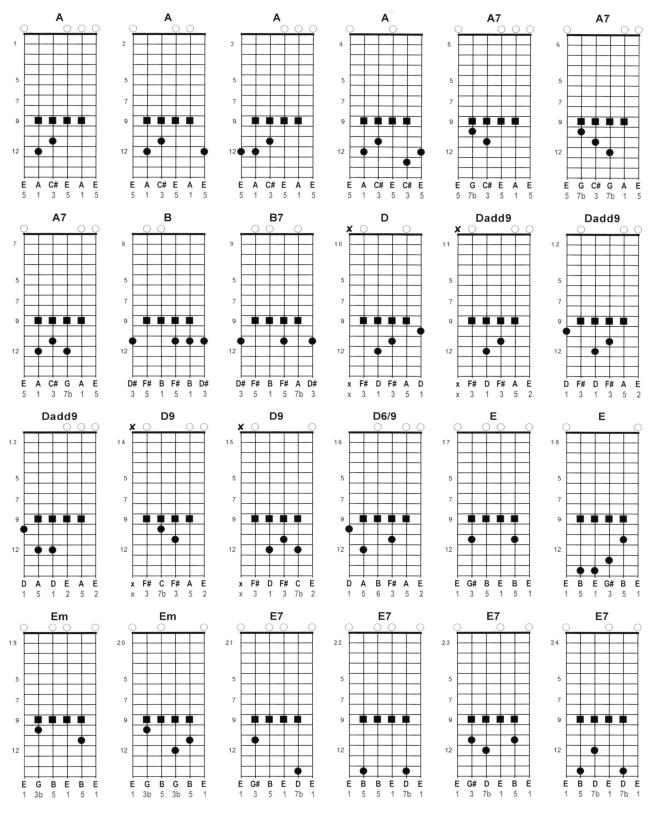

TUNING: E A D G C E

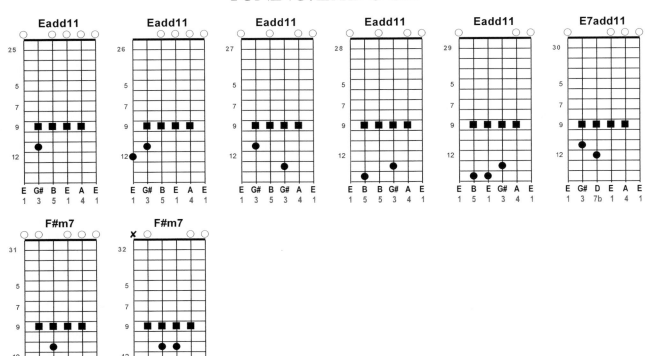

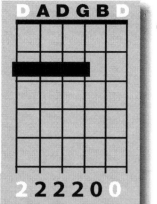

47~ Bottom 4 Double Drop (222200) [DADGBD]

There may turn out to be a nearly permanent trickle of discoveries like this one that involve combining the retuning of more than one string with partial capos. This one has value musically, but it also offers a way of thinking that might lead you to discover something of your own along these lines.

Here you can do some quite interesting things in Am position, that will sound in Bm. There are a number of nice added 9ths and "*minor mu*" versions of the Bm chord that make great fingerpicked chords, and the F#7 chord is a memorable voicing. Dropping the high E string seems to "free" up some sounds, and if you play through the chords here you'll get the idea.

You can even play some cool-sounding blues in E, and the E7, A7 and B7 chords have a nice flavor to them, and can serve as building blocks for a 12-bar blues. The fact that I have included 2 pages of chords shows how much I like this one, even though it is not obvious, nor is it related to a common tuning.

TUNING

D A D G B D

OPEN STRINGS

E B E A B D

Tune both E strings down 2 frets to D

The Bottom 4 Double Drop D.

2 2 2 2 0 0

Some Chords in the Bottom 4 Double Drop D Configuration p.1
TUNING: D A D G B D

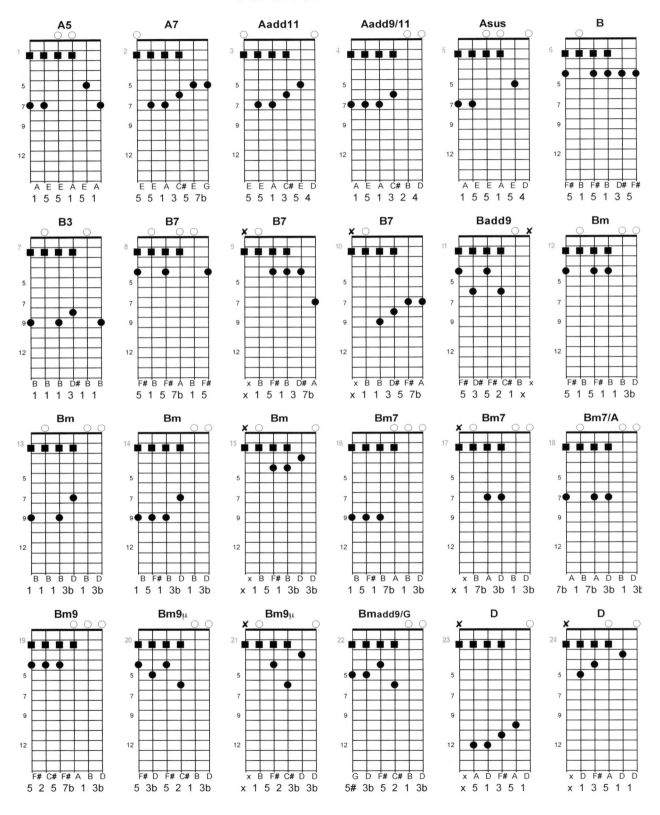

Some Chords in the Bottom 4 Double Drop D Configuration p.2
TUNING: D A D G B D

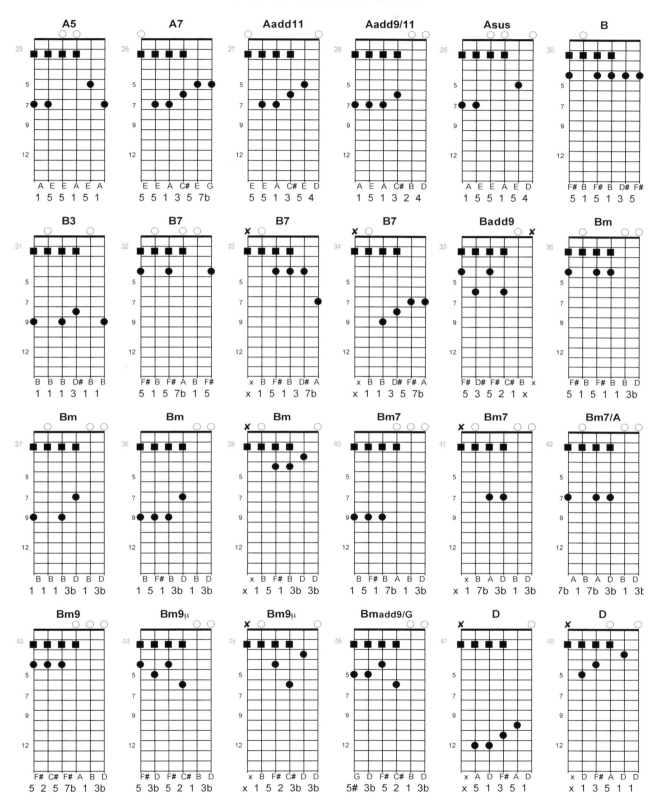

177

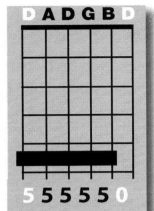

DADGBD

5 5 5 5 5 0

TUNING

D A D G B D

OPEN STRINGS

G D G C E D

Tune both E strings down 2 frets to D

At the 5th fret making the Bottom 5@5 Double Drop D.

48~ Bottom 5 @5 (555550) [DADGBD]

This is a variation of several others in the book, and it yields some great results that some of the similar ones lack. The idea is to lower both E strings to D, in what is often called *"D Modal"* tuning, or *"Double Drop D,"* with the open strings DADGBD. Now the high string adds a D instead of an E on the high end, and that turns out to be really effective in this case.

In the previous configuration, when we played D shapes, we sounded in E with the capo at fret 2, and the E chords get a 7b if you want it. When you play a 4 chord that feels like a G, it's really an A chord, and the generated by the high D note is nice, but on the 5 chord (B) it adds a flat 3rd to make a Bm, which isn't much help in E. Not much happens with the capo at frets 3 or 4 either.

But here with the capo at 555550, good things happen. Play in D, sound in G, you get a 5th on the top end with the high D, the open high 1st string adds a 9th to your 4 chord, and a 1 to your 5 chord.

This is not hard to get used to, and most of these voicings are not available in standard or *Drop D* tuning, which will give you some fresh-sounding music without working too hard to get it.

5 5 5 5 5 0

Some Chords in the Bottom 5 @5 Double Drop D Configuration p.1
TUNING: D A D G B D

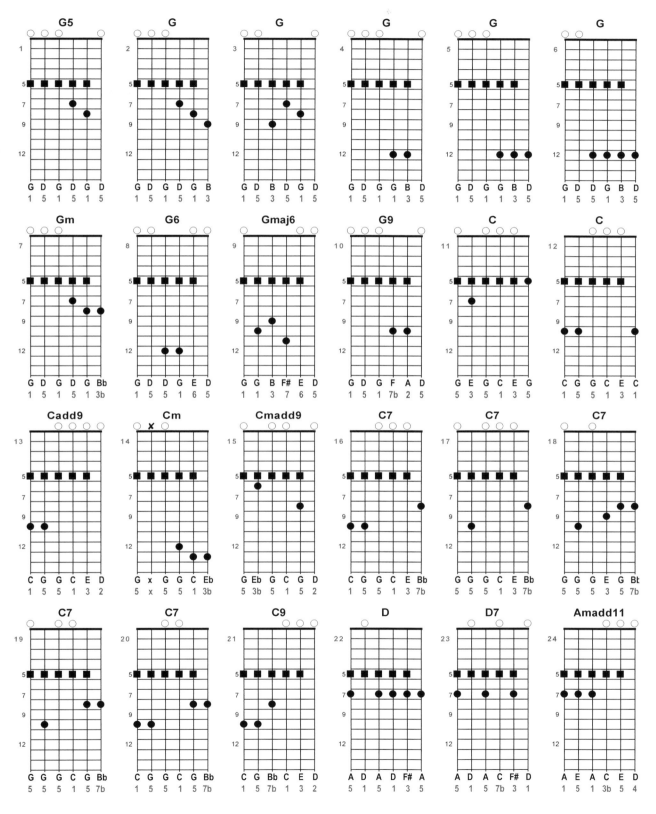

179

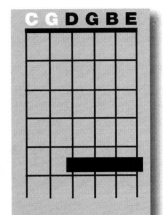

TUNING
C G D G B E
OPEN STRINGS
C G G C E A

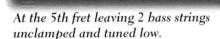

**Tune 5th string down 2 frets,
6th string down 4 to C**

*At the 5th fret leaving 2 bass strings
unclamped and tuned low.*

49- "Low-C" (005555)[CGDGBE]

This is another example of an unusual way you could combine a partial capo with an altered tuning to create some unique effects. It's actually closely related to configuration 077777 which covers the top 5 strings at the 7th fret. Here we capo 5 instead, and also drop the other 2 strings down. You end up 2 keys lower in C, and similar things happen where you get a low bass and a high treble at the same time. In this situation, the geometry of the fingerboard is not the same, since you have re-tuned the bass strings.

Like a few examples in this book, it serves as an example of a way of thinking as much as anything. You could also tune the low strings to D-G in this configuration and play in D position to sound in G or Gm and get some nice music.

Since we have a low C-G under everything, we pretty much are limited to playing in G position and sound in C. The advantage is that you get a very low bass sound and a high treble, and because of the lowered A string (which behaves just like the *Drop A* configuration earlier in the book) you can play the 4 chord more simply. You can play either sweet major key things, or else some rocking blues built around C7-F7-G7 chords. A plugged-in acoustic guitar can sound huge with the low C string, even if it does not in the living room.

0 0 5 5 5 5

Some Chords in the "Low C" Configuration p.1
TUNING: C G D G B E

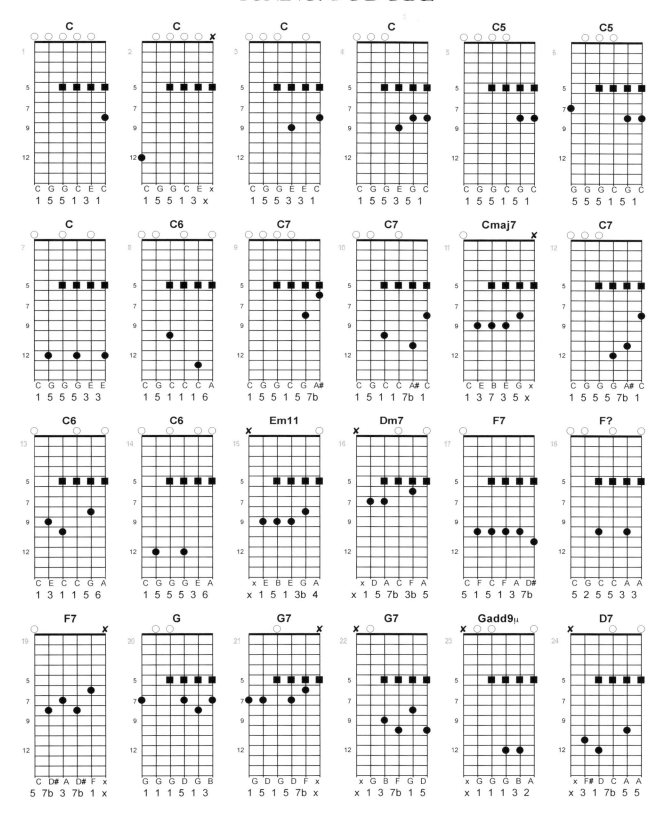

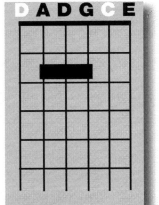

50- DADGCE Esus (022200) [DADGCE]

TUNING
D A D G C E
OPEN STRINGS
D B E A C E

Tune 2nd string up 1 fret, and 6th string down 2 frets

The Model 43 capo put on from the treble side in the DADGCE tuning. It usually works better to attach this capo from the bass side, but it is doable either way.

This is not obvious, or related to any common open tuning, but has a surprising amount of musical value. If you already spend a lot of time in *Drop D* tuning, then all you need to do is sharp your B string to C and pop on an *Esus* capo, and some nice things happen. It may take quite a while before people stop finding things like this, where you retune a couple strings as well as capo a few. They can be useless, amazing, or everything in-between.

If you play in D position, you will sound in E. The B string sharped to C adds a flat 7 which is easily combined with the high E to form a bluesy D9 chord. My favorite thing to do here is to play in Gm and sound in Am, and there are some nice Em & Dm chords. The top 4 open strings form an Am chord, so you only need to fret the bottom 2 strings to make Am. You can also play in Am and sound in Bm.

I also like to play in G major position and sound in A. The extra notes and colorations that happen to a number of the minor chords are quite nice, and there are also a number of more extended chords floating around that are not typical of what you usually hear with a partial capo, especially an Esus.

This is not easy, and takes some understanding of the guitar as well as some pretty hard left-hand fingerings.

0 2 2 2 0 0

Some Chords in DADGCE Esus p.1
TUNING: DADG C E

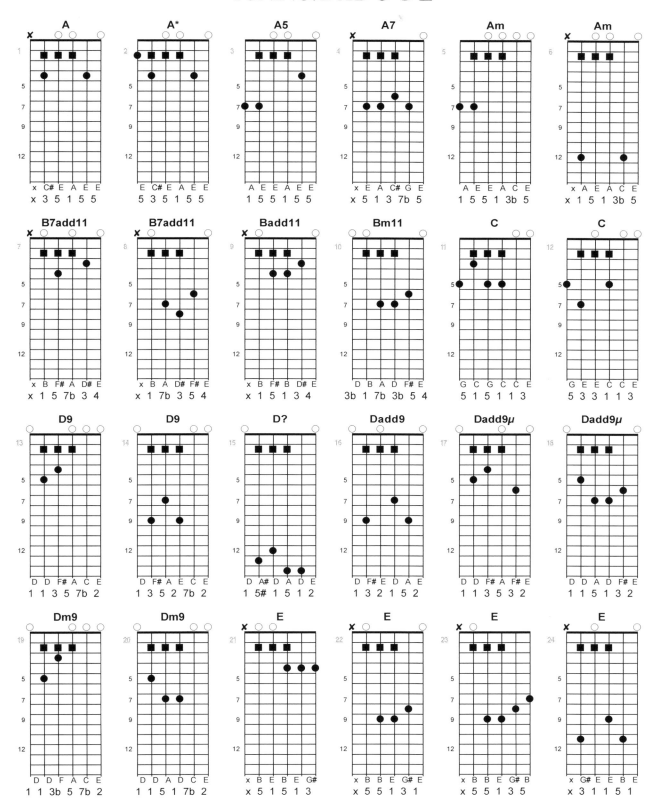

TUNING: D A D G C E

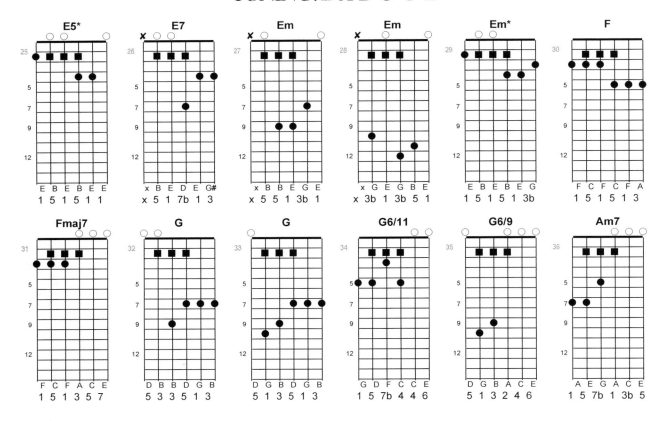

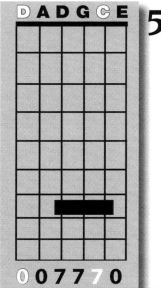

D A D G C E

51~ Drop D /A@7sus (007770)[DADGCE]

TUNING

D A D G C E

OPEN STRINGS

D A A D G E

This one seems pretty odd, with 2 strings retuned and a high partial capo, but it is surprisingly fun and useful, and one of my all-time favorite partial capo "recipe" creations. I have included a large number of chords for this section, in hopes that people will recognize its value and use this.

It is closely related to the 007770 and *Drop D A@7* configurations. It has all the properties of the *Drop D A@7*, which means basically 5 things:

- Low bass combined with high treble
- Droning, open-string resonance
- Cascading harp-like scales on the middle strings
- A lot of *mu* chords (p. 40) and overlapping notes from inner strings that create some unusual melodic situations as well beautiful voicings.
- Plays in D, not E.

For some reason, a lot of the chords are easier to play and sound better, and that slight difference on the B string helps a lot, even though it does add another level of confusion if you are used to standard tuning. The fact that chords #1 and #47 are 3-string barre chords with open low bass roots is very useful.

In Volume 2 of this book we look at some closely-related configurations that add a second capo at fret 5 below the 7th fret capo.

I use this mostly on my 6-string banjo, and it sounds absolutely perfect to my ears, and I can play all sorts of down-home tunes, including Carter Family classics and fiddle tunes, with very intuitive and simple fingerings.

Tune 6th string down 2 frets to D

Tune 2nd string up 1 fret to C

The Drop D A@7sus configuration.

TUNING: Drop D (D A D G C E)

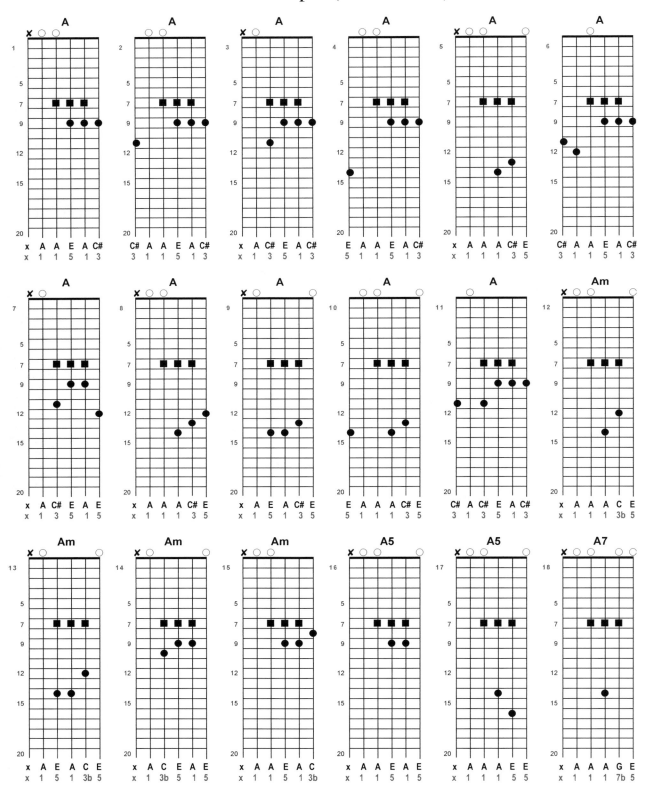

TUNING: Drop D (D A D G C E)

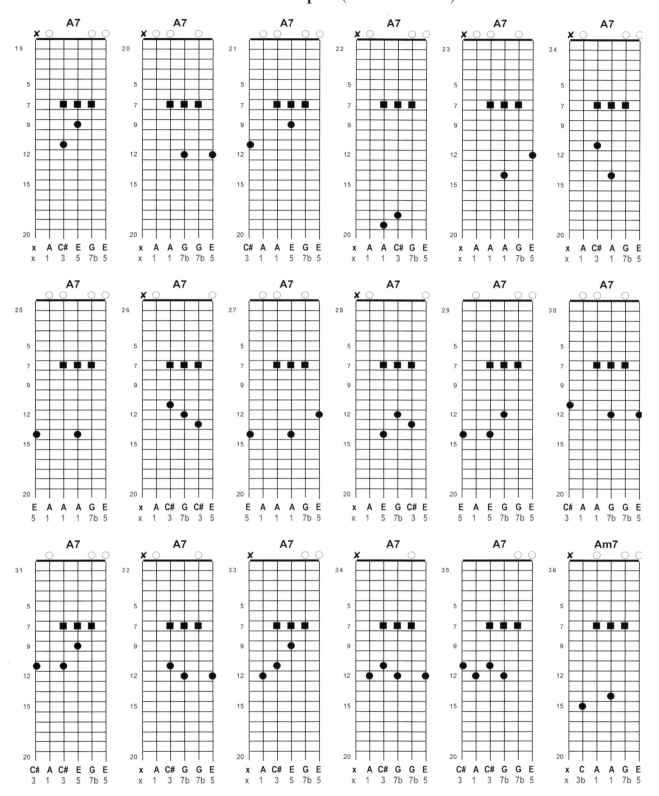

187

Some Chords in Drop D A@7sus p.3
TUNING: Drop D (D A D G C E)

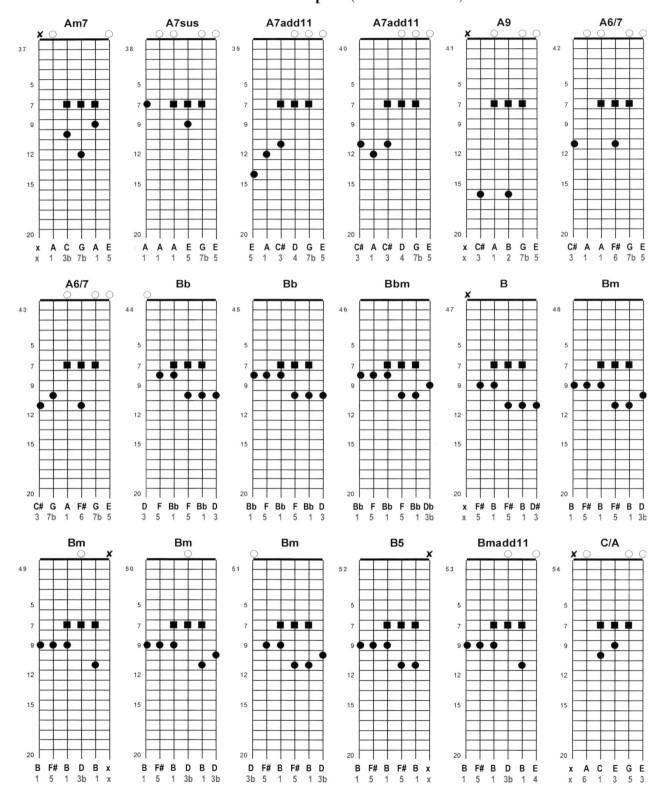

188

Some Chords in Drop D A@7 sus p.4
TUNING: Drop D (D A D G C E)

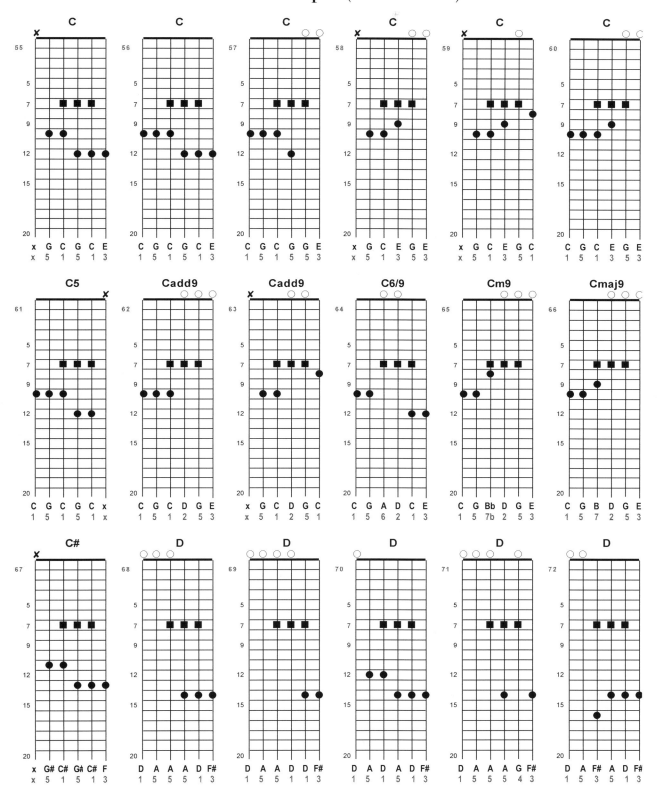

189

TUNING: Drop D (D A D G C E)

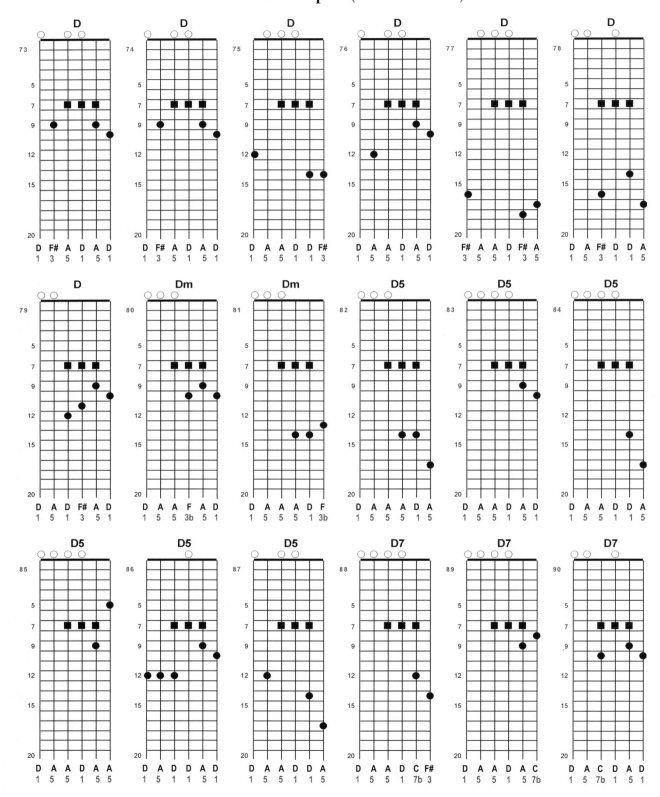

TUNING: Drop D (D A D G C E)

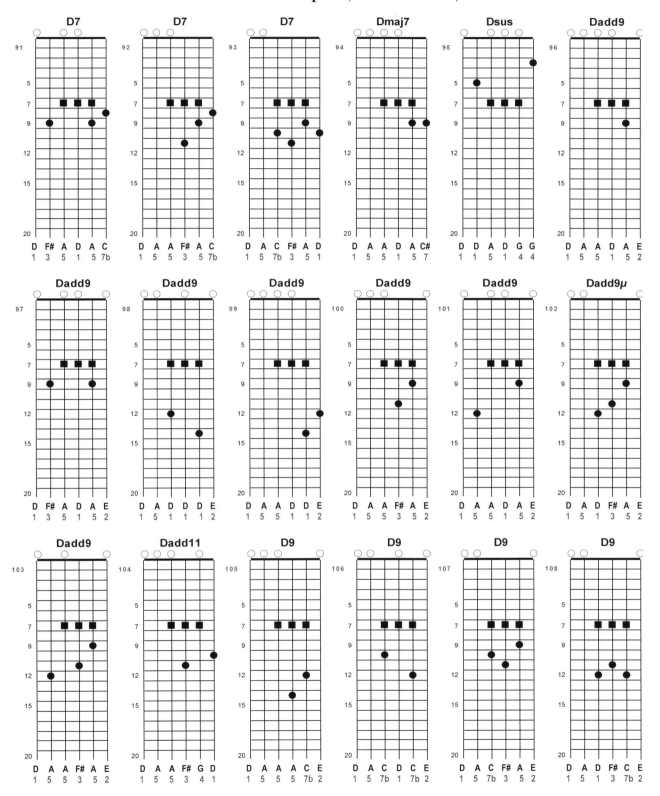

TUNING: Drop D (D A D G C E)

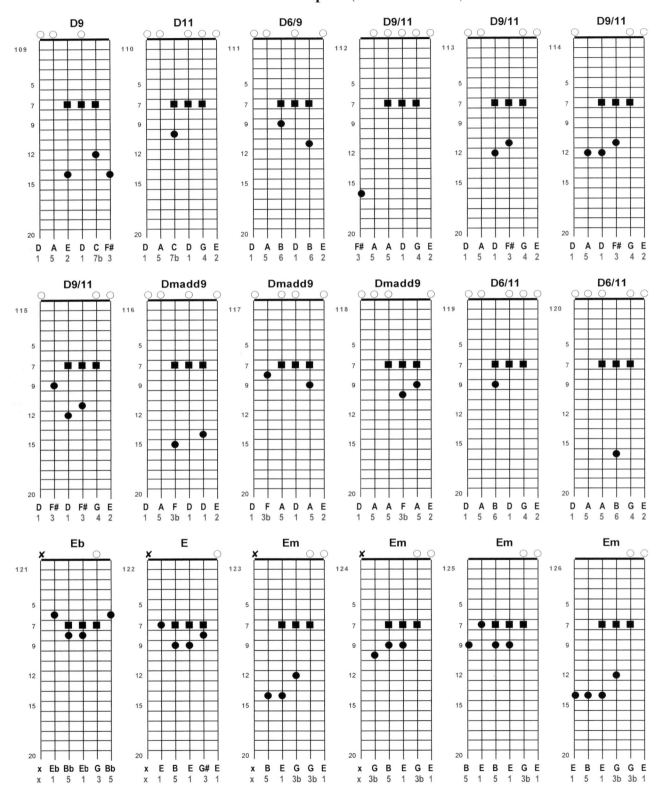

192

TUNING: Drop D (D A D G C E)

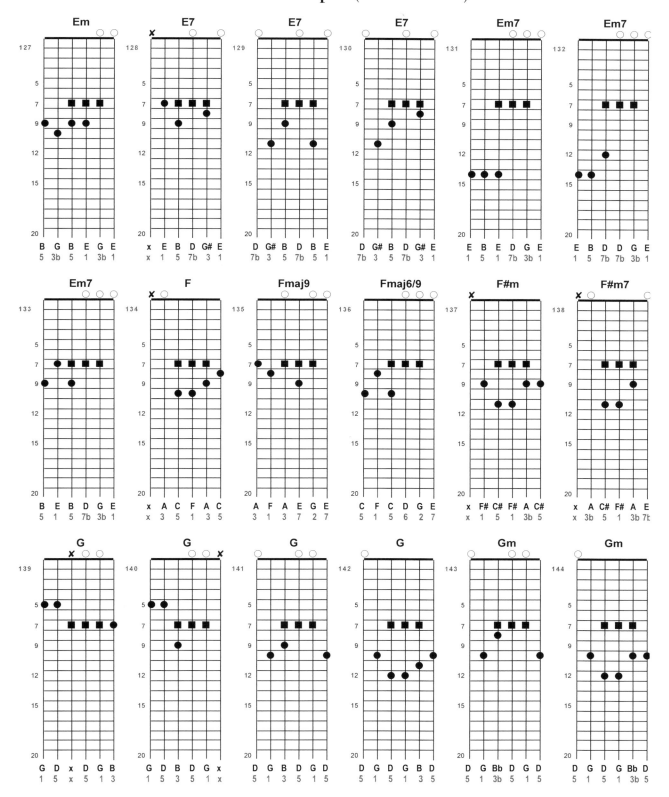

TUNING: Drop D (D A D G C E)

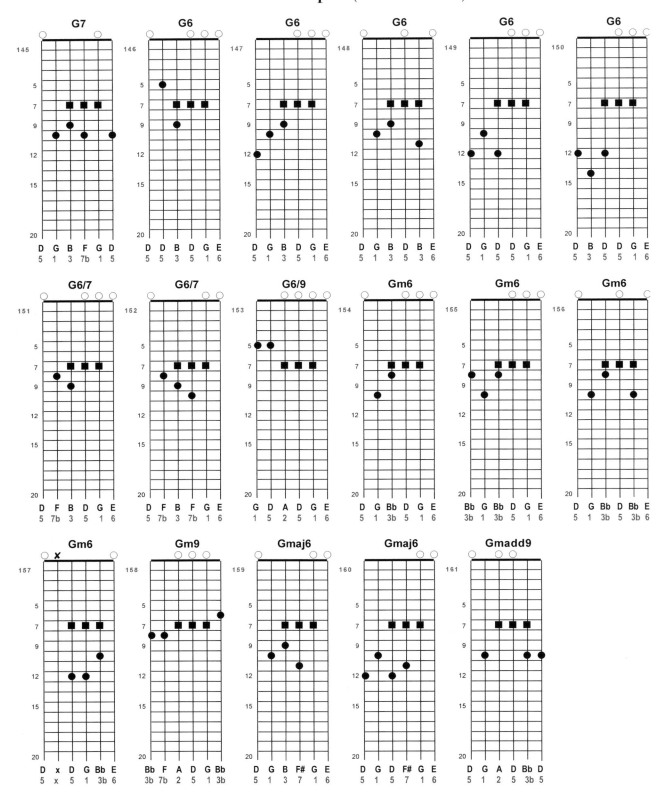

TUNING
E A D E B B

OPEN STRINGS
E B E F# B B

**Tune 1st string down 5 frets, and
3rd string down 3 frets**

The Jones Esus configuration.

52~ The Jones Esus (022200)[EADEBB]

Here is an unusual tuning & capo configuration that is intended to mimic the sound of an even more unusual tuning (D A D E A A) used by English acoustic guitarist Nic Jones on a song titled *"Humpback Whale"* on his epic *"Penguin Eggs"* CD. This capo configuration sounds a whole step higher than that tuning. It was a song that my friends and I were intrigued with, and this offers a way to imitate some of his unique guitar sound. (I should have called it *"Humpback Whale"* configuration but thought that might sound odd.)

I present this here not to urge you to try to perform that song, but again as an example of the kind of things that can happen when you start with an odd tuning. It is also an example of what we can expect people to keep finding for years after we have all tried every partial capo idea we can think of.

Instead of the more drastic retuning that Nic Jones uses, you can get a lot of the same flavor and sound by only retuning 2 strings instead of 4: drop the high E string down to B so it is a unison with the 2nd string, and then drop the G string down to E.

The chords here have an eerie and beautiful sound. This one would be an interesting Saturday morning guitar project for any of you who think you have tried it all. You can't really "understand" this tuning, you just do it. The combination of the odd tuning and the partial capo is thoroughly confusing, but delightful nonetheless. You can play songs in E with versions of the E, A and B chords, and also play in B with the E as your 4 chord and the F# as the 5 chord, or else play modal songs in B with the E, A and B chords.

I used this in 1992 in my recording of *"Oh Marie"* on the CD *"Circles"* and just played rhythm chords with the simple 1, 4 and 5 chords in E. Start with the one-finger B5 chord for your 1 (chord #9), and use the one-finger E (#1 in the chart) for your 4 chord and the one-finger *F#7sus* (chord #20) for the 5 chord. You can also use the E as your 1 and play versions of E-A-B for a 3-chord song. They generate a mood that you can't get with a "normal" *Esus* configuration, though I must confess that I usually perform *"Oh Marie"* without doing this, since it takes some effort to get into this tuning.

0 2 2 2 0 0

Some Chords in the Jones Esus Configuration p.1
TUNING: E A D E B B

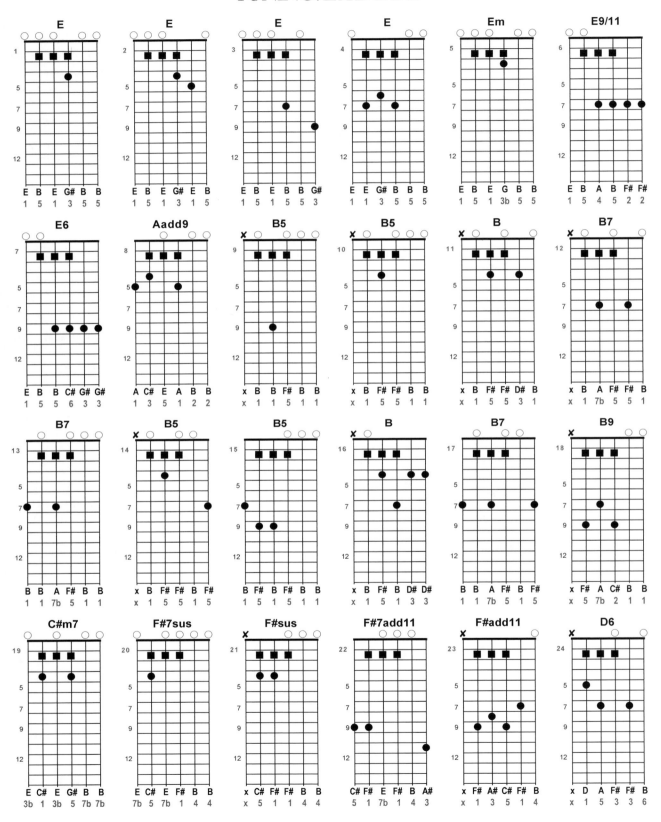

111100

TUNING

E A D G C F

OPEN STRINGS

F B♭ E♭ A♭ C F

53~ Perfect 4ths Tuning (111100)[EADGCF]

An increasing number of guitarists are using what is called *"Perfect Fourths"* or *"P4"* tuning. Though they are mostly jazz and rock lead guitarists, Windham Hill records founder Will Ackerman used it for a tune on his very first acoustic recording that launched the influential record label in the early 1980's. Stanley Jordan has used it for years also.

The thinking behind it is that standard tuning is a compromise, where the guitar is "almost" tuned in intervals of 5 frets (a musical 4th) except for the top 2 strings. Instruments in the violin and mandolin family are tuned in perfect 5ths (7 frets between all strings,) while only the bass guitar is tuned in perfect 4ths.

If you sharp the top 2 strings each 1 fret up to C-F, then the scale and chord geometry take on a new level of organization. Players who embrace P4 tuning find it much less confusing to solo in all keys all over the neck. It is very hard to play even a few open chords, however, and a partial capo can help this a lot. Some P4 devotees are even modifying their fingerboards to build this idea into their guitars. If you capo the bottom 4 strings up a half step, then the open string relationship becomes the same as "standard" tuning, and it is once again easy to play a lot of open chords, as well as enjoy the new freedom of the P4 scale geometry.

Tune 1st string up 1 fret, and 2nd string up 1 fret

You can play some nice-sounding blues in E and A, and there are some new voicings of the 9th chords that are very welcome. If you play in P4 tuning, this is something you need to try.

The drawback here is that you lose a fret of the fingerboard, and the capo puts you in F and Bb instead of E and A. Some players are even having special nuts made that make the bottom 4 strings longer by one fret so that you don't need to use a partial capo and so you still sound in E.

The 111100 configuration in P4 Tuning.

111100

TUNING: E A D G C F

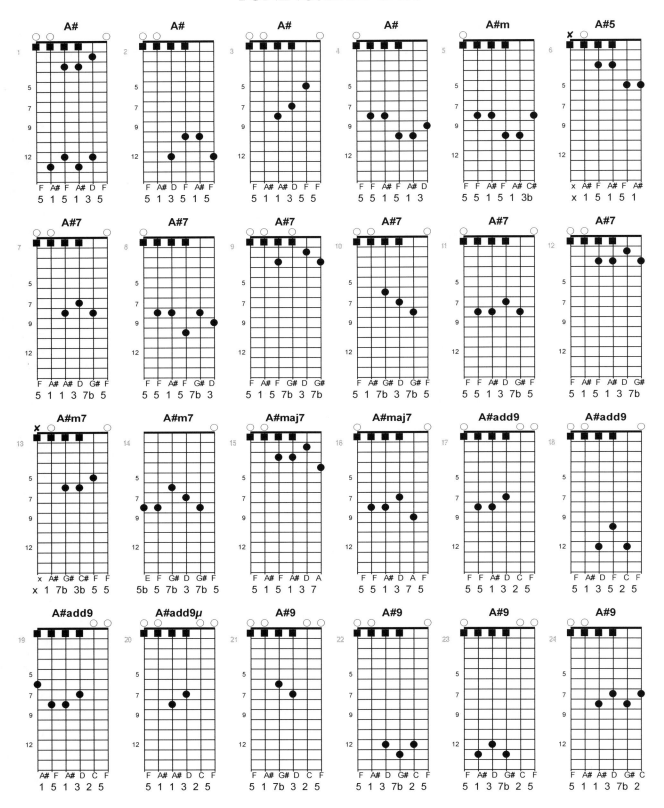

TUNING: E A D G C F

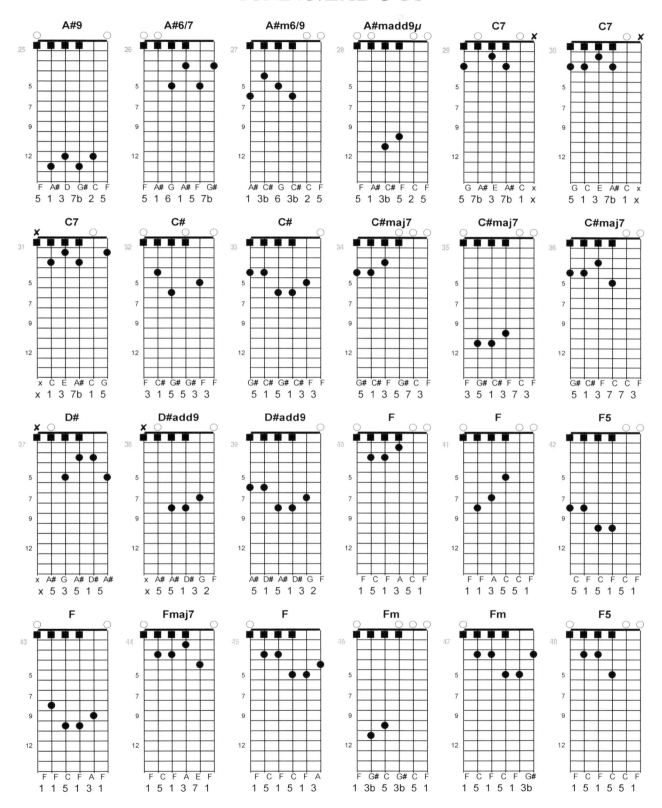

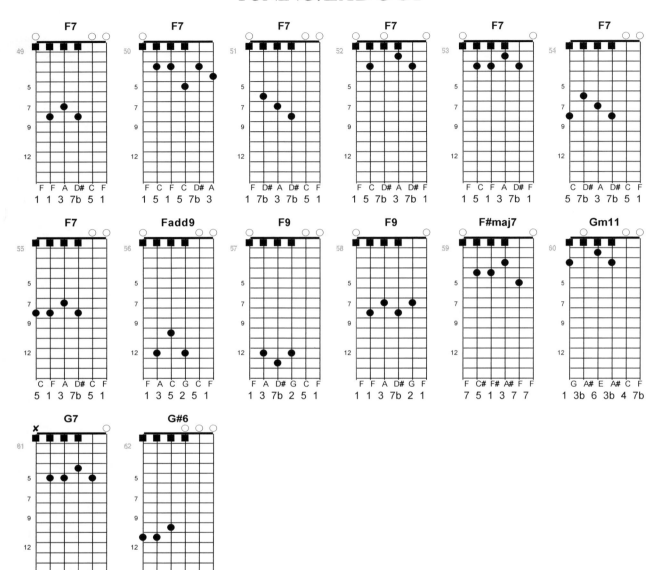

SECTION 3

Using Multiple Partial Capos

More partial capos in standard tuning can open up some new musical possibilities

- Multiple partial capos are not as vast or fruitful a world as the one you get when you combine partial capos with changes in tuning, but there are a lot of great things you can do.

- It may take decades before people have tried a significant number of combinations of tunings and capos to find the ones that are musically useful. There is a lot of unexplored territory.

- Actually, more capos is not always better, but it makes a nice way to show off, and offers new possibilities. More capos means you are tying up more fingerboard with capos.

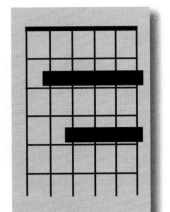

54~ B6 (024444)

This one has some unique and interesting chords and voicings that are not hard to play, and makes a rich sound that combines low drones and high treble strings. I call it B6 because the open strings form that chord. It has a lot of depth, and works for jazzier songs than a lot of partial capo situations. Some of the 6th and 9th chords in the charts here have a pop music sound to them, and are quite unlike the droning and open-tuning sounding partial capo chords you usually encounter.

You pretty much just play as if you are in C or G and see what happens with the open bass strings. This will cause you to sound in either E or A. You can play in a minor key also with good results. This configuration is great for songs that are built around a tonic major 7th chord, since it only takes one finger to make a very full-sounding Emaj7, and you can do this at the nut (chord #12-13) or higher up (#11).

I discovered this one early in my partial capo research; it was in my 1980 *"New Frontier in Guitar"* partial capo book, and it has been in the instructions to the *Third Hand Capo* for 30 years, though I confess to not using it myself in concert or a recording even though I keep meaning to since I like it.

Model 65 and 43 capos forming a B6 configuration- 024444.

0 2 4 4 4 4

TUNING: Standard

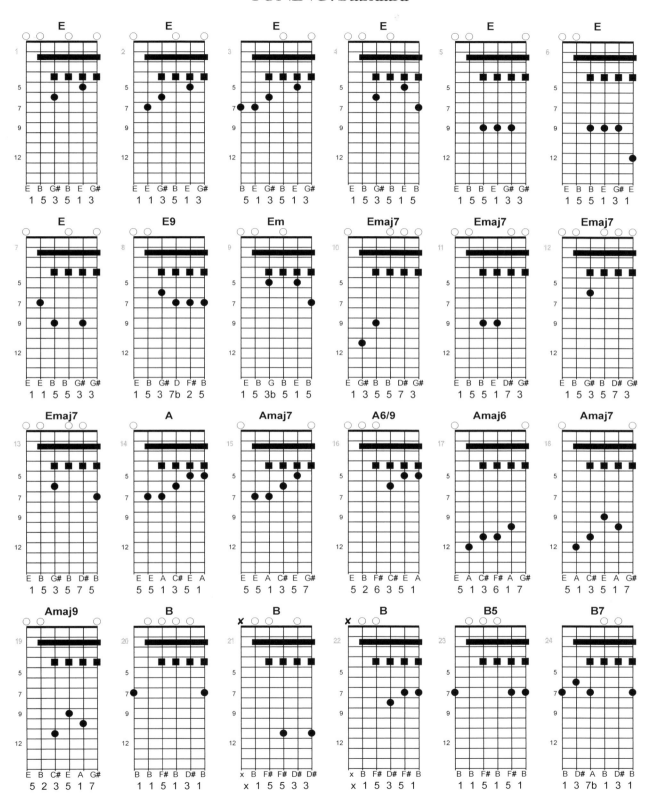

TUNING: Standard

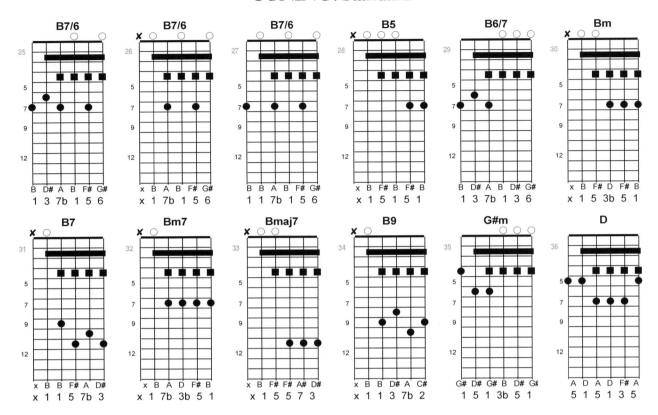

PARTIAL CAPOS AND INTONATION

Intonation is the word for the ability of an instrument (or a singer or player of variable pitch instruments) to play correct pitches. The theory and science of musical pitch, the definition of what it means to be "in tune," and the skill and craftsmanship involved in making instruments are all surprisingly complicated, yet worth mentioning here.

Not all guitars are capable of playing in tune. The shape, size and placement of the bridge, nut, frets and saddle combine with the neck shape, bow and angle to create a very complex system. It is probably a fact also that in recent decades, guitar manufacturing has become a more precise operation, and modern guitars generally play in tune better than old ones. The ***compensated saddle*** has probably done more than anything to improve guitar intonation. On most guitars now, the saddle is not straight, and the 6 strings are not exactly the same length. A big reason why partial capos have become much more popular in recent years is probably that it challenges the intonation of a guitar. Older guitars might not have been able to produce proper notes with capos all over the neck, and people may have tried the idea in the past and not liked what they heard. Tune your guitar, then compare the *Esus* and *Open A* configurations, and you'll probably want to re-tune the B string for each.

204

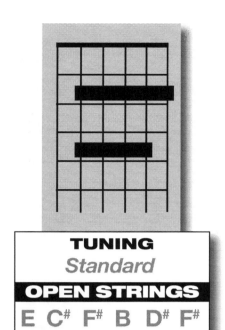

TUNING
Standard
OPEN STRINGS
E C# F# B D# F#

55~ 044442

Another member of the large "2 capos at frets 2 and 4" family, which numbers over a dozen. This one leaves the bass E string open but adds the F# on the high string. Here the lower capo clamps the upper 5 strings. Since the bass E string is open, you are probably going to want to play in E or B, which means using C or G positions.

If you play in C position, you end up in E and the high E string adds a 9th on top of the chord. Playing a Cmaj7 shape (which means leaving the B string unfretted also) gives you an easy but unusual major 9th chord (chord #19), which has the 7th and the 9th scale notes added to the major chord. Like a lot of partial capoing, you play in familiar keys and the capos add some extra notes to the chords that sometimes add and sometimes detract from the sound. It's fun to experiment.

The top 3 strings are musically close together, and when arpeggiated against chords in the bass end they can sound great. You can extend this idea by moving the fret 2 capo up or down a fret, to change the added F# note to either an F or a G. I didn't chart out a page of chords for this, though I might in future editions.

A Model 65 at fret 2 and a Model 43 at fret 4 forming the 044442 configuration.

0 4 4 4 4 2

TUNING: Standard

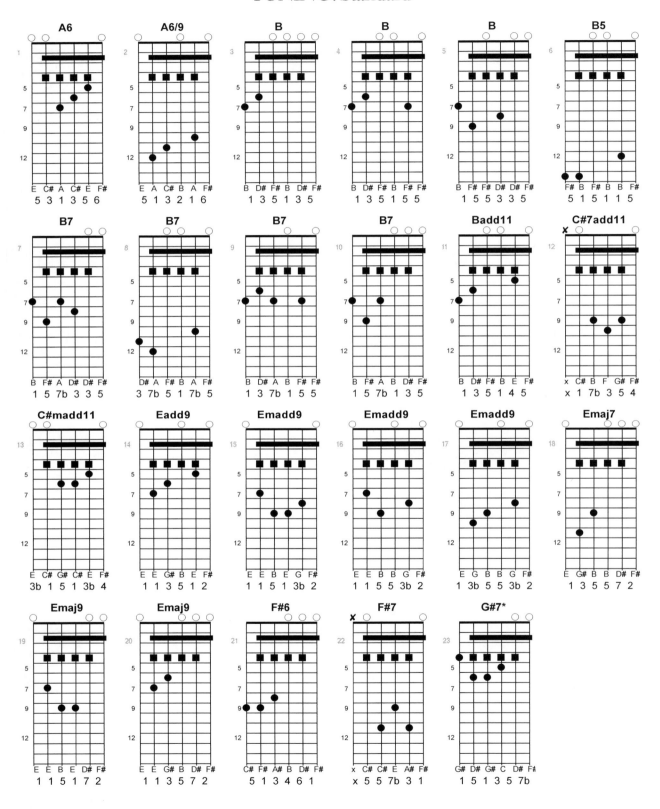

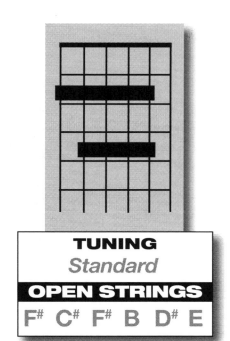

56- Drop E-Modal (244440)

This configuration is only slightly different than the B6 and some of the other "2 capos at frets 2 and 4" family in this chapter. It leaves the open high E string open but not the low E. It appears to have been invented by New Hampshire songwriter Cosy Sheridan and to my knowledge first appeared in her song "*Sharp Objects*" on the **Quietly Led** CD in 1992.

Your strongest musical options here are to play in either G position (to sound in B) or to play in Am to sound in C#m. There are a number of nice B chords (they feel like G chords to you) and also the F# family, which feel like D chords.

Since you don't have the bass E string ringing, if you play in E or B, you can take advantage of the F# bass note and use 2 chords (F# bass) and 6 chords (C# bass) since those are your open bass strings.

When we play in C position we have the disadvantage of the dissonant interval on the treble end, which complicates the issue of sounding in the key of E, because you would have an E and Eb adjacent to each other, and not much in the way of useful open bass strings. A song with a really strong 2 chord might work, since the C chord shapes play normally, and you have that low F# sitting there to support an F#, F#m or F#7 etc.

You could also play in D position and sound in F#, though the A chord shapes that would generate a 5 chord in that key are pretty weak. You'd be better off playing modally, and use the D G and C shapes to play *Mixolydian* in F#, though only the G chord shapes (sounding a B chord) give you any musically interesting and obvious voicings.

All in all, I would not think this would be useful for more than a song or two.

TUNING
Standard
OPEN STRINGS
F# C# F# B D# E

Model 65 and 43 capos forming the 2 4 4 4 4 0 configuration

SUSPENDED AND 11TH CHORDS

The *suspended* chord (which is sometimes called *suspended 4th*, and written *sus* or *sus4*) is an important chord in guitar, and it is especially relevant to the partial capo because so many of the widely-used capo configurations involve suspended chords. It usually resolves back to the 1, but it can be a bridge to the 4 chord also. "Officially" a "suspended 4" chord has a 4 but not a 3, and if they are both present in the same octave it is often called an "*add11*" chord, which better describes the chord structure. The 4th and an 11th are the same note name. "Officially" an 11th chord also has a 7th and a 9th, but since there are 6 notes in a full 11th chord, there are few of them on guitar that aren't missing some of the 6 notes. It is not clear always when to call it *11* or *add11*.

Even this gets fuzzy when there may be a 4 in one octave and a 3 and a 4 in another. Is it a suspended 4 with an added 11? You decide, because I can't. There are some chords I have labeled *sus* that you might want to call *add11* and vice versa. Don't sweat it, or call the "chord police."

244440

TUNING: Standard

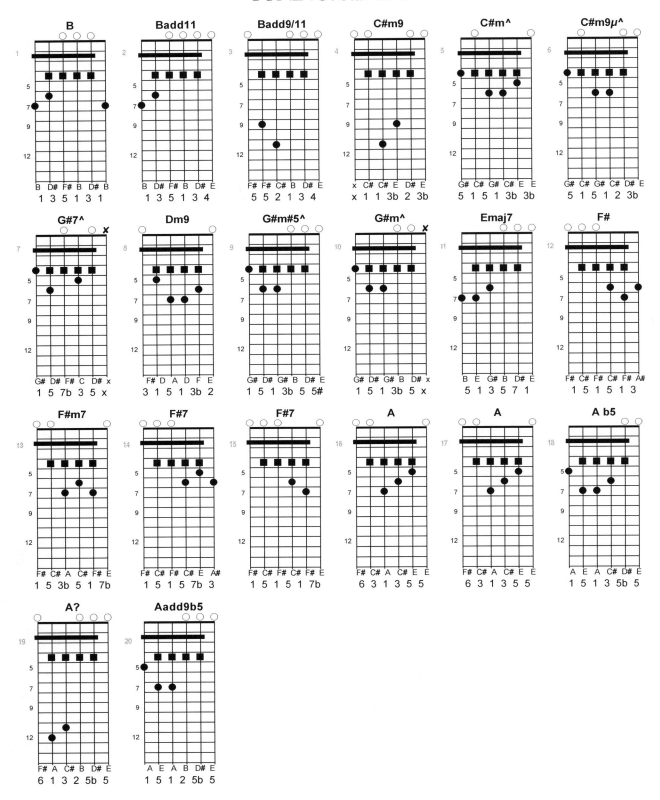

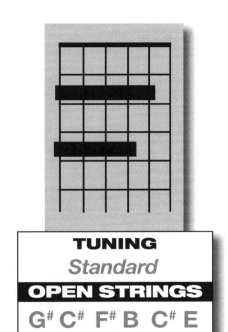

57~ 444420

With the high E drone it makes a little more sense to play in C position to sound in E than it does to play in G position to sound in B, though they both work.

The defining feature of this kind of multiple capo set-up is that you get large number of overlapping chords, where the notes on the middle strings are in the same octave but on different strings from the top strings. There are a lot of the so-called "*mu*" chords (p. 40), and a nice 9/11 (chord #2). The best way to use these kinds of chords is in arpeggiated playing, and fingerpicked things can have a very harp-like sound, with cascading runs. Some of these chords can sound like a whole song by themselves if you fingerpick them really fast and drive the notes against each other.

The top 3 strings sound the notes B-C#-E, which are scale notes in both E and B, so you can even play thumb melodies on the lower strings and just roll the top three strings against the moving bass notes for a really striking sound.

There are several configurations in this section that work like this and they all have slight advantages and drawbacks.

A Model 65 at fret 2 and a Model 43 at fret 4 making the 444420 configuration

4 4 4 4 2 0

TUNING: Standard

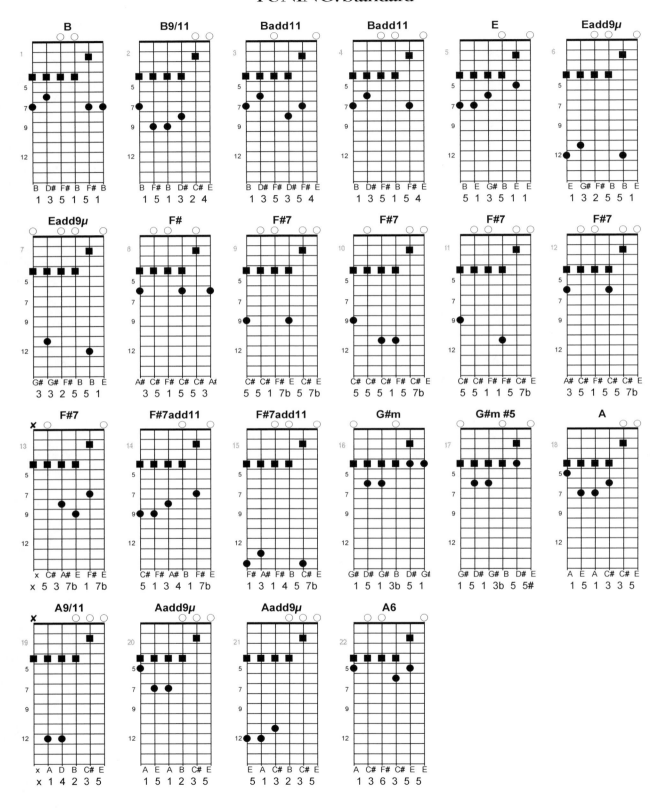

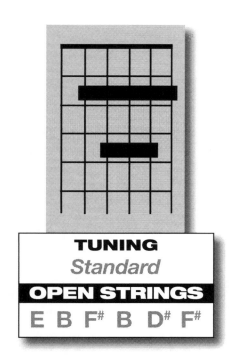

TUNING
Standard
OPEN STRINGS
E B F# B D# F#

58- Almost Open B (024442)

This one also appeared in my 1980 "*New Frontier in Guitar*" book, though I don't think I ever recorded anything that uses it. It is primarily useful for playing in G position to sound in B, though you can also play in C position to sound in E. It is not significantly different from the 0 2 4 4 4 0 configuration that follows this one or from the one I call B6 (0 2 4 4 4 4), which is not in this book. Some key chords end up with some distinctive voicings based on the high E string.

Like a lot of partial capo configurations, some of these chords need to be arpeggiated to have much musical value, and can sound pretty dissonant when strummed.

Model 43 and 65 capos forming an "Almost Open B" configuration

0 2 4 4 4 2

Some Chords in 024442 p.1
TUNING: Standard

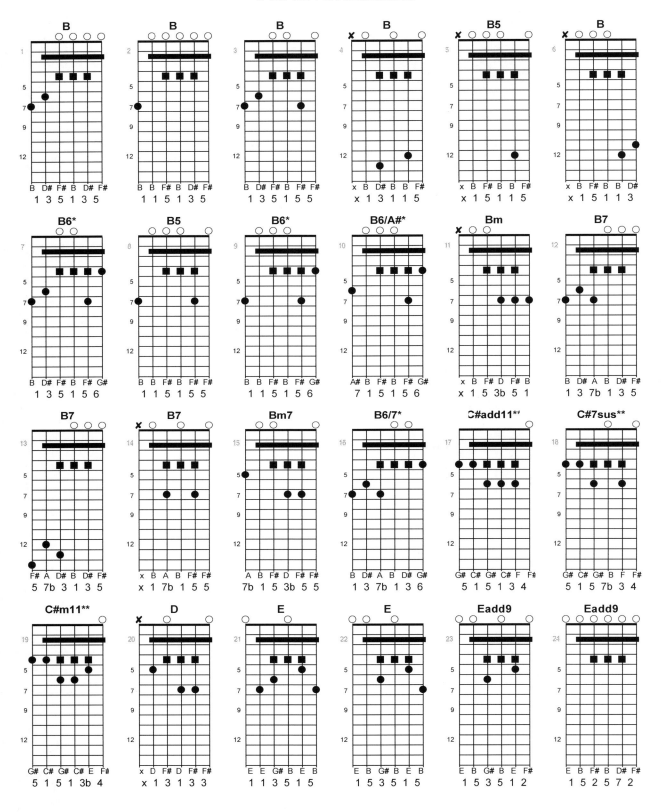

TUNING: Standard

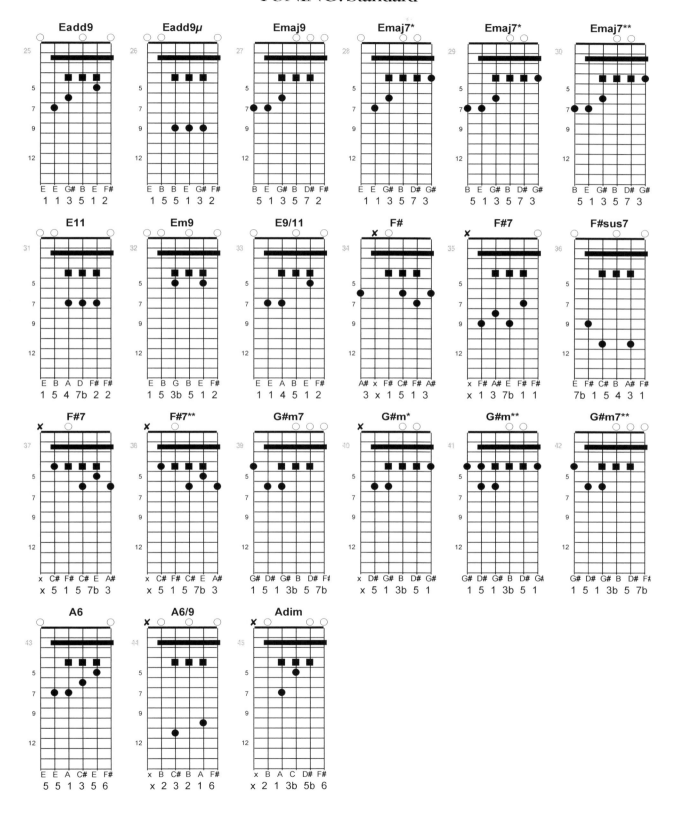

59- 044422

0 4 4 4 2 2

TUNING
Standard

OPEN STRINGS

E C# F# B C# F#

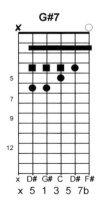

Model 65 and 43 capos at the 2nd and 4th frets making the 044422 configuration.

0 4 4 4 2 2

This is here more for completeness than musical value. Randall Williams puzzlingly presented it as the very first example of a double-capo configuration in his book, and I would put it near the bottom on the list of usefulness for 2 capos. It's best to play in C position, to sound in E, though you might have success playing in G position and sounding in B and get a song out of it somehow.

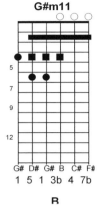

G#m11

G# D# G# B C# F#
1 5 1 3b 4 7b

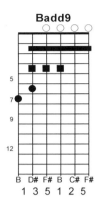

Badd9

B D# F# B C# F#
1 3 5 1 2 5

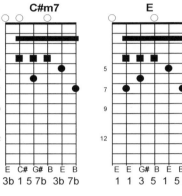

C#m7

E C# G# B E B
3b 1 5 7b 3b 7b

E

E E G# B E B
1 1 3 5 1 5

R
F#5

x C# F# C# F# F#
x 5 1 5 1 1

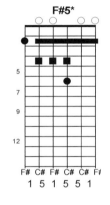

F#5*

F# C# F# C# C# F#
1 5 1 5 5 1

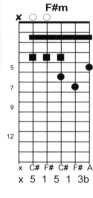

F#m

x C# F# C# F# A
x 5 1 5 1 3b

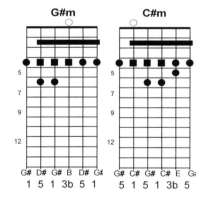

G#m

G# D# G# B D# G#
1 5 1 3b 5 1

C#m

G# C# G# C# E G#
5 1 5 1 3b 5

G

x D G B D G
x 5 1 3 5 1

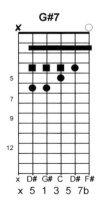

G#7

x D# G# C D# F#
x 5 1 3 5 7b

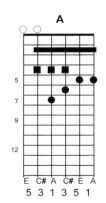

A

E C# A C# E A
5 3 1 3 5 1

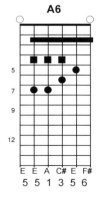

A6

E E A C# E F#
5 5 1 3 5 6

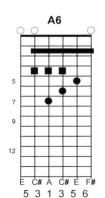

A6

E C# A C# E F#
5 3 1 3 5 6

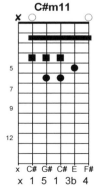

C#m11

x C# G# C# E F#
x 1 5 1 3b 4

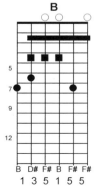

B

B D# F# B F# F#
1 3 5 1 5 5

214

60 – Esus@4 / Open A (044420)

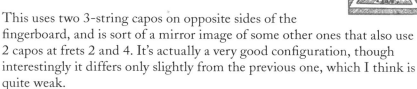

044420

TUNING
Standard

OPEN STRINGS

E C# F# B C# E

This uses two 3-string capos on opposite sides of the fingerboard, and is sort of a mirror image of some other ones that also use 2 capos at frets 2 and 4. It's actually a very good configuration, though interestingly it differs only slightly from the previous one, which I think is quite weak.

Like most of the double capo configurations on frets 2 and 4, your best options are generally to play in G or C position and sound in E or B accordingly. (Or their corresponding minor or modal keys). Because this one has the low C# string, it works better than some of them for playing Am position to sound in C#m. (You could also tune the bass E down to C# and get a big low tonic drone, though you would lose some opportunities on the bass string for fretted chords above the capo.)

This configuration enables you to play a lot of close voicings on the treble strings (including the so-called "*mu*" chords (p. 40)) because the pitches of the 3 open treble strings are within a span of only 5 frets. This allows harp-like chords and scales, and in particular a chord that is rare on the guitar, that contains the scale notes 1-2-3-4-5. Chords #37-38 on the next page both do this, and I call them *9/11μ* chords because they have the 1-3-5 notes of the major chord, plus the 9th (2) and 11th (4) also, all in the same octave. When arpeggiated or fingerpicked these chords are really haunting. This is the only example in this book that contains this chord voicing, out of the **thousands** of chords shown.

A pair of Model 43 capos forming the Esus/A configuration: 0 4 4 4 2 0

This configuration requires two Model 43 partial capos

044420

TUNING: Standard

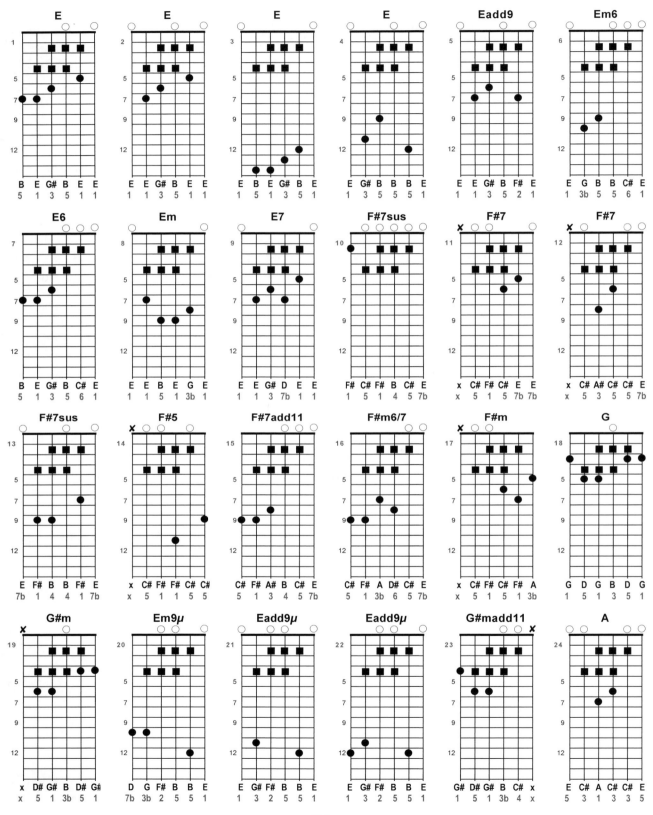

TUNING: Standard

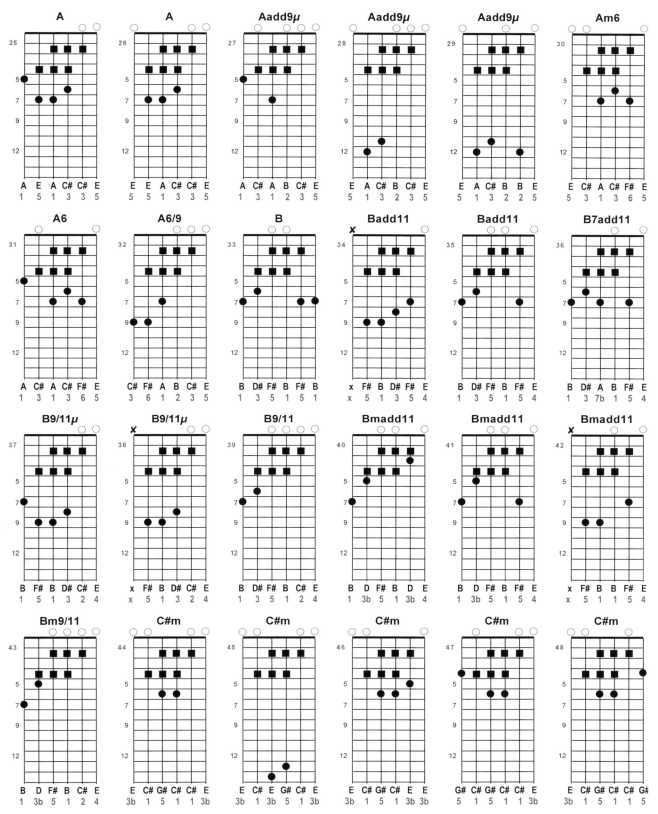

TUNING: Standard

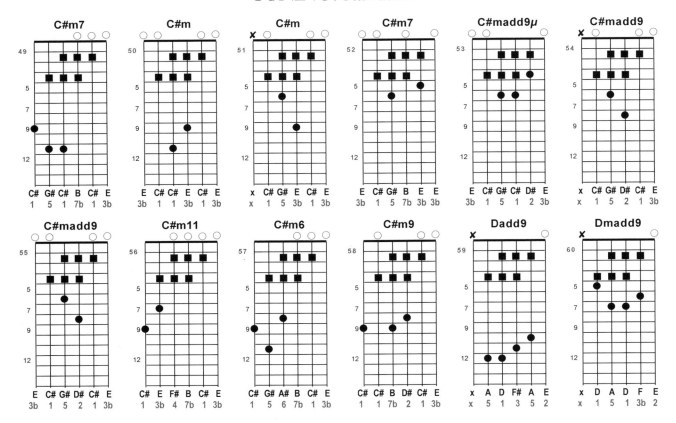

ABOUT PARTIAL CAPO MECHANISMS

Making a perfect partial capo is a harder problem than it seems at a glance. There is a huge range of string gauges, action, string spacing, neck widths, thicknesses and shapes among the guitars of the world, plus variations in fingerboard radius. String height at the 12th fret can be high, so capos end up being bulky in order to provide clearance for all scenarios. People have been trying for years to make a better and a truly universal partial capo. Existing capos are admittedly still a bit clumsy and obtrusive, and we can hope for some improvements.

Single-purpose partial capos are less visible and not as much in the way as universal models, but they are not perfect designs either. The three most common "*Esus*" capos are often too big for narrow necks like *Fender* electrics, or too small for classical necks or 12-strings. Ideally, there should be two or three models of every *Esus* capo to accommodate all the widths of fingerboards, or an adjustable mechanism of some kind. Since it only clamps 3 strings, the *Esus* capo need not compensate for fingerboard radius, which is a problem with longer capos.

Building a mechanism into the guitar seems to make sense, but there are not many players yet who are willing to drill holes and modify their guitars when they can accomplish the same thing with capos that can easily be moved to other frets or to other instruments. If you are "deep" enough into partial capos to want something built-in to your guitar, then you won't be able to play other instruments, which is quite limiting.

The *Third Hand* rotating cam mechanism has been around since 1975, and in 2008 when Peter Einhorn made the new design called the *SpiderCapo*, it still had the same basic drawbacks as the *Third Hand*: it blocks access to the fingerboard, and is very visible. Both capos easily adjust for string spacing, though the *SpiderCapo* doesn't accommodate 12-strings or very curved fingerboards, and requires a special model for classical width necks.

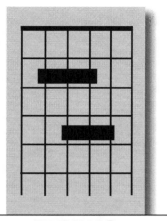

TUNING
Standard
OPEN STRINGS
E B F# B D# E

61- Esus / A@4 (024440)

This configuration uses a pair of *Esus* capos, and yields a few interesting chord inversions, drones and dissonances. The opportunities it offers I think would be more useful for a songwriter than a picker. You can make some textural, arpeggiated fingerpicking instrumental music that has some depth and some chord movement. It is visually similar to one I call *Esus-Asus* (#111), but not nearly as musically useful in my opinion because the top two strings form a dissonant interval D#- E and you pretty much have to fret one of those strings most of the time.

You'll get the best results if you use this to play in G position to sound in the key of B, and to a lesser extent if you play in C position to sound in E. It is possible to get either a strong 1-5 chord change in E or a 1-4 change in B, since the B chord you get when you play in G position is quite full, and the E chord is massive with the low E and B droning underneath. The E chord only requires a couple fingers to form. (Notice that only two of the open strings are not in an E chord, and 2 are not in a B chord.) The fact that both chords can be played with a lot of strings ringing, and only a few fingers to form them allows considerable freedom for melodies, embellishments and extensions to the chords. If you use arpeggiated chords rather than strumming you can minimize some of the flat 5 and flat 9 dissonances that show up, especially in the minor chords.

The chords marked with an asterisk (*) have notes fretted under the capo.

Forming the Double Esus configuration. The capo at fret 2 can be either a 4-string (above) or 3-string (below.)

This configuration requires two Model 43 partial capos

024440

TUNING: Standard

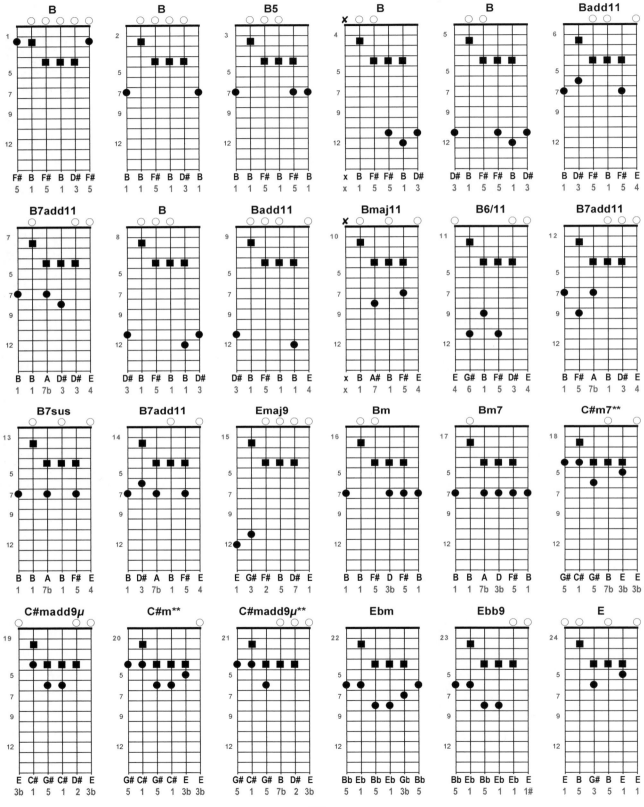

TUNING: Standard

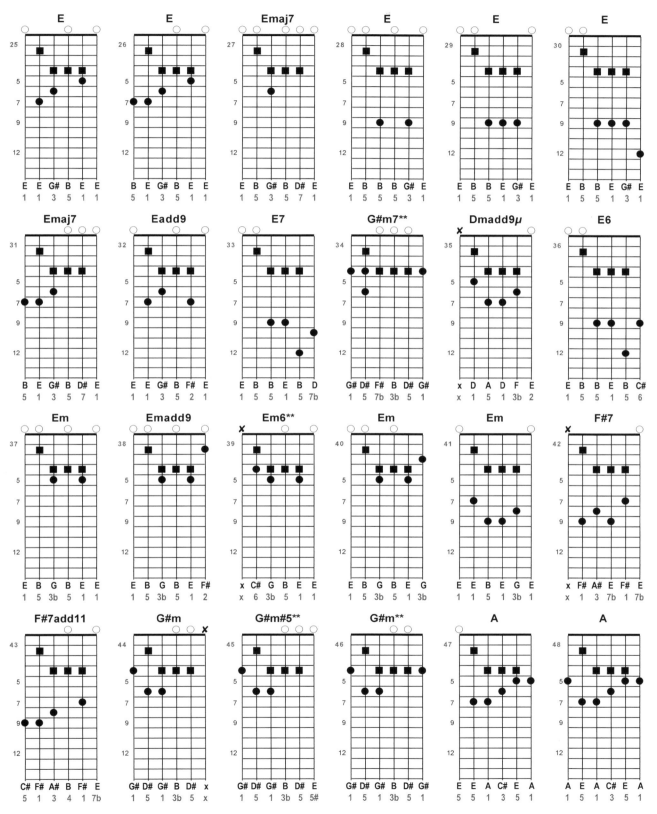

TUNING: Standard

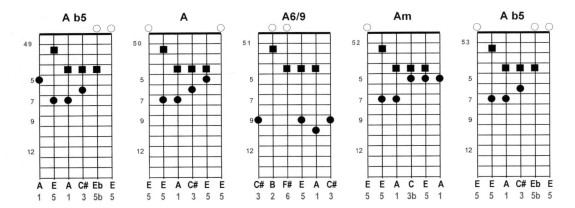

62- 066622

E A D G B E

0 6 6 6 2 2

Model 43 and 65 capos at the 2nd and 6th frets making the 066622 configuration.

0 6 6 6 2 2

Randall Williams introduces this one (along with 044422 we saw earlier) as his 2nd suggestion for multiple capos in his *Partial Capo* book, again an odd choice. Its best use is to play in the key of C# by playing in G position. It's a good example of how some capo configurations are only for "show" and don't have much in the way of musical value. Having the two bottom strings sounding as E and E♭ is not going to open too many musical doors or allow much bass string droning, unless you are looking for dissonance. There are very few ways to add an open string to a common chord, no basic chords with an open root bass note, and little if any musical advantage is gained in my opinion by the very obtrusive presence of two capos that occupy much of the fingerboard.

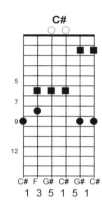

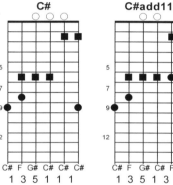

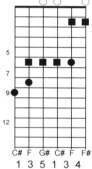

C#
C# F G# C# G# C#
1 3 5 1 5 1

C#
C# F G# C# C# C#
1 3 5 1 1 1

C#add11
C# F G# C# F F#
1 3 5 1 3 4

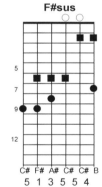

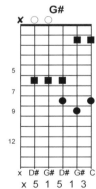

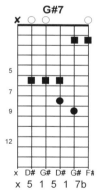

F#sus
C# F# A# C# C# B
5 1 3 5 5 4

G#
x D# G# D# G# C
x 5 1 5 1 3

G#7
x D# G# D# G# F#
x 5 1 5 1 7b

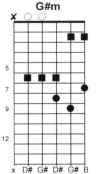

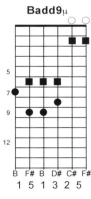

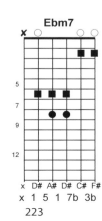

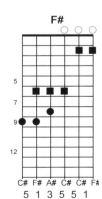

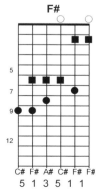

G#m
x D# G# D# G# B
x 5 1 5 1 3b

Badd9μ
B F# B D# C# F#
1 5 1 3 2 5

Ebm7
x D# A# D# C# F#
x 1 5 1 7b 3b

F#
C# F# A# C# C# F#
5 1 3 5 5 1

F#
C# F# A# C# F# F#
5 1 3 5 1 1

223

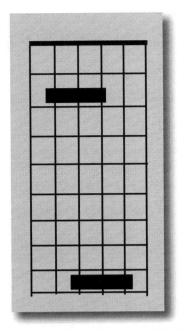

TUNING
Standard
OPEN STRINGS
E B B E G# E

63- Esus / A@9 (029990)

This one resembles 009990 (#25) but uses a second *Esus* capo at fret 2 to add the B note on the 5th string, while still leaving the high E string open. This allows you a full-sounding 5 chord (as well as a 1 chord) when you play in E. I sometimes call a sub-group of them (which includes this one) the EBB configurations, because the bottom 3 strings are those letters.

Most likely you would think like you were playing in G above the higher capo, so your 4 chord would be a C shape and the 5 chord a D or D7 shape. Some very interesting chords become available in this manner, and you can do some nice walk-downs on the bass strings below the capo. If you keep a finger at the 5th fret of the high E string, and then move down from fret 7 to 5-4-3 of the 5th string it makes a nice cadence against an arpeggiated A-G#-E on the three treble strings.

Like most of these situations that involve a capo at the 9th fret, you probably need an electric guitar or a cutaway acoustic to do this. You also may find that you have intonation problems with the capo this high up.

A pair of Model 43's at 029990

This configuration requires two Model 43 partial capos

0 2 9 9 9 0

224

TUNING: Standard

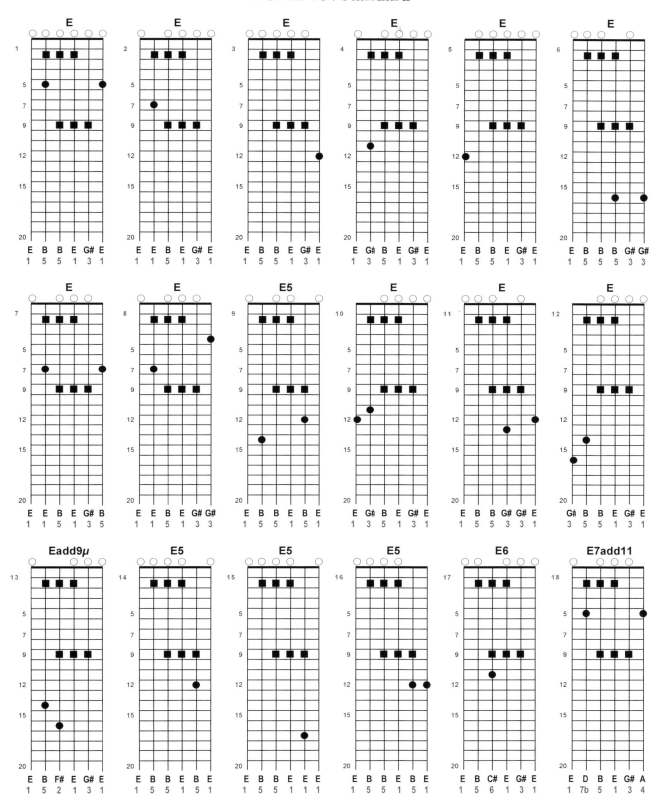

TUNING: Standard

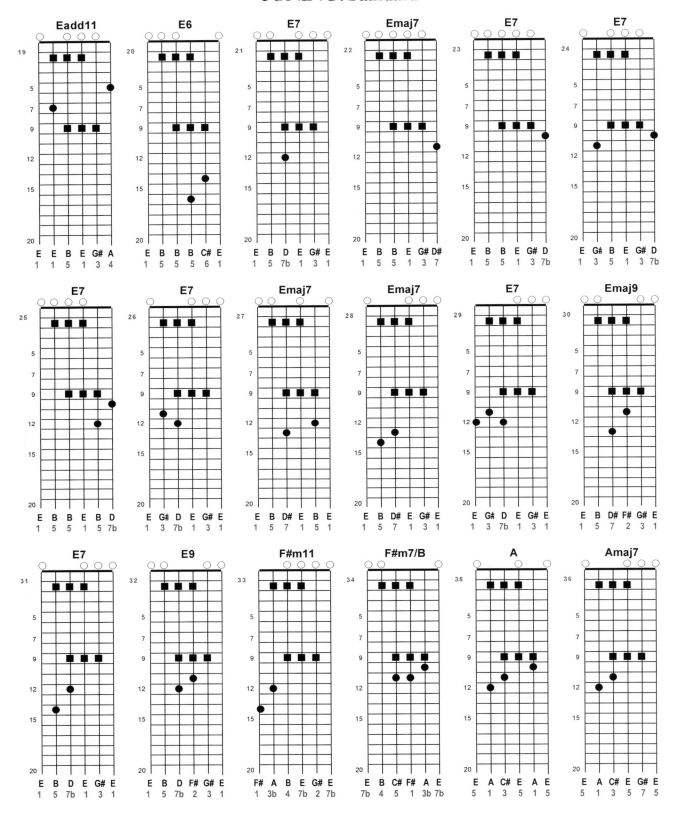

TUNING: Standard

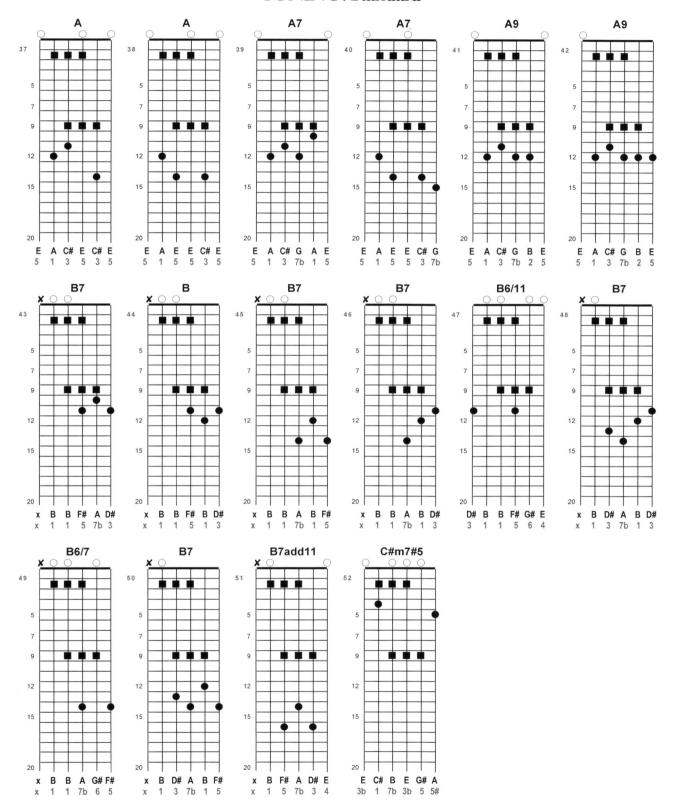

64~ 029999

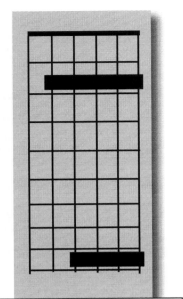

TUNING

Standard

OPEN STRINGS

E B B E G# C#

This one is again a little exotic, because it takes two partial capos and the 2nd capo is so high up, but it is quite fun and generates some nice sounds with the low bass and the super-high treble at the same time. You might have intonation problems, and you really need a cutaway guitar to do this. It's nearly impossible with just a 12-fret neck.

It is a little surprising how good the chords sound, because when you play in G position (and sound in E yet again) you have very low root bass notes on all 3 basic E-A-B chords, that you just play as normal G-C-D. The G shape chord has 2 bass strings open. (Chord #1) The C shape (#10) and D shape (#12-#13) play the same as always but sound better. So it takes very little adjusting to this one, and if you go way up the neck like chord #3, it makes about the widest pitch spread possible on a guitar, with the open low E string played against the 16th and 17th frets of the high strings. It's a beautiful voicing of an E chord you could use on any song.

There are also some nice bass walk-downs you can do on the bottom two strings between the capos, especially starting at fret 7 of the A string and descending down to the capo at fret 2. It's a nice move when you have an audience watching.

With some other types of partial capos you can do some more exploring from this basic set-up, and possibly use an *Esus* 3-string capo at fret 9 and leave the high E string open at either the nut or fret 2 (See Config. #65). You can also go in another similar direction by dropping the bass E to D, and then capo 0 0 7 7 7 7. It is another nice way to sound in D by playing in G position, with a low bass and high treble and only a single capo. A lot of the same chords here would apply there, since it only differs on the bass E string from this one.

You could do this just as well with a pair of Model 43 capos, since the 2nd fret capoed note could be done with either a Model 43 or 65.

Making the 029999 with a Model 43 and a Model 65

029999

TUNING: Standard

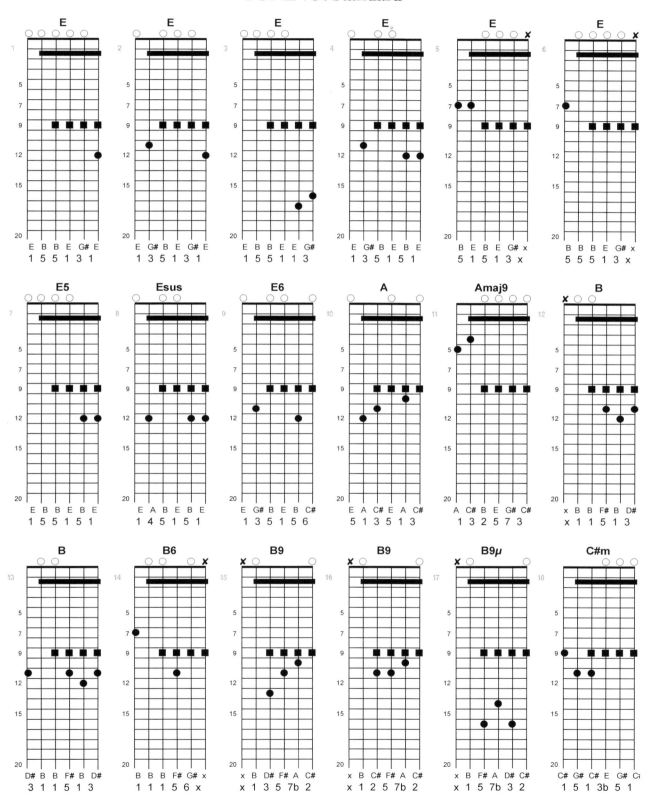

65~ EBB2 (029992)

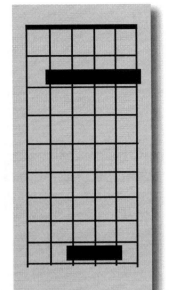

TUNING
Standard

OPEN STRINGS

E B B E G# F#

Only slightly different from the two previous configurations, this uses a second partial capo at fret 2 to add the B note on the 5th string and also the F# on the high E string. You will probably need an electric guitar or a cutaway acoustic to do this, and you may find that you have intonation problems with the capo this high up. You can probably offset a standard capo at the 2nd fret and thus won't need another special capo.

This one has a similar sound and feel to the previous configurations, since it has a low bass drone and most of what you are playing is high up the neck. The added 9th tone (F#) of the E chord droning on the high E string adds a nice effect, which actually is very similar to the "*Drop D 027772*" that appears later.

You can't get much by cross-keying here, and you get the best results if you play in G above the higher capo. That makes the 4 chord as a C shape and the 5 chord a D or D7 shape. Since a lot of the chords have added 9th and 6ths, they will sound best if you arpeggiate rather than strum them. If you play thumb or bass-string melody lines, you can do some nice walkdowns on the bass strings below the capo.

Guitarist Dan Schwartz used this one in 1996 on his instrumental "*RayJoyce!*"

A Model 65 at fret 2 and a Model 43 at fret 9.

0 2 9 9 9 2

TUNING: Standard

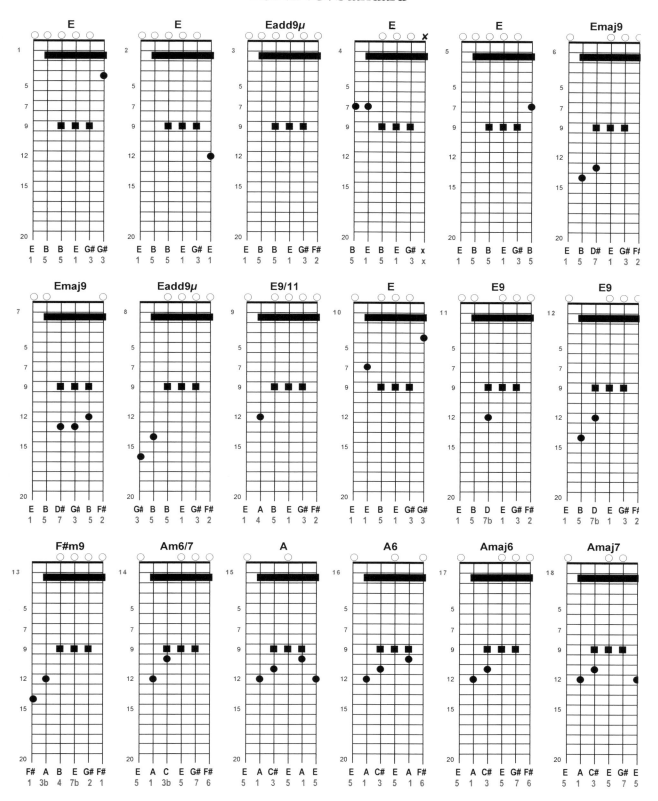

Some Chords in the EBB2 029992 p.2
TUNING: Standard

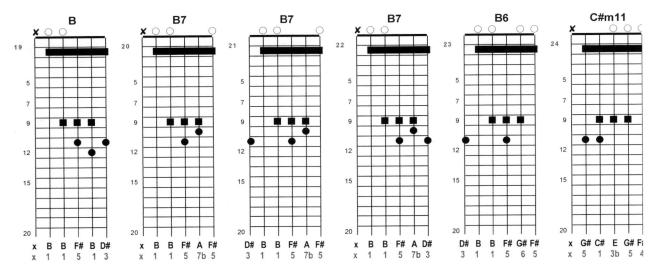

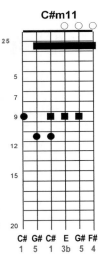

66- 355530

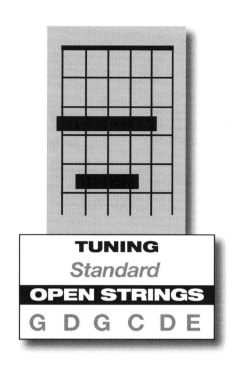

TUNING
Standard
OPEN STRINGS
G D G C D E

This one is very similar to the 555530 configuration (#67,) and it also resembles the triple capo 155530 (#70). They all allow close-voiced chords, interesting colorations, and flowing harp-like melodic lines against different bass notes.

Here it shifts the keys you are strongest in toward G and C, since it can take advantage of the G-D-G bass strings. When you play in D position, it sounds in G, and because of the double capos, you get a lot of "*mu*" chords (p. 40) and harp-like scales on the treble end. The G chord shape makes the dreamy Cadd9μ (#10,11) for example.

You can also play some nice things in E and A positions, which sound a 4th higher in A D, respectively.

A Model 65 and 43 making the 355530 configuration

355530

TUNING: Standard

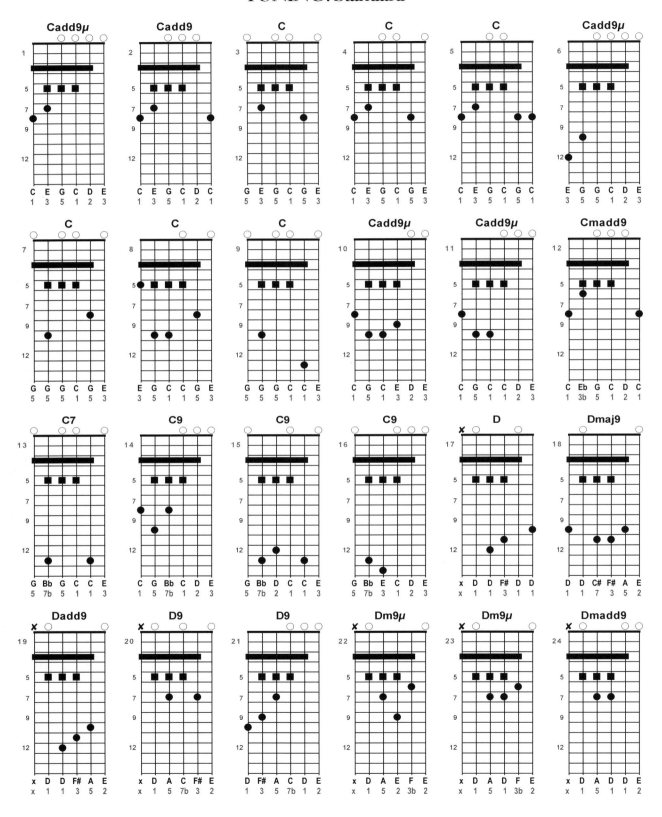

234

Some Chords in the 355530 Configuration p.1
TUNING: Standard

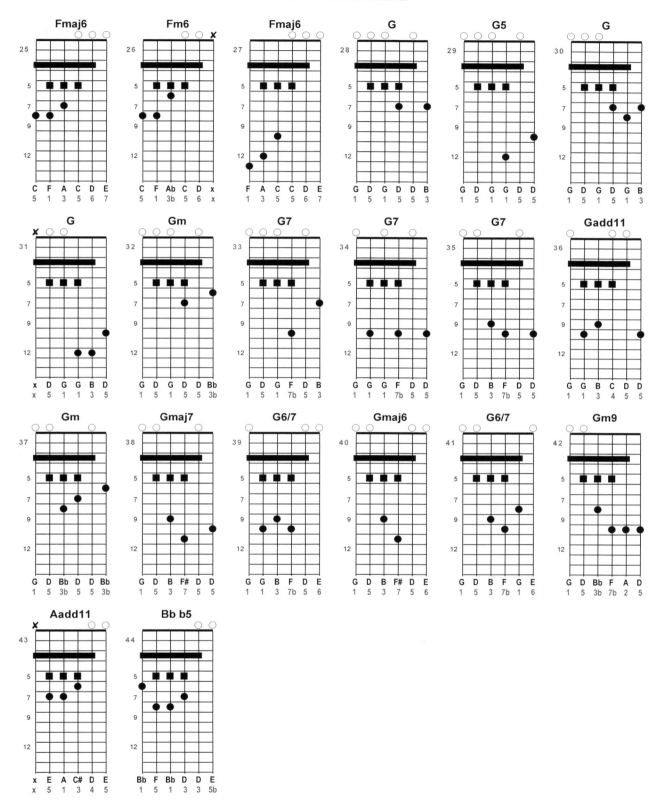

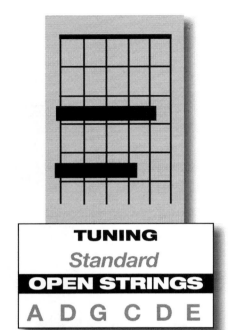

TUNING
Standard
OPEN STRINGS
A D G C D E

A Model 65 and a Model 43 making the 555530 configuration. You could also use 2 Model 43's.

67- A Minor 11 (555530)

Like the previous idea, this one works differently than the B6 setup (#54), since the staggered-capo effect is now in the treble and not the bass. I call it the *Am11* because the open strings form an A minor chord with added 7b and 11 notes. It's not a great voicing of that chord, and the 6 open strings don't sound a very distinctive or coherent chord, but there is nice music to be found here.

Since the top 3 open strings are the notes C-D-E, there are now a wealth of harp-like scales and close-voiced "*mu*" chords (p. 40) available. Instead of droning the bass strings like configuration 044444 (#8) you now use the capos for adding notes to chords and scales in the treble end. Since your highest capo is at fret 5, you can keep track of what you are doing pretty well, since everything you play comes out a musical 4th higher, which is like moving over a string.

You can play in a number of keys and get good results. G position is maybe the most obvious one, and the capos will cause you to sound in C. If you play in E or Em position, you will sound in A or Am, and the chords are so good that I put them first in the chart. You can generate the "*mu*" effect with the Dm chords also due to the open high E that can be added to them. Am position causes you to sound in Dm, which works well also, and you can get a nice Gm chord (by playing a Dm,) and the other chords commonly found in that key all have nice sounds.

Chord #1 is one of the rare and interesting 1-2-3-4-5 chords that I call 9/11. (You can't really do this in standard tuning, so there is no common name for the chord.) This one plays right up the A scale in order with 2-3-4-5 on the top 4 strings. If you set up a fingerpicking pattern and weave it around in that chord it sounds amazing. Chord #4 that I call the minor 9/11 plays up an Am scale. I call chord #6 the "*Eleanor Rigby*" chord because when arpeggiated it plays the opening riff of the song.

5 5 5 5 3 0

TUNING: Standard

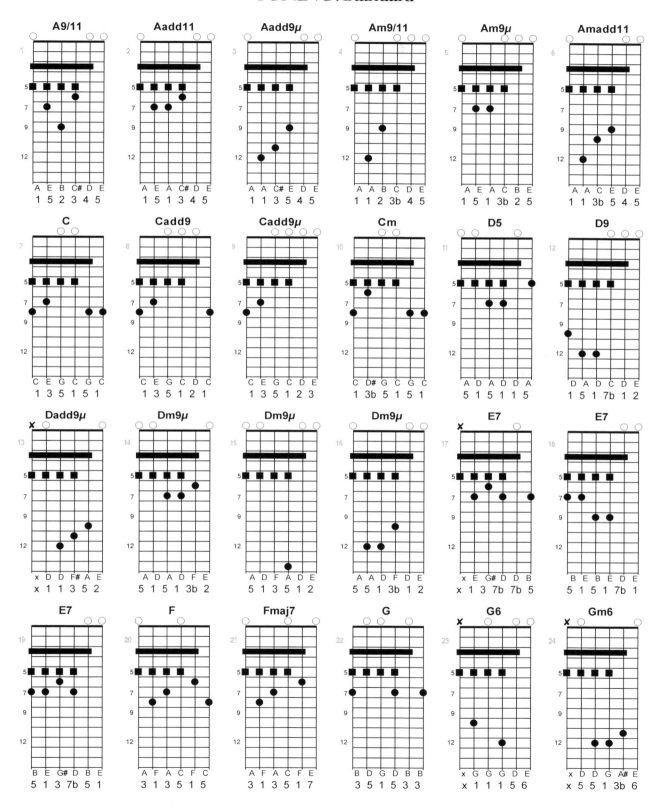

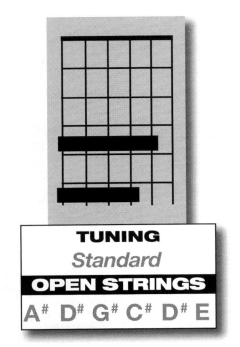

TUNING
Standard
OPEN STRINGS
A# D# G# C# D# E

68~ 666640

Since we are looking at multiple shortened capos in standard tuning, here is another in this same category. This one is just a half step higher than the previous one, and it has a similar strategy, to generate overlapping voicings in the treble. It makes the most sense here to play in G position, which because we are in a capo 6 situation translates to C#. But the high E string is the minor 3rd of that chord, so we really want to play in Gm position and sound in C#m. This is a better situation for a songwriter or for creating an arrangement of a song, rather than a picker.

Like similar set-ups, we get cascading chords on the treble end that really only work when they are arpeggiated. The open 2nd string adds a 9th to a C# root chord, so there are some great "minor add9" chords. The top 3 open strings play the first 3 scale notes of the C#m scale, and when arpeggiated against a moving bass line they can sound really striking.

This is not a hugely useful configuration, but it is a bit unusual and entertaining, and worth spending some time playing with.

A Model 65 at fret 4 and a Model 43 at fret 6 making the 666640 configuration.

666640

TUNING: Standard

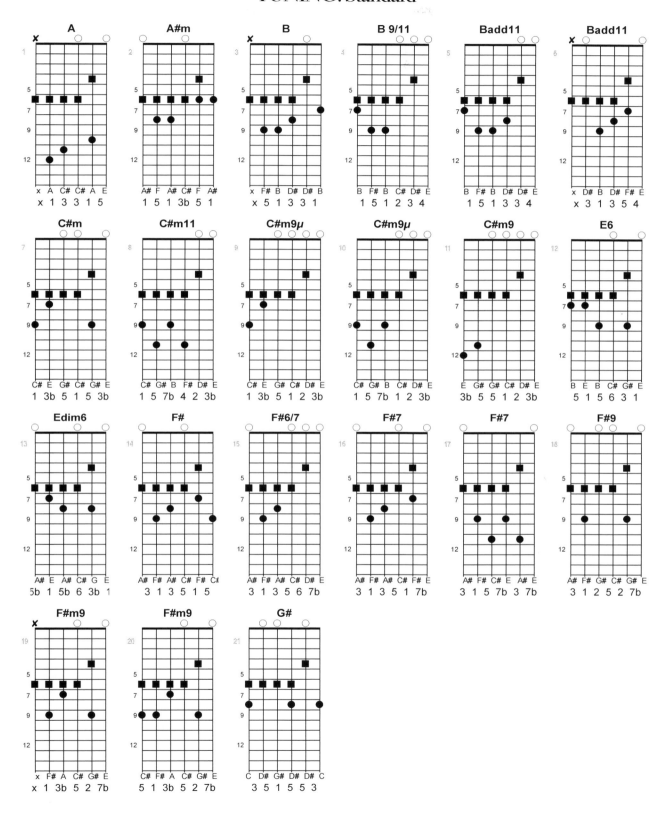

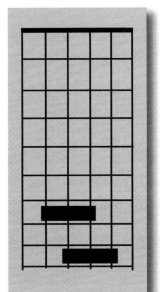

69- Esus@7 / A@9 (079990)

This is related to a number of other configurations, and a member of the surprisingly large *"A@9"* family of capo configurations. Here we use the second partial capo at fret 7 to add another E bass note on the 5th string. I sometimes call a sub-group of them (which includes this one) the EEB configurations, because the bottom 3 strings are those letters.

This one is less mysterious than some of the others that resemble it, since the capos form an open E chord and there are 4 open E strings. All the droning notes are part of an E major chord. So you don't have the lingering droned 4ths or 9ths that you sometimes get with double capos. It might be a nice way for a very young child to learn some chords and have a pleasant guitar experience, since the frets are really short, the fingerings are standard tuning, and when you strum all 6 strings open it makes a huge, bright sound.

Like a number of these 2-capo situations, you could also tune the B string up to C and gain something. You would then play in G position, and sound in E, or else play in C and sound in E.

A pair of Model 43's making the 079990

This configuration requires two Model 43 partial capos

0 7 9 9 9 0

Some Chords in the Esus@7/A@9 Configuration
TUNING: Standard

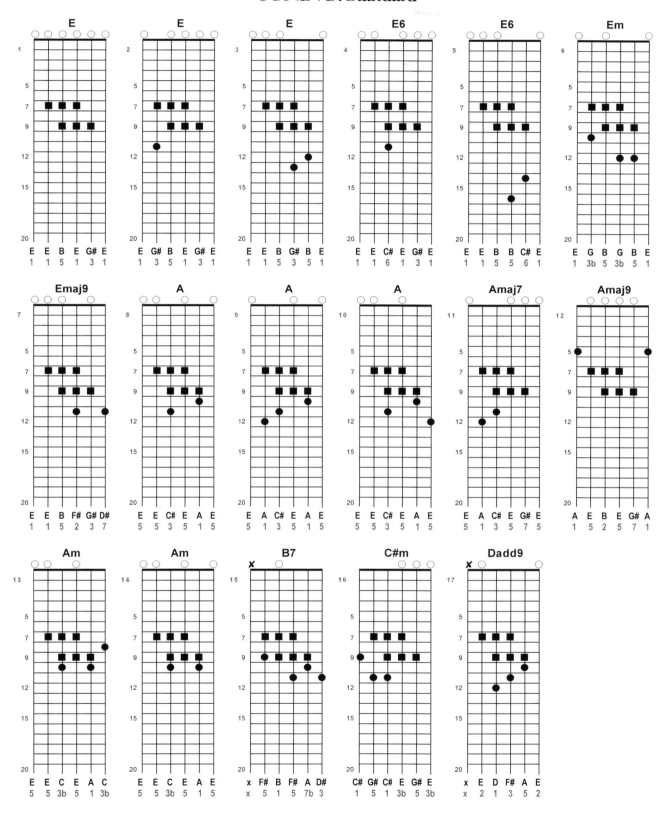

241

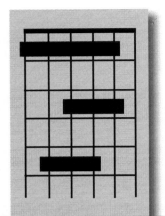

TUNING
Standard
OPEN STRINGS
F D G C D E

70~ 155530

Author's Favorite

This one takes a while to set up, but it is really fun, and it is one of the few 3-capo configurations I have found that is really musically useful. You could have some real fun and add a full capo at fret 1 to give you a grand total of 4.

It is related to some earlier configurations like 355530 (#66), and again features a lot of harp-like ideas, flowing melodic options and overlapping "*mu*" chords (p. 40) and the like. The F bass note on the 6th string opens up the possibility of playing in F. Then the C-D-E notes on the top 3 strings then create a new set of sounds, especially when arpeggiated against some bass notes. The fact that the open strings in this set-up have 5 notes (C-D-E-F-G) that are common to both a C, Dm, and F scales means that you can play in those keys with bass notes and flowing melodies. The D-G bass notes also means that you can play in G *Mixolydian or* D *Dorian* modes and use the C scale against the D or G bass root.

Since you are still in standard tuning, you pretty much think like you are playing in C, to sound in F, or play in G position and sound in C. As usually happens with partial capos, your chords get a new set of notes added to them. You get a great Fmaj6 chord with no effort, or by playing in G position (sounding in C) your treble strings make an add9μ. (Chord #4)

Because you have a strong D bass note, you can play D family chords, either as minors in the key of F or try some things in Dm. The Dm-C changes are beautiful.

A set of Liberty "Flip" Model 65 (fret 1) and Model 43 (frets 3 & 5) making the 155530 configuration.

This configuration requires two Model 43 partial capos

1 5 5 5 3 0

TUNING: Standard

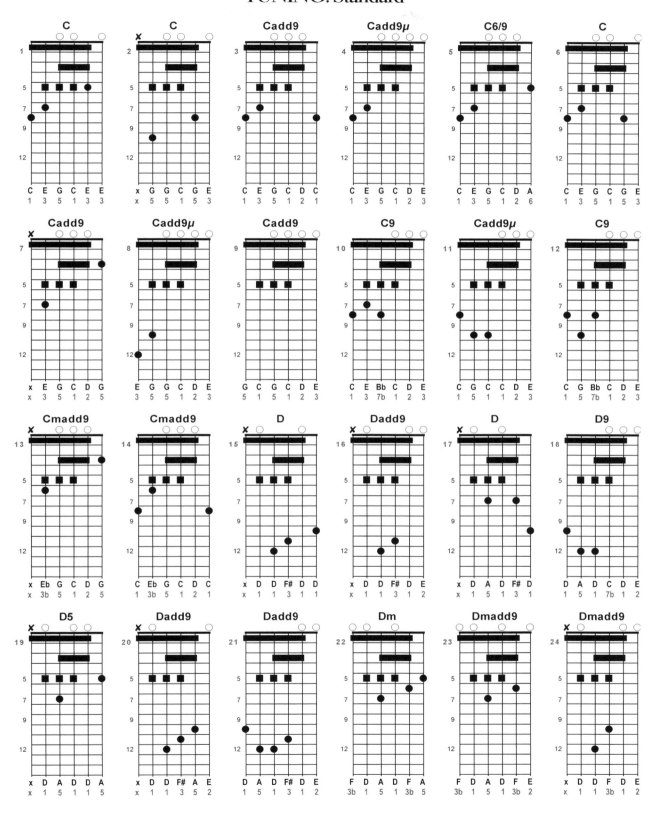

TUNING: Standard

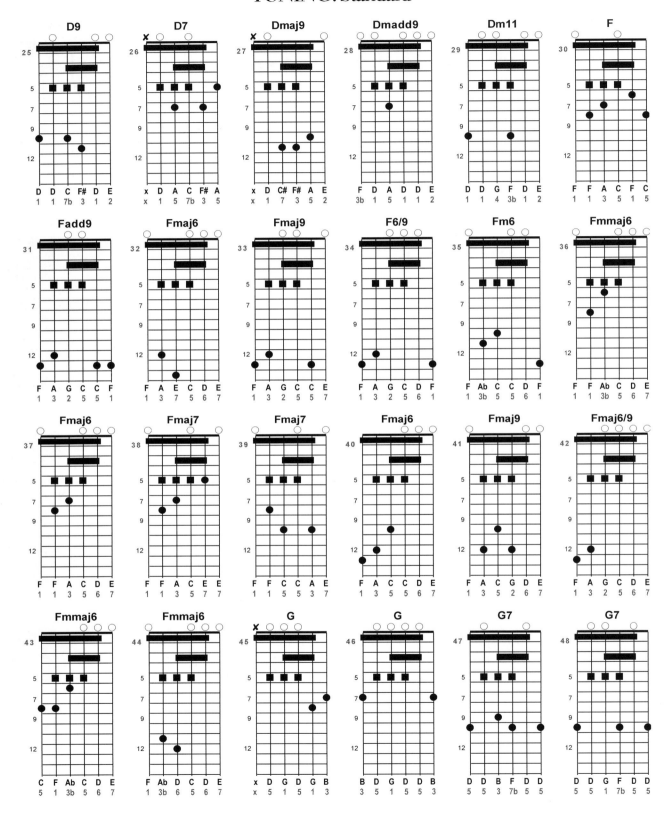

Some Chords in the 155530 Configuration p.3

TUNING: Standard

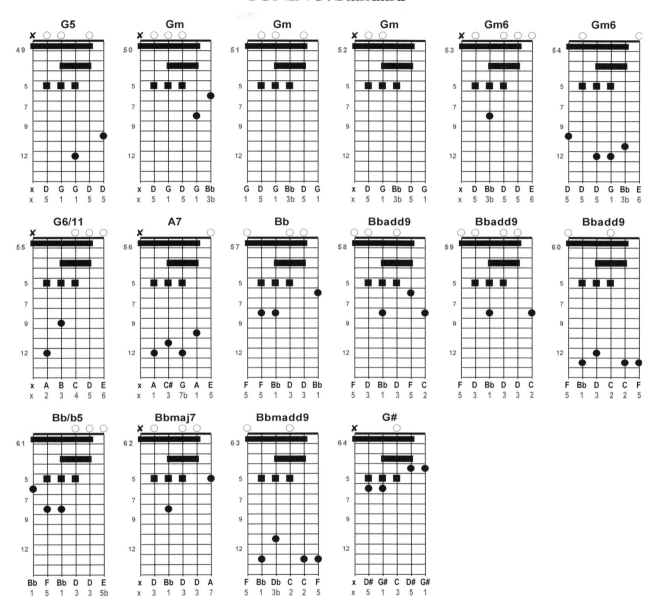

Thanks for sticking with me! In Vol. 2 of this book we'll look at dozens of ways you can use Liberty capos with open tunings. Here are 3 of those ideas from that book that involve deeper levels of combining capos with tunings.

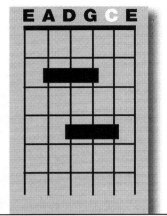

TUNING

E A D G C E

OPEN STRINGS

E B F# B E E

71~ Esus/Asus (024440)[EADGCE]

Another member of the big "2 partial capos at frets 2 & 4" family, this is identical to the 024440 (#61) except the B string is retuned to C. Since this combines the *Esus* configuration in the bass with the *Asus* tuning I call it *Esus/Asus*. I think it is more fruitful than "plain" 024440, if you can handle the retuning. It also leaves the open high E string open to the nut, and some interesting things happen. As you might expect, you could play in G position to sound in B, though the 5 chords (F#) are not easy and a little thin. The best use of this configuration, probably, is to play in C position, and sound in E. You can also play modal (*Mixolydian* or *Dorian* mostly) songs in B, which use the same basic C position chords as you would use playing in E major.

The F family chords (they are A chords actually) are particularly interesting and a personal favorite of mine. The sharped B string frees up a finger, which breaks up the life-long tyranny of the F barre chord shape tying up all 4 of your fingers. A usual F chord shape gets an added major seventh (E) when the high E string is unfretted, but here when you do it, you are instead adding an E to an A chord. So you are essentially playing in C, and your F-shape chord leaves the top 2 strings open, which gives you a lot of new freedom to add melodies or extra notes.

This configuration requires two Model 43 partial capos

A matched pair of Model 43 capos forming the Esus/Asus configuration.

Tune B string up 1 fret to C

This configuration is also effective for songs that need either a strong 1-5 chord change in E or a 1-4 change in B. You also get a lot of interesting voicings that you would not expect. The E chords in general are rich, and take a only a couple fingers to form. The added 6th 7th, 9th and 11ths present a lot of nice options. If you can learn to reach over the capo there are some very nice 2, 3 and 6 chords available, which usually is not the case in partial capoing.

0 2 4 4 4 0

TUNING: E A D G C E

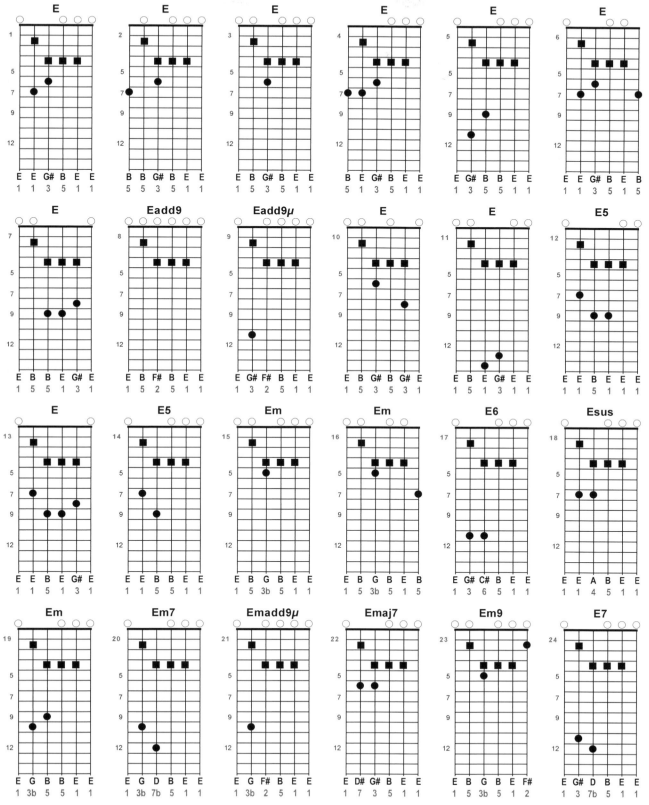

TUNING: E A D G C E

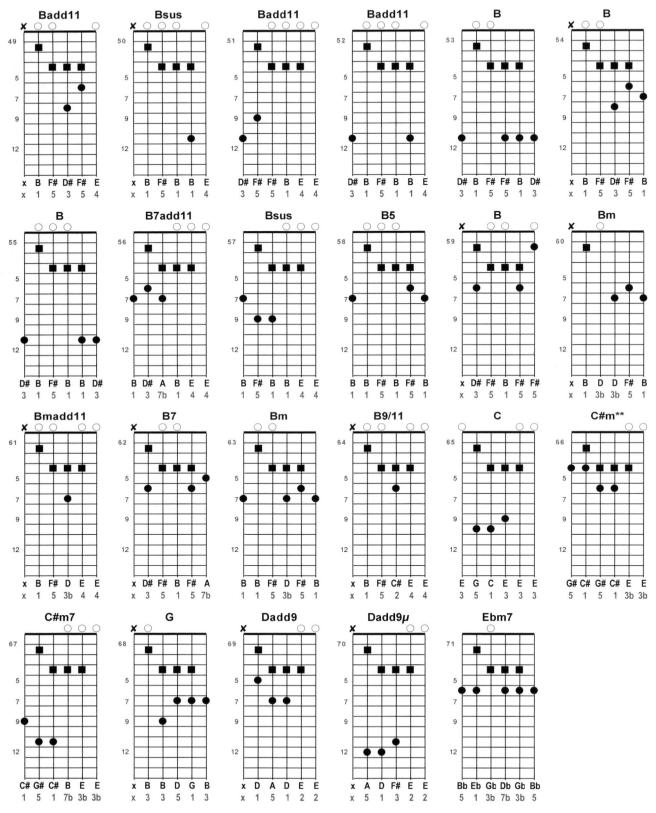

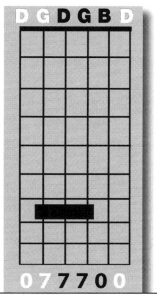

72- Open G 077700 [DGDGBD]

Here is a quick way to get some fresh sounds in *Open G* tuning with an *Esus* capo, and a "sneak peek" at things in Vol. 2 of this book, where I show you dozens more ways to combine tunings and partial capos.

If you play in "regular" G position, you'll sound in D, and there are some great chords and unique voicings. The G7 chord (#40) that runs off the chart is the only voicing like this I have found in tens of thousands of guitar chords.

It's not easy to get a good A chord, so 1-4-5 songs in D are hard to make sound right. Be imaginative and enjoy some of the combinations of chords like #21-#42.

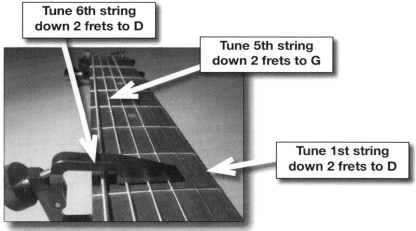

At the 7th fret making the Esus@7 configuration in Open G tuning.

077700

Some Chords in Open G 07770 p.1
TUNING: Open G (D G D G B D)

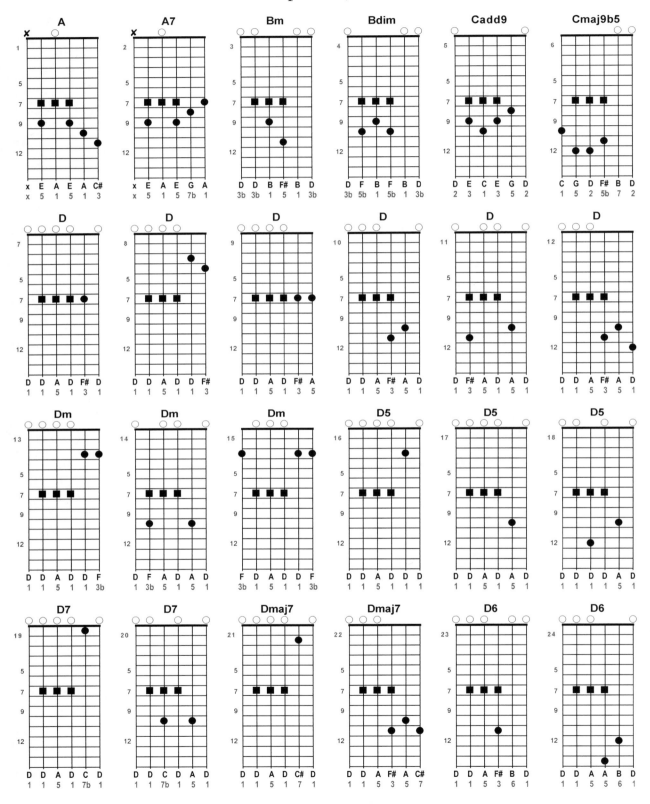

250

Some Chords in Open G 07770 p.2
TUNING: Open G (D G D G B D)

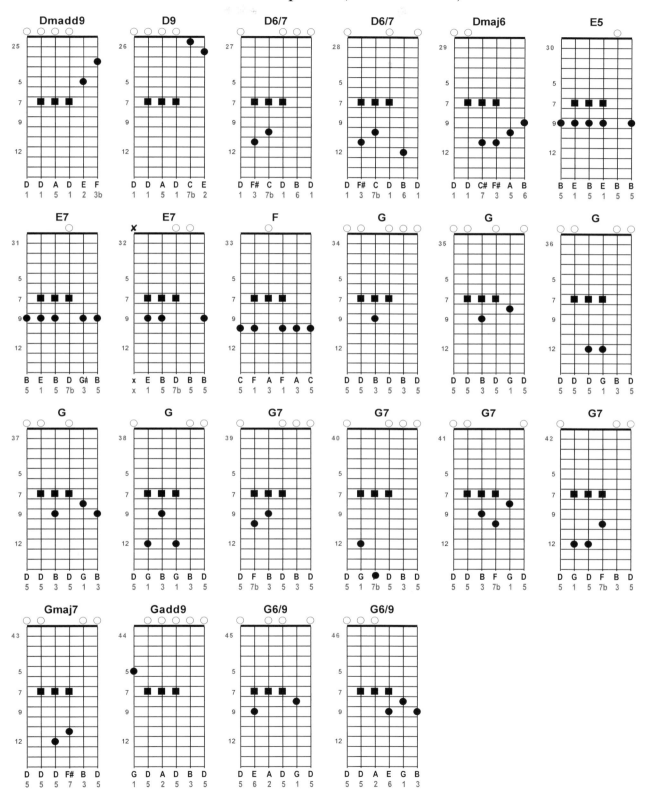

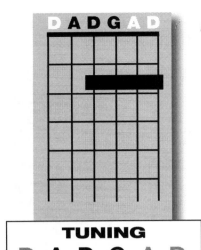

TUNING
D A D G A D
OPEN STRINGS
D A E A B E

Author's Favorite

My book "*Secrets of Partial Capos in DADGAD Tuning*" shows 27 ways to use partial capos in this tuning. 17 of them can be done with a *Liberty* capo, and the other 16 appear in Vol. 2 of this book.

A lot of guitarists seem to feel that if they already use altered tunings, they do not need to learn about partial capos. This is reinforced by the fact that many explanations of partial capos describe it as a substitute for using tunings. The truth is that partial capos and tunings are not the same thing at all, though at a glance they might seem to be. And we are steadily learning that combining the two of them, though confusing, can yield another powerful but bewildering "guitar hyperspace" of new chords and resonances.

DADGAD has become a very popular guitar tuning, and it makes sense that people are using partial capos as a way to expand the musical possibilities that arise if you have your guitar in a tuning like this. I first saw guitarist Al Petteway doing this configuration. It's a winner, and a great example of how to put a tuning and a capo together.

The open strings with the capo this way give you a D A E A B E, which is closely related to the mysterious and lovely C G D G A D tuning probably invented by English guitarist Dave Evans in the 1960's, and recently adopted, explored and popularized by American guitarist El McMeen and some others. If you raised (or capoed) that tuning a whole step it would also be D A E A B E. There are some other simulations of this tuning using standard tuning or *Drop D* tuning and a universal capo, but this is better.

Tune 1st, 2nd & 6th strings down 2 frets

The DADGAD Top 4 configuration.

Most of the possibilities here involve playing in the key of A, or related modal keys. There are a lot of modal A5 chords, and modal scale patterns also lie conveniently across the fingerboard. In fact, it is easy to play all sorts of modal or "power chords" (chords with no 3rd, that are neither major or minor) in this tuning/configuration, since a number of them land conveniently under your fingers (see chord diagrams) and DADGAD tuning allows you to barre anywhere and add one finger above the barre to make a "power chord."

This is a good way to give you some new musical options once you have already put your guitar into this popular tuning, and it gives a performer a way to do several more songs without changing the tuning or risking every song having a similar sound. You could, for example, perform a DADGAD piece in D, then one with this partial capo configuration in A, and then another DADGAD piece after that.

0 0 2 2 2 2

Some Chords in the DADGAD "Top 4 @2" Configuration p.1
TUNING: DADGAD

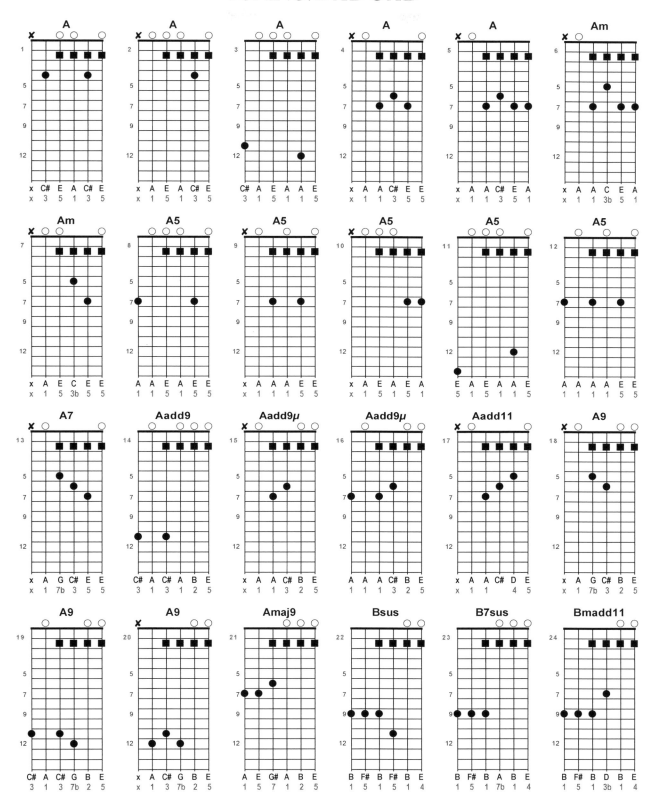

TUNING: DADGAD

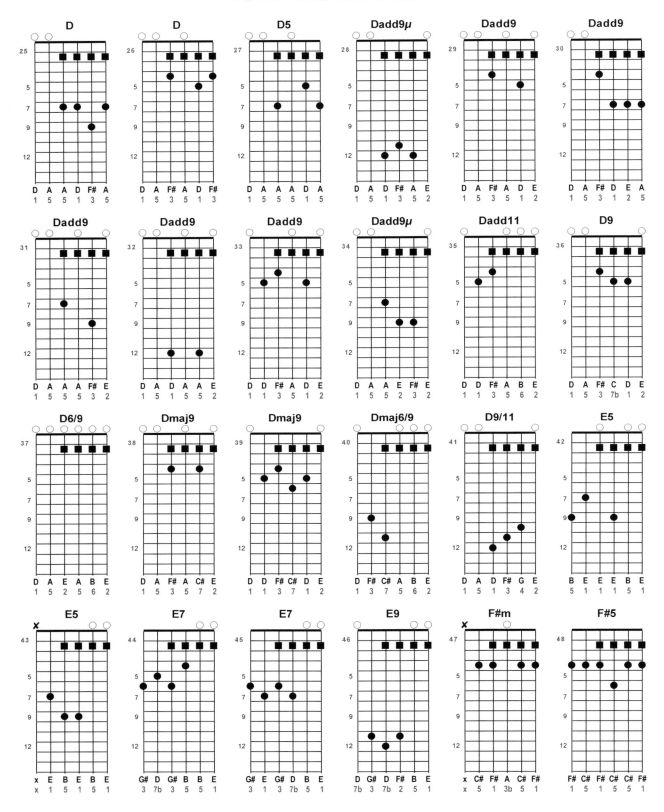

254

SECTION 5

Appendix: Other Partial Capo Topics

This book is thick enough already, and it would be possible to add another hundred pages to discuss the history of partial capos, artists who use them, and how they can be used to play various kinds of new music.

- Here is a quick overview of how it is possible to use partial capos to play simplified guitar chords. It no longer requires hours and hours of practice to master the chords for simple songs. Anyone, including very young children can play good-sounding chords right away with a partial capo. I have written several books on this subject.

- People with hand injuries or fewer than 4 working fingers can play things on a guitar they never dreamed they would be able to. This is very exciting.

- As partial capos get more widespread, there will be problems deciding how to notate music we play with them. I have tried to explain this problem here.

Simplified Guitar With Partial Capos

To page through this book it is not at all obvious how useful partial capos can be to beginners. Partial capos allow a number of easy and useful ways to simplify chord fingering, making it easier to start playing real songs with full, 6-string chords. This is the subject of several of my other books, but is worth a mention here. Partial capos may also be the most useful idea ever in learning to fingerpick. I hope to publish some of that.

An age-old problem in guitar is that even basic chords require 3 and 4 fingers to play, and countless people who want to strum basic chords fail to master the basic chord changes. Even the D-A7 chord change that most beginner methods start with is not something that a motivated adult with good dexterity can master right away. Other common approaches to beginner chords involve only playing 3 or 4 of the strings on the guitar, and they are not musically very rewarding. Avoiding strings with the strumming hand is not really a beginner skill, and incomplete chords played by beginners tend to sound pretty unmusical.

Children have typically not been able to start playing guitar chords until the age of 12 or 13 when their hands are larger and strong enough to press the chords down. For children to play campfire-style guitar, some programs use open-tuned guitars, which causes a new set of problems, while offering only limited advantages. Open tunings are restricted in keys and chords you can play, only certain songs sound right, and even simple 6-string barre chords in an open tuning are too hard for beginners & children.

Guitar programs for children have commonly involved either single-note melody (not realistic for most people), using electric guitars with much lighter strings (not really troubadour/campfire-type guitars), or smaller-scale instruments, that have many thorny problems.

It no longer requires intense practice to master basic chords for even the simplest songs. Essentially anyone can play good-sounding chords right away with a partial capo, and quickly learn to play a large number of common and popular songs in the musical keys that the capos allow access to.

My 1982 book *"Duck Soup Guitar"* marked the first publication of this idea, and it outlines a number of clever ways to use partial capos to play 1 and 2-finger chords on simple children's songs. It presented a very easy and effective "pre-guitar" experience, with the result of allowing full-sounding chords instantly. Not only is this useful for adults who have trouble with standard tuning chords, but very young children and people with hand injuries or less than 4 working fingers on their left hand can have a rewarding "campfire guitar" experience.

The 2-Finger Guitar Guide (2014) is an in-depth examination of all the advantages, possibilities and drawbacks of dozens of common tunings, partial capo configurations and hybrid tunings (combining a partial capo with an altered tuning) and how they can be used to play 2-finger guitar chords to accompany songs. It introduces my discovery of the *Liberty Tuning*, which is a simple hybrid tuning that unlocks a remarkable hidden world of simplified guitar.

Liberty Tuning is itself the subject of several other books. *The Liberty Tuning Chord Book* is an encyclopedia of thousands of chords in *Liberty Tuning*, that shows where to find all the playable chords hidden in this confusing but ground-breaking new guitar landscape. *The Liberty Guitar Method* shows how to play great-sounding 2-finger versions of 15 iconic songs from Bob Dylan, John Prine, Hank Williams, The Beatles, Johnny Cash, Chuck Berry and others. None of these songs has ever been considered a "beginner song," but in this tuning, the chords are all simple geometric 2-finger shapes that even young children can master almost instantly. *Liberty Guitar for Kids* shows how children as young as 4 can strum full chords on an adult guitar in keys they can sing in. The *Liberty Guitar Song Train* book shows how to play all 56 of the 2-chord songs in my 4-CD *Song Train* project with only 2-finger chords.

The *Song Train* was intended to provide a large and interesting repertoire of easy but great songs to give beginners some more compelling material than nursery rhymes to pull them into playing basic guitar. The addition of the *Liberty Tuning* concept to this body of music makes it another quantum level easier to play good-sounding beginning guitar chords right away.

Using Liberty Capos on Other Instruments

The *Model 43 Liberty* guitar capo will work nicely as either a full or a 3-string partial capo on a number of other smaller instruments, especially 4-stringed fingerboards like ukulele, mandolin, and banjo. This includes baritone ukes, tenor banjos, and octave mandolins.

These suggestions are by no means a thorough representation of what you can or should do, and there will need to be another book or two to investigate the musical possibilities.

UKULELE

0222

MANDOLIN

(full capo)

0222

BANJO

0222

0555

(full capo)

0777

Other Types of Partial Capos

Beginning with the *Shabram Chord-Forming Capo* in 1976, which I renamed the *Third Hand Capo* in 1980, there have been a succession of partial capos that have appeared. The *Shubb c7b* was the first single-purpose capo, and it showed up in 1995. There are now about 20 kinds of partial capos, made by 8 different manufacturers, and for the most part they all have certain advantages and significant disadvantages.

These devices were designed and manufactured by a number of people and companies, who generally knew little of the breadth of the partial capo universe, even though they were investing considerable time, money and energy into making and selling their capos. I have owned, used, sold and studied all these capos for many years, which led me to develop the *Liberty* capos.

Liberty FLIP capos do everything these 3, 4, and 5-string capos can do, and do them better.

Only the universal and the *G-Band* capos can do things that the *Liberty* capos cannot, and those **two types have the most problems fitting guitars properly, staying in place, and getting in the way of your music.** Only a handful of valuable musical ideas lie outside of what the *Liberty* capos can do, and my advice is to just stick with the ideas in this book. They will keep you busy for the rest of your life and lead you to an amazing amount of music.

SHORTENED 4 OR 5-STRING CAPOS

Planet Waves "NS Ukulele Capo Pro"

Kyser Drop D

Shubb c8b

Planet Waves "Trio"

Planet Waves "Triple-Action"

G-7 Newport #5

Kyser K-Lever "Drop D" (GREEN)

Third Hand

SpiderCapo

UNIVERSAL
CAPOS

3-STRING "E-SUS"
CAPOS

Kyser "Short-Cut"

Shubb c7b

"G-7 Newport #3"

Kyser K-Lever "DADGAD" (BLUE)

Kyser K-Lever "Open G" (WHITE)

Kyser K-Lever "Double Drop D" (RED)

1 & 2-STRING
"G-BAND"
CAPOS

Woodie's G Band Model 1

Woodie's G Band Model 2

3-String "Esus" Capo Comparison Chart

Legend (Brand & Model —>):
- ••••• = works perfectly
- •••• = quite well/most of time
- ••• = reasonably/OK
- •• = poorly/ sometimes
- • = barely/sort of/might work
- x = not at all

Feature	Liberty FLIP Model 43	Shubb c7b	Kyser Short-Cut	Kyser K-Lever "Open G"	Kyser K-Lever "DADGAD"	Kyser K-Lever "Double Drop"	G7 Newport #3	Third Hand	Spider Capo
Retail price	$32	$27	$27	$56	$56	$56	$40	$25	$40
Weight	.7 oz	1.7 oz	1.3 oz	1.6 oz	1.5 oz	1.6 oz	1.4 oz	1.1 oz	1.2 oz
Easily adjust tension	••••	••	x	x	x	x	••••	•	•
Attractive appearance	••••	••	••	•	•	•	••	x	x
Attaches from either side	••••	••	••	•	•	•	•	••••	x
Access notes under capo	••••	••	••	••	••	••	••••	••••	•
Reach around & over the capo	••••	••	••	••	••	••	••••	••••	x
Good with wider fingerboards	••••	••	••	••	••	••	••	••	•
Good for narrow (i.e. Fender) necks	••••	•	••	•	x	•	x	••	••
Can shorten/trim if needed	••••	•	••	•	x	x	•	••	x
Works well with thicker necks	••••	••	••	••	x	x	x	••	•
Works well with thin necks	••••	••	••	••	•	•	•	••	••
Works well at higher frets (7-9)	••••	••	••	•	•	•	•	••	••
Good with higher action	••••	••	••	••	•	•	x	••	••
Good with heavier string gauges	x	••	••	••	••	••	••	••	••
Works well on nylon-string/classical	••••	x	x	x	x	x	x	••	•
Works well on 12-string	••••	••	••	••	x	x	••	••	x
Is useful on banjo/mando/uke	••••	•	•	•	•	•	•	••	x
Clamps 4 inner strings	x	x	x	x	x	x	x	••••	••••
Clamps 4 outer strings	••••	x	x	x	x	x	x	••	••••
Does Liberty Tuning Version 1	••••	•	•	•	•	•	•	••	••••
Does Liberty Tuning Version 2	••••	x	x	x	•	x	x	•	••••
Fits easily in your pocket	••••	••	••	•	•	•	••	•	•
Attaches quickly	••	••	••	••	••	••	••	••	x
Move mid-song to another fret	•	•	•	x	x	x	•	•	x
Change configuration while attached	x	x	x	x	x	x	x	x	••
Stores on headstock	•	x	x	••	••	••	x	x	x

4 & 5-String Shortened Capo Comparison Chart

Legend:
- ● ● ● = works perfectly
- ● ● ● = quite well/most of time
- ● ● = reasonably/OK
- ● = poorly/ sometimes
- • = barely/sort of/might work
- x = not at all

Brand & Model →	Liberty FLIP Model 43	Liberty FLIP Model 65	Shubb c8b	Kyser Drop D	Kyser K-Lever "Drop D"	Planet Waves "Trio"	G7 Newport #5	Third Hand	Spider Capo
Retail price	$33	$33	$27	$25	$56	$27	$40	$25	$40
Weight	.7 oz	.8 oz	1.9 oz	1.4 oz	1.6 oz	.8 oz	1.7 oz	1.1 oz	1.2 oz
Access notes under capo	●●	●●●	●●	●●●●	●●●●●	●●●	●●●●	●●●	●●●●
Reach around & over the capo	●●	●●●	●●	●●	●●●	●●	●●●●	●	x
Easily adjust tension	●●●	●●●	●●●	x	x	x	●●	●●	x
Attractive appearance	●●	●●	●●	●	●	●●●	●●	x	x
Good with wider fingerboards	●●	●●	●●	●●	●●	●●	●●	●●	●●
Good w/ narrow (i.e. Fender) neck	●●	●●	●●	●●	●	●●	●●	●●	●●
Good with thicker necks	●●	●●	●●	●●	●	●	●	●●	●
Good with thin necks	●●	●●	●●	●●	●	●●	x	●●	●●
Good with higher action	●●	●●	●●	●	x	●	x	●●	●●
Good with heavier string gauges	●●	●●	●●	●●	●●	●●	●●	●●	●●
Can clamp just 4 outer strings	●●	●	x	x	●	●	x	●●●	●●●
Can clamp just 4 inner strings	●●	x	x	x	x	x	x	●●	●●
Also works as a full capo	x	x	x	x	x	x	x	●●	●●
Works well on nylon-string/classical	●●	●●	x	x	x	●	x	●	●
Works well on banjo/mando/uke	●●	●●	●	●	●	●●●	●●	●●●	x
Works well on 12-string	●●	●●	●	x	x	●●	x	●●●	●●
Fits easily in your pocket	●●●	●●●	●●	●●	●	●●●	●	●	●
Change configuration while attached	x	x	x	x	x	x	x	x	x
Attaches quickly	●●	●●	●	●●	●●	●	●	●●	x
Move mid-song to another fret	●●	●●	x	●●●	●●	x	x	x	x
Stores on headstock	●●	●●	x	●●●	●●	x	x	x	x

261

Partial Capos & Notation

It took musical notation, and specialized guitar notation centuries to evolve, and I suspect there will be some confusion and experimentation before the guitar world adopts any kind of standardized way of describing in writing how partial capos are used. Partial capos bring up and complicate a number of issues in notation, and it's worth trying to take a closer look at some of the problems that arise, even though it's hard to wrap your mind around the problem. Some pretty smart people, and people who know a lot about guitars and guitar notation have failed to grasp this issue at first glance, so don't feel bad if you have trouble.

The first notation problem is that so many people and capo manufacturers refer to partial capo configurations as "tunings." Apparently they are unclear on the idea that partial capos and tunings are different concepts fundamentally, that partial capos can easily be used in any tuning and are not just imitations of them.

Even the nicknames of the most common capo configurations have been inconsistent from the outset. In 1980 I started referring to the capo position that forms an A chord as "*Open A*," yet the Kyser company has insisted on calling their specialized capo that forms an A chord an "Open G." Likewise, they call the Esus capo a "DADGAD" capo, which I think is misleading, since it is used most often in standard tuning, and the way it works only slightly resembles DADGAD tuning. The open-strings generated by an *Esus* capo have the same relationship as the open strings in DADGAD tuning, but there are few similarities other than the general "open-tuned" droning flavor of 2 environments.

I have had some success getting people to use a numeric system of 6 digits to describe standard tuning partial capo ideas, so an *Esus* would be notated as 022200 and an *Open A* as 002220. This works fine for multiple capos, whether they are full or partial, and only becomes cumbersome when you capo above the 9th fret, which is rare, or when you use a non-standard tuning.

Creating a single alphanumeric code "word" that described the tuning and the capo together would make some sense, though musical notes do not have simple and consistent names, and there are more than 10 of them so a numeric symbol for the pitch of the open string would not work either. I call the 022220 capo configuration in DADGAD tuning a "DADGAD 022220" and to avoid the endless monotony of numerals I may also call that one "Middle 4 @2 in DADGAD." I also use the words Top and Bottom combined with numbers, since it is clear

what they mean, and easy to say things like "Top 4 @7" or "Bottom 5 @3."

Another highly confusing aspect of partial capo education is that you have to say things like "Play what feels like a G chord, and it will sound as an A." That is exactly what you do in a lot of instances, but the language gets thick when you describe things constantly this way. Even if it looks and feels exactly like a G chord, it may say A on the chord diagram, and all the notes will show at the bottom of the chord diagram the way they actually sound, with A, C# and E notes. It is not hard to keep track of things with a single capo at the 2nd fret in standard tuning, but when there are multiple partial capos on higher frets it's much more difficult to stay oriented.

Partial capos themselves are confusing, and discussions like this of how to describe and communicate to other players what is going on are also confusing. When you look at the issues of how to write both standard notation and tablature, the confusion kicks up to another level.

It is unfortunate that at the beginning of the acceptance of this idea into the guitar world at large, there is already inconsistency and disagreement among partial capo users. It seems almost trivial at first glance, but the issue is deceptively hard to understand. I am in complete agreement with the idea that it is best to notate guitar music with both a standard notation staff and a TAB staff below it, and have done all my work to date this way. Unfortunately, both TAB and standard notation have problems with partial capos.

The problems of partial capo books will get worse as more people transcribe more arrangements into musical notation. I am now uncertain if there is any reasonable way to universally notate partial capo music so that one method will make sense to all people. If you are planning to publish some written music yourself, at least take the time to read this carefully. Do your best to make an informed decision, rather than just doing the first thing that occurs to you. We really need to have a convention and a public debate & discussion, but I don't have high hopes this will happen any time soon.

Computer Software

There have been notation problems since the beginning of partial capo usage, but now that people are primarily using software to generate their TAB and notation, it won't be clear what to do until the software companies make some changes in their products to allow for the idea of partial capos. Software has generally allowed different tunings, and different numbers of strings, but so far I am not aware that anyone has taken to time to remedy this so the system can also accommodate partial capos.

If you are a partial capo user who writes or reads guitar arrangements, you might want to try to understand the problem, and perhaps write some letters or emails to your favorite software makers and urge them to take this problem seriously. I have tried in vain many times to get their attention, and it will take more than just one or two people asking them for it to get done.

Standard Notation

Guitar music is usually written on the staff in standard notation, and as more music gets arranged and written with partial capos, it will not be totally clear what to do. If you write the music the way it "feels" to a guitarist who knows how to sight-read music, it will not "look like it sounds."

It was my conclusion in 1983 when I published my first arrangements with a partial capo, and I still believe now that it is important to make sure the standard notation reads as it "sounds," not as it "feels". This is unlike the way classical guitar publishers generally deal with non-standard tunings, (primarily *Drop D* tuning) where sheet music is generally written as it feels, so that you "pretend" you are in standard tuning, and thus the notes on the bass string do not read as they sound.

The widespread use of altered tunings plus this new issue of partial capos, combined with the vast number of people who do not actually read music on the guitar make writing the music as it sounds a better choice to make. Sticking to this decision complicates other choices we have to make, unfortunately.

The fact that the standard notation people and the classical guitar community already cannot really use their notation system for non-standard tunings underscores the seriousness of this issue, and also brings up the difficult question of who is going to decide how to notate partially capoed guitar music. The final answer might end up being determined by the most popular TAB-generating computer software, and the choices they have made. As of this writing, none of the music publishing software (such as *Finale* and *Sibelius*) allow the user to compensate for one or more partial capos.

Notating TAB

When I wrote my guitar books for partial capo, I wrote the TAB (tablature) numbers to show the notes the way they "feel" (with the capo as the 0, but strings open to the nut also notated as 0, with occasional negative numbers for TAB below the capo.) Computer software for guitar notation does not know about partial capos yet, and people are using several different methods now, including

counting from the capo as 0, or counting everything from the nut, or even hybrid systems where open bass strings are counted from the fret where the capo is placed. This means that in an Esus capo situation, a one-finger E5 chord could be notated at least 3 different ways Notice the TAB numbers under each chord:

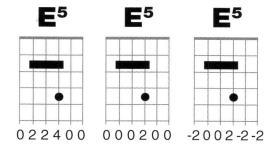

I usually plead the case here that TAB should be counted from the capo and not the nut, since it is certainly more intuitive to do it that way when you use most of the capo devices out there. So I would choose the middle of these three, where there are 5 "open" strings and one fretted note on the 3rd string. I think a 0 in the TAB should mean that the left hand does not fret anything, and it could be caused by the nut or a partial capo.

Because computer software isn't set up for partial capos, a number of people (including fingerstyle guitarist Chris Proctor) have published music that counts TAB from the nut. In 2009 I started using a *Woodie's G-Band* capo in some of my music, and it throws another wrench into this thinking because it only capos 1 or 2 strings, and it does not really become the new nut for the guitar like other partial capos do. When it is combined with other partial capos, it becomes unclear whether to count from the nut or from the capo that most "feels" like the nut.

In the case of the common capo configurations on fret 2 it is not obvious which is better, but there are many other ways of partial capoing where the issue is clearer. Imagine capoing at the 5th, 7th or t fret and leaving one open string. It would not make sense to the player to think that a G chord there was 10-9-0-0-0-10. Your instincts as TAB reader would make it 3-2-0-0-0-3 just like you always play it. Same thing when you capo at 1st fret and capo all except the G string, which I do a lot. There is no question that as a player you usually think of the capo as the nut whenever you use a capo, partial or not.

We also use a partial capo a great deal to teach beginners and intermediate players, and when they play, they are thinking the capo is the nut even more than do more advanced players.

Notation/publishing software is generally set up so the TAB is generated and thus inextricably linked to the notes on the staff. Here is an example: the opening section of my arrangement of *Frere Jacques:*

The first note is an open 3rd string (here shown in "*Half-Open A*" configuration 002222) with capo 2 would notate on the staff as the real A note that it is, and a TAB value of 0, and the second note B is 2 frets above the capo so it gets a TAB value of 2.

Notice in measure 3, the first pair of TAB ZERO'S that you play as "open strings," an A bass note which is a true open string, and the "open string" 2nd string playing the C#. That note "feels" like an open string because it is clamped by the capo and you're not fretting anything.

If you do not tell the computer that the guitar is retuned and let the computer generate the TAB, the 2nd note being a B will cause the computer to put a 4 into the TAB on the 3rd string, not the 2 that is shown here. (To me it feels like it should be a 2 and not a 4).

If you tell the computer your guitar was actually tuned to E-A-E-A-C#-F#, which is what the capo makes your open strings with the capo 002222, it solves one problem and causes another.

The 2nd fret above the capo on the G string will either be generated by your TAB software as a 2 if you tell the computer it has been retuned, or a 4 if you don't. Telling the TAB software you retuned would make the unfretted and fretted notes on the capoed strings come out "right," but for fretted notes on the uncapoed strings the TAB wlll feel "wrong" to many people. This would happen in measure 3 in this example: when you played the low A note (open 5th string) and the C# on the 2nd string feels like an open string but has TAB value 2. In this example the middle two bass string notes have TAB numbers 5 -7 in the above example, but here the computer TAB would call it a 7-9. See the issue? Here is the same example as above notated this way, counting from the nut, so you can compare the TAB. The first quarter notes in measure 3 seem counter-intuitive and really should be both zeros because you don't fret with your left hand on either note.

The workaround of telling the computer you are in a different tuning when you are just using a partial capo gets your TAB right on some strings, but it blows up when you use an altered tuning and a partial capo at the same time, which many of us do.

If you instead count TAB from the nut, essentially by telling the computer that you don't have either a capo or an open tuning, then all the TAB numbers come out "right" except the capoed open strings. (These are important notes, and a big part of the reason we use partial capos.) The first 2 notes of this arrangement would be 2-4. It's deeply intuitive to use a zero "0" TAB for an unfretted note, whether it is a true open string or clamped by a capo. Because the partial capo is all about celebrating those new capoed open strings, it feels "extra right" to notate them as TAB zero notes. There could be a new notation invented that puts a box around any TAB number that was fretted by the capo. This would essentially mean "open string."

Notating "Behind-the-Capo" Notes

There is also the even-thornier issue of how to notate under and behind-the-capo frettings, and what to do if the capo is moved in the middle of a song.

For behind-the-capo notes, a negative number is the obvious choice, except that in sloppy printouts and photocopies the minus sign can vanish or merge with the string line. Even trickier is the issue of how to notate things fretted at the same fret as the capo. It is not a 0, since that means the nut. I like to call notes fretted behind the capo as negative numbers -1, -2, and I use a zero with a slash for the notes at the same fret as the capo. This is done as a "theta" (option-O on Mac keyboards) ø, which is somewhere in all computer keyboards and all common fonts. In some typefaces, though, it gets confused with a zero which programmers have put a slightly different slash through for years to distinguish it from a capital O. There is no way to avoid some confusion.

I recommend drawing the partial capo on the TAB, which makes it clearer, and which would solve the problem of the moving capo also. (Some spring-clamp capo users who use Kyser partial capos take advantage of the quick action of the capo and move the capo in the middle of a song..) Notating this would not be much more confusing than a key change in standard notation. Just draw a new capo diagram on the TAB line and keep going.

Here is the first page of my *Esus* arrangement of Stephen Foster's "*Hard Times Come Again No More.*" Notice the 2nd note in the piece is an F# that is TAB ø "under the capo" note at the 2nd fret of the E string. The 3rd note is G#, which would be fret 4 in standard tuning, but it has TAB of 2 since it is 2 frets above an *Esus capo.*

Hard Times Come Again No More

Some Partial Capo Math

How Many Partial Capo Configurations Are There?

To figure how many ways you can put a partial capo on a guitar...

We don't count "0 0 0 0 0 0" which is no strings clamped, and we don't count clamping all 6 strings which is a full capo.

If we solve for

X= *the number of configurations*
C= *the number of capos*
F= *the number of frets on the instrument*
S= *the number of strings on the instrument*

I have not done the math to figure out how many combinations can be done with mixed or multiple Liberty capos.

With one capo it is pretty easy...

Just 2 to the S power minus 1, since each of the S strings can be either up or down. So 2 to the 6th power, minus one = 64-1= 63 with at least one string capoed

This means a 6-string guitar yields 63 configurations of one partial capo at each fret. So on a 12 fret neck one universal partial capo can clamp 63 x 12 = **756** configurations, and **882** for a 14-fret neck. It's not easy to get a capo on many guitars at the 14th fret, so it's safe to say **there are at most 756 ways to put one capo on a guitar, in each tuning. For acoustic guitars it's really 63 x 9 frets= 567 possibilities.**

For a *Liberty* 3-string capo, there are 2 ways to put it at each fret= 24 ways in 12 frets, 18 ways in 9 frets. The 4-string side goes 3 ways at each fret= 36 in 12 frets or 27 in 9 frets. So a single *Model 43* can go 60 places on a 12-fret neck, or 18 + 27= 45 choices in 9 frets on an acoustic guitar, in each tuning.

The math is a lot harder when you use multiple capos, since if more than one capo clamps the same string, only one of them does anything.
"f over c" is "f things taken c at a time" if you remember the formula from math class long ago

So with 2 capos we get 66 x 728= **48,048** configurations

$$\text{Then } \mathbf{x} = \begin{pmatrix} f \\ c \end{pmatrix} \left[(c + 1)^{s} - 1 \right]$$

and with 3 capos we get = **900,900** configurations
For 12 capos we get = **4,826,808** configurations.

You can also get this same number more easily by thinking like this: The 1st string has 13 different fretting choices on a 12 fret neck (since we count the open string)-- so a 2-string instrument would have (13x13)-1 combinations, and thus a 6-string guitar would have (13x13x13x13x13x13)-1= 4,826,808 configurations. So a 14-fret guitar would yield (15x15x15x15x15x15)-1= 11,390,624 configurations. (531,440 for 9 frets)

This means there are theoretically millions of ways to put partial capos on a guitar fingerboard– in every different tuning! Because strings break if you tune them sharp, and they lose tone if you loosen them more than 3-4 frets, the permutations of partial capos is mathematically larger than that of just tunings. There are roughly 5x5x5x5x5x5 tunings (15000+) that you could try with a standard set of strings. I generally find a few dozen useful ways to use capos in each tuning, which leads me to estimate that there are roughly 2000 musically useful capo configurations for every 100 tunings. Since there are about 100 tunings in use, my current research represents less than 10-20% of the total size of the "hidden world" of partial capos on a 6-string guitar.

THE SONG TRAIN (2007) is a landmark resource for beginning guitarists by Harvey Reid & Joyce Andersen. 4-CD boxed set with 80-page color hardback book, contains 56 one & two chord songs. Half the songs are copyrighted, by the likes of Bob Dylan, Hank Williams, Chuck Berry etc, so it offers beginners easy but great songs they can play. Folk, blues, gospel, rock, celtic, country and gospel songs, and an amazing cross-section of American music. **www.songtrain.net**

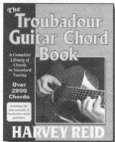

THE TROUBADOUR GUITAR CHORD BOOK (2013) The best, most complete and readable standard-tuning chord encyclopedia, and an essential new reference tool. A monumental and important new work that may never go back on your shelf. Unlike other large chord books that are tailored for jazz guitarists, the *Troubadour Guitar Chord Book* features over 2900 open and closed-string voicings, optimized and selected for solo acoustic and troubadour-style guitarists.

THE BIG DADGAD CHORD BOOK (2014) The best, most complete and readable chord encyclopedia in DADGAD tuning, with 2500 chords mapped out. Another indispensable reference book for anyone who plays in this popular tuning.

MODERN FOLK GUITAR (1984) The first college folk guitar textbook. A unique and comprehensive 325 page guitar handbook for the adult beginner, that remained in print for 30 years. Used in the music departments of numerous universities to train music teachers. Many have called it the ultimate beginning folk guitar book. Hopefully will be re-printed again, and may become a digital book in 2015.

DUCK SOUP GUITAR: *Beginning Guitar With Super-Easy Chords* (1982) A little-known but revolutionary beginning guitar method. Shows how to use a partial capo to simplify guitar fingerings for beginners and people with special needs. Contains 28 children's songs with chords, notes & lyrics, and shows 6 clever ways to use a partial capo for easy chord fingerings. Anyone can play full-sounding guitar accompaniments instantly. Before *Liberty Tuning* this was what you could do with simplified guitar. It's now obsolete.

SLEIGHT OF HAND (1983) The first book of partial capo guitar arrangements, still in print. 16 solo guitar arrangements using a universal partial capo. Intermediate to advanced level, mostly for fingerstyle guitar, but has 2 flatpicked fiddle tune arrangements (*Sally Goodin'* and *Devil's Dream*) In TAB and standard notation. *Suite: For the Duchess, Für Elise, Scarborough Fair, Minuet in Dm, Flowers of Edinburgh, Simple Gifts, Sally Goodin', Irish Washerwoman, Pavanne, Minuet in Dm, Red-Haired Boy, June Apple, Jesu Joy of Man's Desiring, Devil's Dream, Sally Goodin', Scherzo, Shenandoah, Greensleeves, Sailor's Hornpipe, Fisher's Hornpipe*

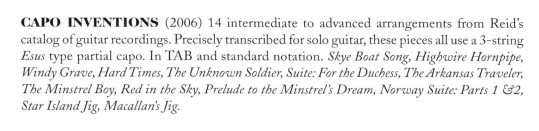

CAPO INVENTIONS (2006) 14 intermediate to advanced arrangements from Reid's catalog of guitar recordings. Precisely transcribed for solo guitar, these pieces all use a 3-string *Esus* type partial capo. In TAB and standard notation. *Skye Boat Song, Highwire Hornpipe, Windy Grave, Hard Times, The Unknown Soldier, Suite: For the Duchess, The Arkansas Traveler, The Minstrel Boy, Red in the Sky, Prelude to the Minstrel's Dream, Norway Suite: Parts 1 &2, Star Island Jig, Macallan's Jig.*

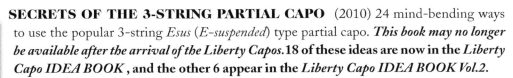

SECRETS OF THE 3-STRING PARTIAL CAPO (2010) 24 mind-bending ways to use the popular 3-string *Esus* (*E-suspended*) type partial capo. *This book may no longer be available after the arrival of the Liberty Capos.* 18 of these ideas are now in the *Liberty Capo IDEA BOOK*, and the other 6 appear in the *Liberty Capo IDEA BOOK Vol.2*.

MORE SECRETS OF THE 3-STRING PARTIAL CAPO (2013) 27 more ways to use 3-string *Esus* (*E-suspended*) type partial capos. *This book may no longer be available.* 12 of these ideas are now in the *Liberty Capo IDEA BOOK*, and the others aret in the *Liberty Capo IDEA BOOK Vol.2*.

SECRETS OF THE 4 & 5-STRING PARTIAL CAPOS (2011) Another treasure trove of ideas, for the *Planet Waves*, *Shubb*, or *Kyser* shortened 4 or 5-string capos. (Also valuable for *Third Hand, Liberty "Flip"* or *Spider* universal capos.) Most people who have one of these capos know a few ways to use them. Here are an amazing 47 ideas that use a 4 or 5-string capo to generate new music. Over 1600 chords. *This book may no longer be available after the arrival of the Liberty Capos.* 30 of these 47 ideas are now in the *Liberty Capo IDEA BOOK*, and the other 17 appear in the *Liberty Capo IDEA BOOK Vol.2*.

SECRETS OF THE 1 & 2-STRING PARTIAL CAPOS (2012) How to use the unique *Woodie's G-Band* 1 and 2-string partial capos. 33 clever ways to use these capos in a number of tunings and in combination with other partial capos, with over 1100 chords. 98 pages are packed with photos, ideas and capo knowledge that is only available here. Even the makers of the capos don't know about these ideas.

SECRETS OF PARTIAL CAPOS IN DADGAD TUNING (2012) Most people think of partial capos as a substitute for open tunings, and don't realize that they can be combined. Harvey Reid shows you over 25 ingenious ways to use partial capos to expand the musical possibilities of DADGAD tuning (4 of them use the similar CGDGAD tuning.) Get new chords, fingerings, voicings, resonances and unlock a new, mysterious world of new music hiding in your fingerboard. If you use DADGAD tuning a lot, you need this book.

SECRETS OF UNIVERSAL PARTIAL CAPOS (2012) 45 ways to get new music from your guitar that can only be done with universal partial capos. This hidden world of music in your fingerboard includes a number of tunings and combinations with other partial capos. Over 1500 chords. Packed with photos, clear explanations and capo strategy will save you years of searching. **Because the *Model 43 Liberty* capo clamps 4 middle strings, 13 of these ideas are now in the *Liberty Capo IDEA BOOKS*, *Vol. 1-2*.**

SECRETS OF PARTIAL CAPOS IN DROP D TUNING (2014) The most common tuning is *Drop D*: D A D G B E, and like any tuning, it can be combined with partial capos to add another dimension to the guitar. This book presents 24 ways to use one or more partial capos of all types to generate more new music.

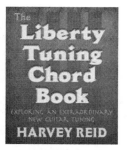

THE LIBERTY TUNING CHORD BOOK (2013) In his partial capo research, Harvey Reid discovered a simple new guitar tuning that introduces a remarkable geometrical symmetry and simplicity to the guitar fingerboard that no one ever dreamed existed. Here is a thorough examination of what this amazing tuning can do, with over 1200 chords, sorted, mapped out and organized to help you find your way in *Liberty Tuning*. Lots of tips, advice & clear explanations. For guitar teachers, beginners and anyone who already plays guitar and wants to learn about this important discovery.

THE LIBERTY GUITAR METHOD (2013) Total beginners can play music like never before. It's easy to do and sounds great. Learn to use *Liberty Tuning* to play great-sounding, simple 2-finger chords to songs by Bob Dylan, Hank Williams, John Prine, Johnny Cash, Chuck Berry, The Beatles, Adele, and more. You won't believe it 'til you try it. *Hush Little Baby, This Land is Your Land, Your Cheating Heart, A Hard Rain's A Gonna Fall, Amazing Grace, The Cuckoo, Folsom Prison Blues, Angel From Montgomery, Maybellene, Let It Be, Imagine, Someone Like You, The Wedding Song, House of the Rising Sun*

THE LIBERTY SONG TRAIN (2013) Learn how to use *Liberty Tuning* to play all 56 two-chord songs in the epic *Song Train* collection with just 2-finger chords, in the same keys as they were done on the *Song Train* recordings. Beginning guitar has never been easier. Careful explanations, with lots of helpful tips, strategy and advice. If you have the *Song Train* 4-CD collection, you need this companion book.

THE 2-FINGER GUITAR GUIDE (2013) A careful study of simplified guitar chords, this book takes you through each of the common tunings and partial capo configurations that can be used to play simplified guitar chords. Learn the advantages and disadvantages of each of 28 different guitar environments, including the amazing *Liberty Tuning* and related hybrid tunings. If you have a shortage of fingers on the fretting hand, or if you work with hand injuries, special music education or music therapy, this is the definitive guide to showing what can be done musically with just 2 finger chords.

LIBERTY GUITAR FOR KIDS (2013) It's a huge breakthrough in children's guitar. Children as young as 4 can learn to strum simple 2-finger *Liberty Tuning* chords and play guitar like never before. Classic traditional plus modern children's songs arranged in keys young voices can sing in. No need to wait until the children grow bigger or waste your money on crummy small children's guitars. Learn how even small children can instantly start strumming songs on adult guitars. It's really amazing. *London Bridge, Row Row Row Your Boat, Farmer in the Dell, Hush Little Baby, This Land is Your Land, Oh Susannah, Standing in the Need of Prayer, Hey Lolly Lolly, Comin' Round the Mountain* and more.

About the Author

Harvey Reid has been a full-time acoustic guitar player since 1974, and has performed over 6000 concerts throughout the US and in Europe. He won the 1981 *National Fingerpicking Guitar Competition* and the 1982 *International Autoharp* contest, and has released 30 highly-acclaimed recordings of original, traditional and contemporary acoustic music.

He is best known for his solo fingerstyle guitar work, but he is also a solid flatpicker (he won Bill Monroe's *Beanblossom* bluegrass guitar contest in 1976), a versatile singer, lyricist, prolific composer, arranger and songwriter. He also plays mandolin and bouzouki. Reid recorded the first album ever of 6 & 12-string banjo music, and his CD ***Solo Guitar Sketchbook*** made GUITAR PLAYER MAGAZINE's Top 20 essential acoustic guitar CD's list. His CD ***Steel Drivin' Man*** was chosen by ACOUSTIC GUITAR MAGAZINE as one of **Top 10 Folk CD's** of all time, along with Woody Guthrie, Ry Cooder and other hallowed names. His music was included in the blockbuster BBC TV show *A Musical Tour of Scotland*, and Reid was featured in the Rhino Records **Acoustic Music of the 90's** collection, along with a "who's who" line-up of other artists including Richard Thompson, Jerry Garcia & Leo Kottke.

In 1980 Reid published *A New Frontier in Guitar,* the first book about the partial capo, and in 1984 he wrote ***Modern Folk Guitar***, the first college textbook for folk guitar. Quite possibly the first modern person to publish and record with the partial capo, he is almost certainly the most prolific arranger and composer of partial capo guitar music, and is responsible for most of what is known about the device. He lives in southern Maine with his family.

Made in the USA
San Bernardino, CA
20 March 2017